DEVELOPING
THE NAVAL
MIND

DEVELOPING THE NAVAL MIND

Benjamin F. Armstrong and John Freymann

NAVAL INSTITUTE PRESS
Annapolis, Maryland

This book has been brought to publication with
the generous assistance of the U.S. Naval Academy
Faculty Development Fund.

Naval Institute Press
291 Wood Road
Annapolis, MD 21402

Library of Congress Cataloging-in-Publication Data
Names: Armstrong, Benjamin, author. | Freymann, John, author.
Title: Developing the naval mind / Benjamin F. Armstrong, and John Freymann.
Description: Annapolis, Maryland : Naval Institute Press, 2021. | Series: Blue & Gold
    Professional Library | Includes bibliographical references and index.
Identifiers: LCCN 2021017759 (print) | LCCN 2021017760 (ebook) |
    ISBN 9781682476031 (hardcover) | ISBN 9781682477359 (pdf) |
    ISBN 9781682477359 (epub)
Subjects: LCSH: Naval art and science—Philosophy. | Naval education—United States.
Classification: LCC V19 .A76 2021 (print) | LCC V19 (ebook) | DDC 359.001—dc23
LC record available at https://lccn.loc.gov/2021017759
LC ebook record available at https://lccn.loc.gov/2021017760

♾ Print editions meet the requirements of ANSI/NISO z39.48-1992
(Permanence of Paper).
Printed in the United States of America.

29 28 27 26 25 24 23 22   9 8 7 6 5 4 3 2

Dedicated to
the memory of
CAPT. OWEN THORP III, USN, PHD
who taught us that being
an officer, a leader, and a scholar
are all the same thing.

Contents

INTRODUCTION
DEVELOPING THE NAVAL MIND

E very naval officer has a memory of the first wardroom leader or ready room mentor who took an interest in them and their professionalism. Not the shine on their shoes or the technical knowledge needed for success, and not their memorization of procedures but instead their genuine intellectual engagement with the ideas and philosophies of naval officership. Those officer-teachers are out there, leaders who also served as professors of practice, who want to exchange ideas and debate the key questions of the day around the wardroom or work center with a cup of coffee, or at the Officer's Club with another beverage. We all also remember the opposite examples, the mocking of a junior officer for reading the *Economist* and "trying to be smarter than everyone else," or the insistence that young service members stop learning about strategy or "subjects above their pay grade" and instead keep their noses in their technical manuals and tactics publications and think only about their qualifications.

If the naval profession is going to keep pace with the social, political, and technological changes of the twenty-first century, it is time to reassess how we think about the idea of professionalism. More than how recently you had a haircut or how you wear your uniform, professionalism has higher ethical, personal, and strategic elements that are often best honed through reading, reflection, and group study. The nature of war is constant, but the character of war is ever changing, and understanding that change and developing the methods and innovations needed to deal with it require Sailors and Marines who are able to deal with and even thrive in complexity. Understanding the nature and character of the challenges they face requires women and men capable of strategic and ethical reasoning. It requires officers, Sailors, and Marines who view their job as intellectual as well as physical, a job of thinking alongside action. If it is true, as we are often assured, that the rate of change is accelerating, and the modern world is presenting new and complex challenges, then the discussions, debates, and conversations in our wardrooms, ready rooms, and work centers must also pick up the pace and gain a renewed focus.

This book is about education and the naval profession, about the development of the naval mind and the creation of officers, Sailors, and Marines with wide interests and the ability to do more than simply comply with established procedures and checklists. Today's naval educational enterprise—the curricula in Annapolis, Newport, Quantico, and Monterey and in programs like the Reserve Officer's Training Corps and the Navy College Office—offer vital services to the development of our Sailors and Marines. However, the genuine development of the Navy and Marine Corps as learning organizations, instilled with the capacity for real critical thinking, requires more than just a brief tour at a naval college or university. It requires a consistent effort at personal study and development as well as the active mentorship and group learning available only in operational units and shore commands. Naval learning is a career-long process, and the demands of the twenty-first century require nothing less than a continuous focus on our own professional improvement. This book is a guide for that process and an initial point from which to begin charting your own course.

In the decade before the outbreak of World War I, then-commander William Sims wrote an article for the Naval Institute's *Proceedings* entitled "Cheer Up!! There Is No Naval War College." Sims had completed the course of study at Newport, and he had done so well that the staff selected him to remain for an additional year to serve as an instructor. But after teaching at the Navy's premier graduate institution, Sims returned to the fleet, and he realized that the topics he had been teaching in classrooms and on the wargaming floor also belonged in the wardrooms of the fleet. Education was not only about professors and accredited and highly developed curricula, it was also a constant professional necessity and belonged in all the ships and units of the Navy and Marine Corps.[1] Commander Sims would become Captain Sims, and eventually Admiral Sims, and would command U.S. naval forces in European waters during World War I. And, although he returned to Newport after the war ended to become president of the Naval War College, he never stopped believing that professional learning and the development of the naval mind was a lifelong pursuit and that they belonged in the fleet just as much as in schools. When we look back at our naval past, it does not take long to realize that this attitude has been a central, if sometimes forgotten, key to the very concept of naval professionalism.[2]

We offer this book as a starting point for naval professionals to reclaim the heritage of personal professional study and group learning that has helped to define the most successful naval forces in history. While the best officers may be professors of practice, only a very small number of U.S. naval officers are professors by trade. We have had the privilege of being part of that group, sent to graduate school to study history, philosophy, and navies and earn our doctorates; to teach midshipmen at the Naval Academy in seminars and classrooms; and to help administer educational programs. But we remember the wardroom discussions and ready room debates that shaped our views of professionalism before the Navy selected us to become permanent military professors. Like Admiral Sims before us, we recognize that professional learning cannot wait for or stay in the classroom. *Developing the Naval Mind* is an effort to return to the ideals of our Navy and Marine Corps' past, illustrated by the history of organizations like the U.S. Naval Lyceum and the U.S. Naval Institute and imbued with an ethos that embraces dynamic learning and experiential development created by group discussions and personal study.

Our approach in the following chapters stems from our conviction that discussion is a tremendously powerful tool for forming, developing, and clarifying one's own ideas. Of course, it is essential to read, learn, and think alone wherever home and work life permit. Solitude—harder and harder to come by in our digitally distracted age—can facilitate concentration and creativity. But people also need to think in community, in dialogue with others. As Aristotle observed more than two millennia ago, speech is a fundamentally human trait, and we use it not merely to communicate emotion and information but also to reason, to think. That is, we reason not in monologue but in dialogue. By discussing ideas with other people, we are challenged to speak precisely, which pushes us to clarify what we claim to think or believe. When pressed hard, we are forced to examine our own assumptions, often so deeply held that we are unaware of them. Sometimes we come up with ideas that we had never thought before.

Discussion as thinking and reasoning—that is the animating concept of this book. The activity itself is beneficial, with or without the delivery of information and data or arrival at firm conclusions.

In the following pages, readers will find chapters and an appendix that work together to provide resources to officers, Sailors, and Marines who desire to learn in the fleet. The chapters in part I are made up of short essays discussing the skills and tools that will help leaders create their own professional seminars in their units either afloat or ashore. This includes a reflection on the history of professional learning, a discussion of techniques for facilitating effective discussions, and some advice on how to manage seminar-style learning. For the Sailors and Marines who are ready to participate in discussions and professional debates, we offer some suggestions for effective reading and methods of personal study to help prepare for the intellectual give and take in a good, deep discussion.

Following this introduction, part I offers a discussion of how to design your own reading list, create your own seminar, and find the resources to encourage further individual and group learning in wardrooms, ready rooms, and work centers throughout the fleet and Fleet Marine Force. Perhaps, after reading and thinking and discussing professional matters, the readers of this book may begin developing their own professional ideas. We hope that's the case! We have also included a chapter that suggests a process to begin writing your own professional article and ways to get involved in the wider discussion of military and naval professionalism by publishing your ideas.

The readings in part II include information that serves the larger goals discussed in the book's opening chapters. The series of readings can serve as the first syllabus for a professional seminar in your unit. The articles selected are a mix of essays on leadership and professionalism as well as subjects involved in naval strategy, operations, and tactics. Each of the articles includes five discussion questions, which we have prepared to help you begin your seminars. We have selected these essays and articles as a starting point, using the historical archive of the Naval Institute's century and a half of articles and essays from U.S. Naval Institute *Proceedings* as an initial point of departure for the journey. Rather than making an attempt at a conclusive or definitive list of readings that will master the subject, this collection is designed to get you started. The appendix includes a series of ideas, suggestions, and "gouge" on professional publishing for those who are interested in pursuing their own work and their own contributions to our maritime profession.

From the age of sail to the modern era, leaders from Matthew Perry to Alfred Thayer Mahan, William Sims to John Lejeune and Ernest King, have insisted that naval learning never stops. It is not just an endeavor for classrooms and accredited institutions. It is the responsibility of every leader to develop the intellectual professionalism of the men and women who serve with them. The sections of this book are offered as a way to set course on that voyage, to ensure that we have leaders prepared to face the ever-changing character of war and that we have Sailors and Marines with the critical thinking skills to address the speed of the modern world. This effort can be taken up by anyone: skippers and executive officers who are searching for a way to add more to the discussions over coffee in the wardroom, department heads who want to learn alongside the junior officers who work with them, or junior officers and noncommissioned officers looking to engage their Sailors and Marines in the higher discussion of the profession. If the Navy and Marine Corps are going to become the learning institutions necessary to address the strategic and technological challenges of the twenty-first century, they will start with learning how to grapple with more than the question of what comes next in the checklist and with developing the intellectual foundations—the thinking and reasoning skills—of the naval profession.

[Part I]
THE SEMINAR

1

RELAX, THERE IS
NO NAVAL UNIVERSITY

At the home of American naval education in Annapolis, Maryland, the third deck of Nimitz Library at the U.S. Naval Academy is about as far away from Bancroft Hall as a midshipman can get. "Mother B" is often claimed as the largest dormitory in the world, where roughly four thousand midshipmen spend a large part of their time in professional development, studying, or sleeping. The library on the Yard has multiple purposes beyond the strictly scholarly. As a nod to modern "student services," in recent years a coffee bar was installed on the first floor, and computers and wireless service offer convenience between classes. The third deck is still generally the quiet place where midshipmen, and in particular the new plebes, can escape for a respite from the prying eyes of upperclassmen. Located at that altitude, alongside the resting plebes, is the home of the Naval Academy's Special Collections & Archives.

A little-recognized but valuable place for historical and professional research, the archives contain a unique and often forgotten part of the earliest history of education in the U.S. Navy. When Secretary of the Navy George Bancroft, a noted historian and professor himself, created the Naval School at Annapolis in 1845, the initial cost of starting the school included the seeds of a library, beginning with a little over two hundred volumes. In this initial group of books was a text published about five decades earlier in Great Britain entitled *An Essay on the Duty and Qualifications of a Sea Officer*, by Royal Navy veteran James Ramsay. The original copy of that book, a third edition printing from 1790, is available for midshipmen, faculty, and researchers to view today. On the pages between the aged covers of the volume we find the English language's very first published reflection on naval professionalism and the requirements of naval officership.[1]

In 1760, a century and a half before the forger and historical con man Augustus Buell fabricated the "Qualifications of a Naval Officer," which he pretended was written by John Paul Jones and which midshipmen have been memorizing for generations despite its false provenance, James Ramsay wrote the original text of his essay.[2] When Ramsay was serving as a surgeon on board one of His Majesty's ships, a friend asked him to provide some advice for a young man who was looking to earn a commission. The original was not much longer than a substantial letter to a friend. In 1789, after several cruises as a chaplain, the Reverend Ramsay was motivated to rewrite and expand his original missive, this time constructing a well-organized and clearly argued treatise on naval professionalism. The expanded second edition appeared in 1790, with the third edition following at the end of that same year with some small adjustments. It remained the most significant publication on the subject for decades and was clearly a required text for the library of any newly founded naval educational institution.[3]

Ramsay's reflection on professionalism runs across a wide sea. He assures aspiring naval officers that they must do more than simply memorize their tasks and learn the step-by-step methods of a ship at sea. He laments that so many officers are capable of the basics of seamanship or navigation, or even combat action, but cannot think creatively or solve more complex problems. This type of officer "knows nothing of the principles of his art; and if any difficulty arises, in which experience has not before suggested a remedy, he can draw none from his store of general knowledge; nor at once apply the fundamental rules of his profession."[4] The way to overcome the risks of becoming this kind of practical officer, according to Ramsay, was to study the profession. This meant dedicating time to not only the doctrine and processes necessary for success on board ship but also personal study in a range of topics to broaden the mind and create critical reasoning skills.

Among the essay's sections on shiphandling, learning how to signal, an admiral's responsibilities, and "French bottoms," the author repeatedly returns to the professional requirement for self-education. He emphasizes the importance of studying history—the history of the service and of one's own nation but also the histories of potential adversaries and allies—to better understand the world in which a navy operates. In addition, as a true liberal arts man, Ramsay reminds aspiring officers of the need to study the sciences and mathematics and to keep up to date on these pursuits. This study might occur on one's own, by reading or working at it while at sea, but also should occur ashore when the officer has slightly more time for a focused pursuit of knowledge.[5]

Reverend Ramsay himself spent many years at sea and, as a chaplain, helped to teach midshipmen, junior officers, and Sailors, about their professional responsibilities. He mentored future admirals and captains and in his spare time was an active and ardent abolitionist who helped move the British Empire toward ending slavery and the slave trade. Two and a half centuries later, his advice is as sound for young women and men who aspire to a naval career in the twenty-first century as it was in the eighteenth. Personal professional study and discussion and group learning with mentors and peers are just as vital as attending the right schools and having the right codes placed in one's service record.

————

Almost two hundred years ago, during the presidency of Andrew Jackson, a period emerged in U.S. naval history that some historians have termed an "age of naval enlightenment." The first two decades after the refounding of the Navy and Marine Corps in 1798 saw four naval conflicts: the Quasi-War with France, First Barbary War, War of 1812, and Second Barbary War. It was a busy time for naval officers. The Jackson years brought a period of relative peace for the U.S. Navy, a period of reflection and professionalization.[6]

With less combat and fewer deployments, officers began considering the details of their service more closely. Sailors assigned to the Brooklyn Navy Yard took inspiration from the lyceum movement that had spread across Europe and created intellectual societies that put on lectures and debates and created libraries. In 1833 they established the U.S. Naval Lyceum in a small building on the base. The organization, dominated by junior officers, wrote in their constitution: "We, the Officers of the Navy and Marine Corps, in order to promote the diffusion of useful knowledge, to foster a spirit of harmony and a community of interest in the service, and to cement the links which unite us as professional brethren, have formed ourselves into a Society, to be denominated 'The United States Naval Lyceum.'"[7] Their effort was twofold. First, they looked to establish a museum of artifacts, art, and curiosities that naval officers collected from their deployments across the seven seas. Second, they established the *Naval Magazine* to discuss the pressing issues of the day. This was not an official naval organization and was not organized by the government but instead was created by officers who believed that being a professional meant studying and learning about the profession. They felt that they could accomplish this best through both personal, private study and group learning.

For two years the *Naval Magazine* was at the forefront of naval profession-alism and criticism. Subjects for discussion included the military promotion sys-tem and rank structure, the introduction of new technology like steam power, the importance of education and a naval academy, and strategic and geopolitical sub-jects. Unfortunately, the maintenance of the museum and building that housed the lyceum appears to have taken up a majority of the funds, and the magazine ceased publication in 1837. But the ideals of innovation and reform were alive. One of the magazine's pseudonymous authors wrote, "The spirit of the times and the necessities of the navy loudly declare that change is requisite. We cannot remain as we are."[8]

The Naval Lyceum lived beyond the last issue of the magazine. It continued to host lectures and talks on the vital naval subjects of the day, and the collection of the museum grew into an important repository. Officers held group discussions, and there were question-and-answer periods after the lectures. The *New York Times* described the lyceum as "a commendable little institution in every sense."[9] The members who began the organization as junior officers rose through the ranks and became important naval leaders of the Mexican-American War and the Civil War. While the *Naval Magazine* receded into the past and the museum lecture series and discussions slowed, the members of the group moved on and commanded Amer-ica's first steam-powered warships and led its growing responsibilities on the global stage. The lyceum, with its dedication to learning and professionalism, established an intellectual foundation for naval officers who looked to improve their service and ensure that the quest of professional knowledge that it embodied did not end.

Following the end of the American Civil War, the United States continued a pattern that has been displayed throughout its history by dramatically cutting back on naval spending. The war between the states, reconstructing the nation in its wake, and the promise of continued expansion westward guided the American populace to a continental focus. This internal focus led to cuts in the size and capabilities of the Navy. Many naval officers saw it as a decade of neglect.

In October of 1873 fifteen of these officers came together on the grounds of the U.S. Naval Academy, just as a group had in Brooklyn. Senior and junior com-missioned Navy officers, warrant officers, and marines, they began as a discussion group to debate naval affairs and national and international issues. They named their group the United States Naval Institute. Many of the early meetings included discussion of papers, which the members prepared and presented, followed by a sometimes raucous group comment-and-discussion session. The papers turned out to be quite good, and the discussion period afterward developed everyone's critical and strategic thinking about the key challenges of the era. The institute's members decided to publish their own journal containing the best of the papers and some of the commentary. In December 1874, they named the journal *The Papers and Proceedings of the United States Naval Institute*, today simply titled U.S. Naval Institute *Proceedings*.[10]

Early members of the institute included officers who would have an enormous impact on the U.S. Navy and Marine Corps. Stephen Luce was one of the first officers to present a paper to the group. He is best known as the greatest advocate for, and founding president of, the U.S. Naval War College. His virtual invention of graduate-level American professional military education has had an impact on strategic thought and military and naval affairs that ripples across generations. Another early member was then-commander Alfred Thayer Mahan. Mahan is known to most students of military history for his strategic writing and his famous book *The Influence of Sea Power upon History, 1660–1873*. He was one of the institute's earliest presidents. He began his publishing career with an essay on naval education in the pages of *Proceedings*. From Civil War officers like Adm. David Dixon Porter to the future leaders of the U.S. Navy in the 1898 Spanish-American War, such as W. T. Sampson and George Dewey, the organization grew rapidly. The articles published in *Proceedings* questioned the status quo and raised American knowledge of naval affairs as the country recovered from the Civil War and returned its attention to the larger world, and to the sea. At the same time, the comment-and-discussion format encouraged professional exchanges between officers and developed group learning.[11]

The Naval Institute and *Proceedings* began primarily as a place for junior and midcareer officers to express their ideas and advocate for reform. Over time it continued that tradition but also became a place for thought leaders, from senior admirals to established academics, to debate the issues with upstart junior officers and military critics who looked to move in new directions. The organization officially adopted the following mission: "To provide an independent forum for those who dare to read, think, speak, and write in order to advance the professional, literary, and scientific understanding of sea power and other issues critical to national defense."

The quest to develop the naval mind and the strategic and critical reasoning necessary to face a changing world is not solely an American effort. In the late eighteenth and early nineteenth centuries, the French navy had developed an elaborate and often formal system of educating officers throughout a career. It was such a complex system that the British naval attaché in Paris once testified that "the

English had no system of naval education, and the French had too much system."[12] Forty years after the group of officers met in Annapolis to form the Naval Institute, another group gathered in discussion in Hampshire, England. These officers of the Royal Navy saw the approach of the Great War and feared that their service was unprepared. They met, as then-commander Reginald Plunkett said, to develop "some means of regenerating service intellects before Armageddon."[13] These British sailors were focused on their own officer corps, which they believed needed a greater understanding of naval affairs and war as the United Kingdom approached the looming conflict.

Inspired by Adm. Sir Herbert Richmond and the noted civilian strategist and historian Sir Julian Corbett, they founded what was originally thought of as a correspondence society. The purpose was to bring junior officers together in discussions for their own self-improvement. In 1913 they began publication of a journal titled *Naval Review*. There was significant official resistance from the newly established Naval War Staff, and in World War I the Admiralty ordered the *Review* to cease publication. However, editor W. H. Henderson continued to collect material and even circulated some of it to members in the original spirit of a "correspondence society." At the end of the war the *Review* began publication again, including the material Henderson had collected, to ensure there wasn't a loss of lessons learned from the conflict.[14]

When publication began again in 1919, Henderson's opening article specifically took inspiration from the Americans' Naval Institute but looked to take a uniquely British tack. Concerns that expressing contrarian views would have a negative impact on the careers of the junior officers, who were their target audience, led to a unique editorial policy. Where *Proceedings* has a clear editorial requirement for authors to write under their own names, and the *Naval Magazine* encouraged the use of pseudonyms, the *Naval Review* elected not to use bylines at all. Articles were considered "from the membership," and the editors diligently protected the contributors. Much like *Proceedings*, *Naval Review* has continued publication into the twenty-first century and helps guide naval thinking on the opposite side of the Atlantic, developing even more naval minds.[15]

The examples provided by Reverend Ramsay's *Essay on the Duty and Qualifications of a Sea Officer*, the Naval Lyceum, the Naval Institute, and the *Naval Review* all point to the key concept that personal study and group learning and debate have been central elements of naval professionalism across centuries. Despite the examples offered to us through history, the U.S. Navy and Marine Corps approach to naval learning and intellectual development in the twenty-first century tends to be focused on classrooms and schoolhouses. Whether attending a war college for mandatory Joint Professional Military Education or taking advantage of the small number of scholarships and opportunities at civilian universities, today's naval officers rarely see education and professional study as something that belongs in the fleet. But it does.

While we are all aware of the dictum that every Marine is a rifleman, and we are often reminded of the "warfighter" responsibilities of Sailors across the fleet, it is also true that every leader is a teacher. And the very best professional officers of the sea services are beyond just teachers, they are professors of practice who bring more than procedural knowledge and a detailed eye for compliance and administration, they approach our profession with intellect and curiosity, and they instill that in the other Sailors and Marines in their wardrooms, ready rooms, and work centers.

2

READING A PROFESSIONAL ARTICLE

JOINING THE CONVERSATION

Naval professionals are trained to read primarily for information. At the very beginning of their careers, they learn the drink-from-a-fire-hose approach to consuming information from messages (printed in all caps), briefings, memoranda, technical publications, operating manuals, instructions, notices, email, PowerPoint slides, websites, newspapers, magazines, and social media. They read quickly to find out what they need to know, absorb it or note it, and then move on. In the age of the computer and the Internet, they use highly advanced search tools to locate what they need extremely quickly, without having to browse or dig around. "Google" has become a verb, and scrolling is now something people do impatiently (where's the BLUF, doggone it?), if they bother to do it all (no time to scroll, click the next link). If people are honest with themselves, they have to admit that a lot, if not most, of their reading activity takes the form of casual scanning while multitasking.

You have decided, however, to participate in a seminar to further your intellectual development as a naval professional. That is a serious undertaking, and it requires a different kind of reading. The naval mind has to read for ideas, concepts, and, above all, argument. To that end, it is helpful to think of reading an article as engaging in a conversation, to imagine yourself as a partner in serious dialogue with the author. At its deepest level, reading is simply a conversation between you and the writer. Of course, reading does not have the immediacy and dynamic give-and-take of in-person conversation because it lacks the richness and nuance of gesture, body language, and tone of voice. Nonetheless, to approach reading as conversation helps you move away from the common notion that reading is little more than the passive absorption of content stored in and displayed by an impersonal medium—a book, a blog, a paper page, a glowing screen. Such a view of reading can lead you to forget that a person, a fellow human being with flesh and blood and thoughts, wrote the words you see on the page or screen. The author is usually a stranger distant in space and often distant in time, so imagine that you are having a dialogue for the first time with someone you've never met and would likely never be able to meet. That's one of the awesome benefits of reading. Serious dialogue requires serious listening, attentiveness, and effort. It is the same with reading for argument. It's hard work, but it can yield wisdom and a sense of deep satisfaction—even joy.

Every article and essay included in this book makes an argument or a professional point that it wants you, the reader, to think about and make your own. Even if you think that what you are reading is a straightforward, simple narrative, there is still a reason the author wants you to read that story, and the choices the author made in telling it constitute an argument below the surface. Naval authors, whether historians, serving professionals, or veterans and contemporary scholars, don't sit down to simply offer you a laundry list of facts that increase the sum total of data stored in your brain. They want you to hear what they are saying and to agree with a certain argument about that topic. Otherwise, there would be very little point to the hard work and time that it takes to write on professional subjects. While reading and writing seem solitary, they are actually a community effort because it takes both the mind of the writer and the mind of the reader to complete the activity. As we already said, it is a conversation.

In this chapter, we offer some advice on how to engage in intellectual reading of naval professional writings. While we write these suggestions with the articles contained in this book's second part in mind, they can also be used generally with respect to everything that your mind consumes, from short pieces on the Internet to entire books.

Part One: Preparing with a Smart Skim

You need to answer two important questions before you can deeply engage in the conversation with the author. First, "what is this about?" and second, "what is the main argument?" A quick and relatively easy way to get provisional answers to these is to skim the essay, article, or book. We say provisional because your thoughts on these questions may not be the same after a close reading of the work. However, everyone needs somewhere to begin.

Start your skim with the easy stuff. Read the title, then look over the essay, and read any of the subtitles or headings inside the work. Sometimes authors use these to demarcate sections of their essay, and quickly reading over them will give you a sense of how the essay is structured. You might also identify what kinds of evidence the author uses. This portion of the skim is also when we academics really "nerd out" by checking over the footnotes, endnotes, or list of sources. The notes convey a sense of the depth of research by showing whether and how extensively the author gives credit to others' ideas and work. An article based on the material in a single book is rather different from an article in which facts or ideas have been corroborated or compared across multiple sources.

After the quick overview, continue the skim by reading for ideas. Read the introduction of the essay. Usually this is the first paragraph, but some authors stretch into a second paragraph, using the first as a "scene setter" and then getting to their point or their argument, in the second. This is where a reader should be looking for the thesis statement, which is academic-speak for what the author is claiming to be the case and why it matters (the "so what"). Once you've read the introduction, skip all the way to the end and read the conclusion. Often an author makes a clear statement of their main argument again in the conclusion. Additionally, a good conclusion will serve as a summary of where the essay has taken the reader. It's the debrief, to use naval jargon. Reading the introduction followed by the conclusion before reading the rest of the essay should help you answer those two basic questions we mentioned above.

If the article was written decades ago, be attuned to context and do not assume that the author's concerns are the same as those of the present. Remember that he or she may have been writing to a different audience in a different time. Who is the author and what does/did he or she do? To whom is the author writing, and when, and where? To what or to whom is the author responding? What are the circumstances, the big events, the pressing issues at the time of writing? These questions will help you develop an appreciation for the author's perspective, which you might even try to adopt in your imagination. For example, it helps to know that William Sims struggled to reform naval gunnery, that he wrote "Military Conservatism" at the end of a long career, that he wrote in 1922 before the U.S. Navy was a world-class force, and so on. It would be unrealistic, therefore, to expect that he could possibly anticipate the circumstances in which today's U.S. Navy finds itself, but it is illuminating to realize that some of the problems he describes have persisted to the present and are at least one hundred years old. Doing just a little bit of background research can aid tremendously in reading and working through an article's argument.

If you have the time and the interest, an additional skimming step can be useful but is not necessary. Similar to reading the subtitles or headings internal to the essay, reading quickly over the first sentence of each paragraph offers a basic navigational chart that tells you where the essay will take you. If the essay is well written, these topic sentences tell you what the rest of the paragraph is about. A complete skim, then, involves reading the introduction, the topic sentences, and the conclusion. It might require a brief detour for background. Such an approach enables you to determine in only a few minutes the topic of the essay, its main argument, and a sense of how that argument will be made. With those pieces of information in mind, you are ready for the main effort: close reading.

Part Two: Close Reading

Begin reading from the start. Yes, read the introduction again. It won't take long, and it will get you into the rhythm that the author has worked hard to construct. Remember to read (i.e., "listen") primarily in order to understand, not necessarily with a view to agreeing or disagreeing. Be teachable; embrace the possibility that the author might expand your knowledge and understanding. Have an open mind, setting aside your own assumptions and biases (easy to say, hard to do). Regarding a controversial topic on which you have strongly held opinions, allow that the author might be right and you might be wrong or at least not entirely right.

Think actively about what you are reading. Look for patterns, similar statements, or repetitions. In addition, look for contradictions or places where the author's argument seems to weaken. Don't meekly or lazily accept the evidence at face value but rather think about how (or even whether) it supports the argument. If something doesn't seem right, make a note of it. You don't have to sort out the contradictions or anomalies immediately, and you will go back to them after you're done reading the essay all the way through. If you are struggling with a text, there may be many reasons for the difficulty. It could be that you are tired or distracted or both. Perhaps the author's prose is full of jargon that you do not know, or its style, coming from a different cultural context, strikes you as antiquated or impenetrable. Maybe you find the author, subject, or text to be offensive, boring, tedious, ridiculous, or irrelevant—or all of those. Be patient and persevere.

It is OK to pause once in a while to see how the pieces of the argument are fitting together. In fact, we encourage it. Take a breath at the end of a paragraph or section and think about what the author has been telling you. Ask yourself about the patterns you have identified and why they are there. Consider whether the author may have intended them. A momentary pause gives you a chance to quickly double back if you realize something was important and want to underline or annotate it. Or perhaps you want to amend or erase a marking because you realize that something you thought was contradictory is no longer so.

Ask lots of questions as you progress through the article, even addressing the author by name. For example, "What are you trying to say here, Al?"; "What are you assuming in order to make this claim, Wayne?"; "Jim, what exactly do you mean by 'transforming leader'?" It can be amusing to indulge in a level of familiarity that you would never in a million years actually assume, but don't get carried away. The adage "Familiarity breeds contempt" applies to reading too, and it is much easier to verge into disrespect when the author is present only on the page or screen. The rules of civil conversation still apply, no matter how distant the parties are in time and space.

The most challenging texts can be the most rewarding. They can push you to see things from a different perspective, cause you to ask questions that have never occurred to you before, challenge you to clarify your own thinking. For that to happen, though, you need to ask yourself why you object to or agree with a certain passage. You have to identify where you find something to be confusing and why, then try to clear up the confusion. Wrestle with the text. Disentangle the knotty parts. Draw diagrams or flow charts to visualize the argument. When reading about geopolitics, read the article with a map or globe or Google Earth nearby. Even go 3-D if you can: for example, when reading Wayne Hughes' "Missile Chess," pull out a chess board and set up and play the game he describes. Good reading is effortful reading, so make the effort and have faith that it will be worth it. You may suddenly find yourself staring at the bulkhead and having to shake yourself free from being deep in thought about a particular point in the essay. That's a great moment because it means that you are engaged in conversation with the author.

As you progress through the article, try bringing other writers into the dialogue. That is, try to connect and compare what you are reading with material you have read before, especially other articles in the seminar. Connecting something you've never read before with things you've previously learned or discussed can help you comprehend and retain both new and old more firmly than otherwise. When you read Dale Rielage's "How We Lost the Great Pacific War," try to make connections between that article and William Sims' "Military Conservatism." This may happen in group discussion too, and so much the better. Of course, relating what you read to your own experience will make the article more personally meaningful, especially if the argument deals heavily in abstract generalities. Use particular cases from your own experience or knowledge of history to relate to and test an author's claims. Be wary, however, of falling into the mistake of assuming that your experience is the sole criterion for the validity of an argument.

If you are stuck on a difficult passage, try putting it in your own words, creating analogies, and using metaphors. Think of examples from your own experience or education that either support or undermine the author's point. Paraphrasing can be a powerful way to clarify not only the author's but also your own thoughts. It can also help lodge the words and ideas of anything you read more firmly in your memory. Be on guard, however, against distorting an author's ideas through inaccurate paraphrase. That will lead to confusion, error, and misunderstanding. Accurate paraphrases can be difficult if you find yourself objecting to an author's ideas, and it can be exceptionally difficult if you don't quite know why you object. You can confidently claim to understand an author (or anyone else, really) only when you can state the author's ideas in your own words in such a way that the author would say "Yes, that's what I'm saying." Of course, it may be impossible to check with the author—for example, A. T. Mahan, R.I.P.—but it is worth making the effort so that one's agreement or disagreement is as clear as possible.

Part Three: The Debrief

Once you have read the entire essay, it is time to reflect on what you have learned. The final step of a good intellectually and professionally engaged reading is to conduct a debrief for both yourself and the author. This is where your markings and annotations will prove their worth because now you will examine not only the article but also your responses to it. Your copy of the article has become a record of conversation between you and the author.

Beginning your debrief takes you all the way back to your initial observations about the work. At the start, you answered two questions for yourself: what was the topic, and what was the main argument. The start of your post-reading reflection should take you back to those observations and help you determine if you were right. It is not uncommon to finish an essay and realize that it was about something slightly different from what you originally thought. Or sometimes you will discover that there is a much clearer thesis statement buried somewhere toward the end of the body of an essay. Determining what the author was actually trying to convey to you, now that you have finished reading all of the essay, can easily move you to modify or entirely change your idea of what the essay was about.

After re-answering the questions about topic and thesis, consider the author's evidence and the logic of the argument. The second part of the debrief is determining not what the essay was arguing but how the author made the argument and then to determine if it was effective. You may have discovered logical fallacies or misinterpretations and inadequacies of the evidence. The author may have convinced you by laying out a clear thesis supported by rigorously logical reasoning. Perhaps the author relied heavily (too heavily?) on a narrative or a story that leads the reader toward the conclusion of the argument.

Finally it is time to consider what you really think about all of this. The first and the second parts of the debrief are focused on the author and what he or she thinks. But as we said earlier, a good professional reading is a conversation. The final element of the process is to determine not only what you think of how the author argued but also what you think of the argument itself. It may be that you agree with the main point of the essay, but you think the author did a poor job of supporting their idea even if you agree with it. Or you might disagree with the argument while admitting that the author's approach was clearly reasoned and impressively researched. Whether you agree or disagree, be able to explain why.

Test your mastery of the reading by boiling it all down. Write a summary of the article and your response to it. Aim for a summary that you could deliver in two minutes or even less (the so-called elevator pitch). What can you omit without sacrificing accuracy? To put it another way, what can't you leave out without distorting the dialogue between you and the author? Can you succinctly state the central claim(s) of the article? Can you identify what you find compelling or unconvincing? If you can craft an accurate, clear summary that answers all of those questions, then you can be confident that you have a solid grasp of the article. Be prepared, of course, to respond to follow-up questions about the author's claims or your own.

After the debrief, reflect on how the article connects with other things that you have read or discussed with your peers. Think about what the essay means for your life as a naval professional. Ask what insights, questions, or points of view you can now add to your store of wisdom. Consider how the ideas relate to your experience in the fleet or your thoughts on leadership, professional conduct, or military strategy, operations, and tactics.

Some Tips and Techniques

Find time. To repeat, good reading is effortful reading. There is no getting around the fact that it takes time, so the most important thing that you can do right away is fence off some time for you to do the reading (and sometimes the re-reading) needed to prepare for discussion. It is prudent not to leave such reading for the end of the day because you will probably be too tired, distracted, and stressed to read closely and think clearly. Pay yourself first. Try starting your day with serious reading, when you are most alert and least likely to be distracted or interrupted. Wake up forty-five minutes to an hour earlier so that you have time to read and think with a (relatively) fresh mind, before the 1,001 tasks and interruptions of the day begin. Resist the temptation to check email and texts before you sit down to read. Take a quick break halfway through for coffee or push-ups—no email!—and then get back to the text.

Find space. Give some thought, too, to choosing a space in which to read. Circumstances might leave you few or no options, especially at sea or in the field, but the idea is the same: minimize distraction to help maximize attention. When it comes to space, preferences vary widely. Some people want as much silence as possible; others prefer a noisy coffeehouse. Some want lots of bright light; others prefer a small cone of light in a dim or dark room. Some want warmth; others want cold. Most prefer to sit—choose a chair that is comfortable but not too comfortable—and a few like to stand. Go with what works best for you. We suggest, though, that your rack is not the place in which to do effortful reading. You will just end up falling asleep a few minutes after you start.

Format and tools. Many of us prefer to read in hard copy, either holding a physical book or magazine or printing out the pages from an online source. Others are perfectly comfortable in the digital world and prefer reading on a e-reader device, tablet, or even a phone. You need to figure out what format works best for you and commit to using it. Although a skim can be done quickly and easily in any format, a close reading requires you to take notes and to mark and annotate the text. If you are reading a physical or digital copy, have by your side a notebook or sheet of paper and a pencil or a pen to write with. If you're a 100 percent digital worker, you'll need to have mastered your device's capacity for annotation, highlighting, and commenting, and don't forget to charge your stylus before you start reading.

Mark up the text. If you have a love affair with highlighters, it's time to break up. Use a pencil instead in order to underline, circle, asterisk, and so on as you read. This facilitates engagement with the text as a conversation with the author, and it makes the text more usable to you during re-reading and discussion. Develop a simple system of marking to help you quickly find passages that are important, problematic, confusing, or simply quotable. Draw a box around the thesis. (No box, no thesis—either there isn't a thesis, or you need to keep looking.) Put an asterisk next to major supporting points. Circle frequently repeated words or phrases—they can be a clue to what the author thinks is important or is struggling with or both. Underline or circle page numbers to locate sections that are especially significant. And so on.

Annotate. You will be an even more active, attentive reader if you annotate as you go, conversing with the author as you comment in the margins or, space permitting, between the lines. (This is another reason to use a pencil instead of a soon-too-dry-to-use neon crayon.) Annotating helps you stay focused on the page and tracking with the argument. There is usually too little space to write extensively, but that is actually a good thing because it keeps you from straying away from the text. It is sufficient to record your reactions, such as: "Good point"; "Really?!"; "Disagree"; "Not shown"; "Need more evidence"; "Does not follow"; "Spot on"; "Wrong"; "Unclear"; "Concur." Use a system of abbreviations to optimize the available space. Also use the margins to refer to other readings and thus enlarge the conversation: for example, "but see Mahan"; "cf. [compare with] Sims 'Mil. Cons.'"; "Stockdale disagrees"; "Turner supports."

Take notes. Actually, take brief notes. If you tend to write lengthy notes, constrain yourself to writing in a smaller space. Fold a sheet of paper in half or use one or two large (5" × 8") index cards. We don't recommend typing notes on a screen unless that function is native to a digital format. If you're reading a paper copy, stay analog. Moving your eyes from paper to screen and your hands from article to keyboard tends to inhibit careful reading.

Look it up. If you encounter a word, a concept, a reference, an allusion that you don't know, look it up. It might be important to the author's argument, and even if it isn't, at least you will have learned something new. Don't try to "wing it" by inferring from context. There are so many free, user-friendly, readily available resources that there is no reason not to invest a little effort in some quick research. Need a dictionary? There's an app for that. Wikipedia? There's an app for that, too. Don't fall into a rabbit-hole of link-clicking, though. If you can't find something in less than five minutes, then note the word or passage for follow-up and move on.

3

BEING IN DIALOGUE
TIPS FOR DISCUSSION AS A PARTICIPANT

When we hear the words "naval leadership," we usually think of things like making hard decisions, giving orders, and a method infused with a bias for action and activity. Discussion, dialogue, and contemplation are often the last things that come to mind. Yet that is exactly what this book is trying to encourage from naval leaders. We want to learn how to use discussion and dialogue to better develop our naval intellect, how to slow down and contemplate the meaning of naval professionalism and the challenges of strategy and maritime policy. Essentially, we want to go against that very bias for action that our naval education and training system is designed to instill in us from day one. This, of course, is both dangerous and a complicated endeavor.

With our professional bias for action comes a relative comfort with, or understanding of, physical danger. But naval leaders must also be willing to deal with and understand intellectual risk. It's complicated because while leaders should retain a bias for action, they must temper it with wise judgment, disciplined imagination, and healthy skepticism. We can indeed think and ponder on our own in whatever solitude we can carve out for ourselves, but it remains a fact that we are fundamentally social beings who have evolved to inform our reason and sharpen our judgment in the company of others. As we have noted, we reason not in monologue but in dialogue. Discussion protects us from trapping ourselves in the echo chamber of our own mind or our professional biases. It keeps us from getting stale, from thinking of ourselves as infallible, and from obsessing over our own ideas. Indeed, discussion does quite the opposite. It keeps us fresh, humble, and open to new ideas and ways of thinking. Discussion keeps naval leaders honest with themselves and with others. Is that dangerous? Possibly. Complicated? Maybe. Necessary? Absolutely.

Most naval officers are educated as engineers and scientists, and we often hold up the scientific method as the bedrock of how we are men and women of reason. But there is another path to reasoning, besides the quantitative collection and analysis of data to prove a theory. Discussion itself is a process of thinking and reasoning. The activity of dialogue itself is beneficial, with or without the delivery of information or the arrival at firm conclusions or scientific facts. In truth, much of what naval leaders have to deal with in their careers is not scientific but instead human. This requires a capacity for ethical reasoning, for strategic reasoning, for working through a problem to a not-quite-perfect but sensible answer. At its heart, this requires us to be human and to interact well with other humans.

As we have already suggested, we do not tend to train or teach naval leaders how to participate in effective discussion, how to build on each other's ideas in dialogue, or how to be contemplative. The purpose of this chapter is to offer some guidelines that might help develop these skills for those who are going to participate in discussion. They are brief and are meant to offer a starting point for a process. As with most things, from practicing the option offense in football to working the landing pattern, we truly learn by practice.

Examples of Dialogue and Discussion

The history of naval thought has clear examples of the kind of dialogue and discussion necessary for the development of a naval mind. These come both from our historical roots and even from fiction. In the captain's cabin of HMS *Surprise*, Capt. Jack Aubrey often engaged his officers in professional discussions over a meal, even giving lessons on the selection of the "lesser of two weevils." The examples of naval intellectual institutions from chapter 1 offer their own precedents in American history.

The Naval Lyceum of the antebellum U.S. Navy and the Naval Institute of the years after the Civil War offer us inspiration. Both organizations were founded as an opportunity for officers to discuss the naval profession. They included commissioned officers, midshipmen, warrant officers, and marines. At the simplest retelling of their founding, they were a group of officers who decided to get together to share their ideas. In the case of the lyceum it was in a free space at the Brooklyn Navy Yard, and in the case of the Naval Institute it was an empty classroom where College Creek joins the Severn River in Annapolis.

At first, the officers who were gathering in Annapolis did not even have a name for their group. It was just something they started doing. But the organization grew out of the need for discussion and dialogue. After getting together, the assembled group felt that they needed some direction, and many of the members had interesting pet projects and ideas they were mulling over. One of the members suggested that someone begin by writing a paper and presenting it to the group, which they could then discuss. This was not a formal search for publication-worthy material, even though this effort would eventually birth the journal *Proceedings*. Instead, it was simply a means to give them all something to talk about. The session of "comment and discussion" was the centerpiece of the developing institute. In fact, the dialogue itself was of such importance that one of the members was responsible for transcribing the give-and-take, and in the early years of *Proceedings* the discussion itself would be printed after the article. This lives on today in the pages of *Proceedings* in a modified form, published under the title "Comment & Discussion," which other journals call "Letters to the Editor." The entire exercise was a voyage of discovery, for the paper's author but also for the participants.

We advocate for this kind of discussion, the voyage of discovery. It is founded on the Socratic principles of dialogue and dialectical exchange. The idea is to keep our minds open, to listen to the other minds in the group, and to build on each other's ideas and reason through them. Being right is not the point, and it is not a debate to score points. This will be a challenge for many of us. We are often used to the version of conversation where, rather than listening, we use the time while someone else is talking to formulate what we are going to say next. To lead these kinds of discussions, you will need to see yourself not as a discussion leader but instead as a discussion facilitator.

Growing a Discussion

While Annapolis remains the home of the Naval Institute, the organization no longer holds the kinds of free-form discussions that were central to its founding. There is another institution in Annapolis on College Creek, however, that offers us another example: St. John's College. The famous Johnnies, as they are known inside the high granite walls of the Naval Academy, have spent decades working to perfect the art of dialogue as well as their croquet skills. In the 1930s, from the other side of King George Street, St. John's initiated the Great Books and dialogue-based learning curriculum it is known for today under the leadership of Stringfellow Barr and Scott Buchanan. In 1968 Barr gave a talk in California on the subject of dialogue and learning through discussion in which he listed ten "rules of thumb" that provide us with a solid starting point for leading an effective naval discussion.[1] What follows here are Barr's guidelines in naval form, and we recommend them as your rules of engagement for participating in productive discussion.

No speeches. There is a temptation, one that is supported by how naval professionals conduct their qualification oral boards and how many of our classrooms work, to aim for a complete and comprehensive response to any question. Instead of responding to a question with shorter observations, which our fellow discussants can build upon, we respond to a question as completely as possible. In short, our bias for action and activity drives us to attempt a complete answer from the very start. However, as Barr writes, "the effort to be too complete is often self-defeating." As a participant, you must avoid the temptation that we all have, professors especially, to rattle on in an attempt to cover all possibilities. Instead, make a brief addition to the conversation and see where that additional piece of evidence or wrinkle takes the group.

Open yourself up to the wild ideas. Barr reminds us that the Greek historian Herodotus claimed that the Persians "deliberated while drunk and decided while sober." This reinforces that, at the start of a discussion, the most outlandish ideas or assertions can often lead in the most productive directions, even if that direction results in eventually reining them in. As naval professionals we are often cautioned to find workable answers or to be practical. But both famed navalists Capt. Alfred Thayer Mahan and Adm. William Sims rebelled against what they called "the practical officer." Instead they insisted that naval professionals need to embrace the spirit of innovation and new ideas.[2] In the case of a professional discussion in your work center, wardroom, or ready room, the wild ideas are often the best ones to start with. As the conversation develops there's always time to sober up and think more about realistic concerns.

Interrupt and ask questions. On the radio, we are careful to maintain discipline and not to interrupt or talk over others. In the polite company of a dinner with your in-laws, it is considered equally rude to interrupt and shout questions at each other. But a good professional dialogue often thrives on the kind of give-and-take that comes from an interruption with a pointed question. This is another place to remember that we aren't talking about monologues. Instead, a quick attempt to clarify or to ask a question that indicates a flaw in the reasoning might seem to derail what the speaker is saying, but it might sacrifice the speaker's monologue for the betterment of the overall discussion.

Embrace the apparent chaos. Keeping things short, interrupting each other, blurting out questions. These discussion techniques may seem to present chaos at first. But then again, a little bit of intellectual chaos can be quite healthy. As with any valuable endeavor, it takes practice to master the techniques of mentally stimulating discussion. As Barr's speech in California points out, "inexperienced dancers on a ballroom floor and inexperienced skaters on an ice rink also collide. Experience brings a sixth sense in Socratic dialectic too." If the discussion seems to take on the rowdiness of a ready room sharing sea stories from the last port call, that might actually be OK. Embrace a little bit of the bedlam at first, and after a few discussions the group is likely to find its battle rhythm of give-and-take and group reasoning.

Pay attention and listen. The quickest way to kill a discussion is to pull out a phone or open a computer. Put it all away. The real measure of a good conversation is how well all the participants are listening rather than what everyone is saying. Without attentive listening, there is a higher likelihood that you descend into a session of mini speeches rather than a discussion. In a dialogue, it really does not matter where the idea comes from or who says it. What matters is that the idea is broached and that everyone hears it and can build on it. There is no enemy in a discussion, no one to battle. So stow the warfighter identity at the door and listen as you participate.

Be ready to disagree. Disagreement is fundamental to the process of a dialectic. However, disagreement is not the same thing as an argument or a fight. Do not avoid disagreement but instead address it head on. It is often the best way to reason toward a bigger idea. Barr warns to avoid the temptation to "agree to disagree" because it is the fastest way to kill a productive conversation that may actually lead somewhere. If things become heated, the group may need to take a breather. Or, if you reach the end of your allotted time, an idea or disagreement may have to be tabled. However, in the interest of developing our naval minds, never let a good and honest disagreement go to waste.

Follow the conversation wherever it wants to go. When you begin a professional discussion, everyone in the group is going to have a preconceived notion of where it is going to go. We will all have an initial plan for what we want to talk about, or what we think is most important from the subject matter. Be ready to give that up, however, as soon as the discussion begins. Barr says it best: "The name of the game is not instructing one's fellows, or even persuading them, but thinking with them and trusting the argument to lead to understanding, sometimes to very unexpected understandings." If, at the end of a discussion, a participant feels that important subjects were not covered, that's a good time to bring it up and perhaps suggest scheduling another discussion to tackle those issues that were left behind. However, do your best to avoid our often-unavoidable naval tendency to instill discipline on the conversation and follow a checklist of topics or subjects.

You facilitate a discussion; you don't lead one. In the early years of the Naval Institute, each meeting was assigned a chair who was responsible for managing the discussion. The chair called the meeting to attention and introduced the speaker who had written a paper and then called on members who wanted to ask questions or make statements in the comment and discussion afterward. This approach is often required in larger settings, such as meetings with more than a dozen people, but it also stifles real dialogue in a smaller group. In our efforts to develop the naval mind, we think that smaller groups are often more productive. For this reason, in the Naval Academy History Department we try to keep our seminar groups to a dozen midshipmen or fewer, while many of our other classes could be twice that size. In a small group, the organizer or convenor of the meeting should see themselves as a facilitator rather than a leader. Part of the job is to keep these ten suggestions in mind, and help your fellow discussants remember them as well with an occasional nudge or kindly worded suggestion. Part of the job is to come up with a couple of questions that you hope will spark conversation and to have them ready. We'll discuss more of this in the next chapter.

Become intellectual wingmen. If we become more practiced at listening, and we in turn begin asking better questions of each other, more than just professional reasoning and learning will happen. There is the possibility that a wholly new group of relationships will begin. Developing our naval minds together can change our identities and can take us from being just shipmates or coworkers to becoming professional compatriots and even eventually developing truly deep friendships. This has the possibility of reinforcing the morale of our ships, squadrons, and units, and in developing a better and deeper understanding of one another, we also become more cohesive and better able to work together in the dangerous situations that define our profession.

Be ready to laugh. This is supposed to be both intellectually developmental and fun. Barr reminds us that our conversations should maintain "playfulness and sense of the comic," just as Socrates often did, and that "the truly relevant jest is never out of order." It's not just a matter of keeping it light but a matter of embracing the sometimes raucous and even downright silly environment that every Sailor and Marine sometimes experiences in their work center, wardroom, or ready room. Sailors and Marines are a bit notorious for sarcasm and a good practical joke, so we aren't suggesting anything that isn't already a part of our maritime culture. But it's OK to have fun, even when tackling serious subjects.

Dead-Reckoning through Your Discussion

The U.S. Naval Academy has a long history with our colleagues from across King George Street. It is a history that has sometimes been tense yet also includes a lot of fun, like the annual croquet match. Some alumni who have spent four years on the Yard might bristle at the idea of adopting the ideas of Stringfellow Barr as a path to developing the naval mind. However, we think that his guidelines are incredibly sensible and they largely mirror our own experience in seminar rooms and classrooms for the past several years.

These ten ideas should be seen as guidelines, however. Each discussion group has its own makeup and will develop its own character as the participants get accustomed to one another. Even when we already know each other in a social or professional sense, we often don't know our shipmates in an intellectual sense. Developing that relationship will help build the group. If everyone is keeping these guidelines in mind, just making an attempt at following them without any sense of perfection or checklist following, the group is bound to have productive and enlightening conversations.

Navigating a professional discussion should be an exercise in dead-reckoning. It will be hard to take exact fixes of your positions. The conversation may drift a little over time. Sometimes we will end up in a different place than we intended. However, as opposed to when we're navigating the ship, in this case dead-reckoning will lead us to new discoveries and new ideas. These are the very things that develop the naval mind.

« 4 »

GUIDING A
CONVERSATION
FACILITATING A SEMINAR DISCUSSION

Most of us have been conditioned from youth by our institutions of education and training to believe that learning takes place in the form of one-way transmission from source to receiver. That is, a "sage on a stage" delivers information, or knowledge, or instruction in a procedure or technique to a group of mostly passive listeners, who may or may not be taking notes according to a system that almost all have improvised because none of them have been taught how to take notes. High school, college, graduate school; SWO training, nuke school, flight school; brick-and-mortar, or online—the teacher instructs and the student learns. In naval terms, the person giving the brief is the expert, and everyone else should learn from them. Results can vary widely. If the instructor or briefer is truly engaging, high-energy, and passionate, and the students are truly interested, motivated, and well-prepared, the lecture can be quite effective. If not, the lecture easily becomes an exercise in excruciating boredom. This type of learning, the academic lecture or naval brief, has dominated the pedagogical landscape for centuries as the chief paradigm for transmitting knowledge. It might not be the most effective mode for teaching and learning, but it seems to do the job most of the time, especially if there is consistency, follow-up, and reinforcement.

Another equally ancient form of learning, though, is bi- or multidirectional exchange in dialogue. A method of instruction based on (relentless) question-and-response takes its name from Socrates. Plato, Socrates' student, wrote dialogues. As Aristotle points out in his *Politics*, human beings use their faculty of speech not only to communicate information but also, and more importantly, to figure out what is true or untrue, good or evil, wise or unwise, useful or useless. We are social beings, and we reason best when we reason together, proposing and refining ideas in dialogue with our fellows. Again, results can vary widely. Dialogue marked throughout by clear communication can lead to just laws, wise policy, winning strategy, and effective tactics. On the other hand, conversation masquerading as dialogue may develop and reinforce groupthink that leads to unjust laws, feckless policy, losing strategy, and ineffective tactics. Before you know it, the group is "on the road to Abilene."

In our military culture we tend to think the domain of the "schoolhouse"—whatever its form—is for learning and thinking, and the domain outside it is for doing. Moreover, military culture tends to treat the two domains as mutually exclusive. This book is therefore countercultural because we think that thinking and learning can and should take place beyond the schoolhouse, and the impracticability of lecture should be no obstacle to that effort. A group of professionals out in "the world" can assume responsibility for its own continuing education. They can think and learn outside the school in a seminar that develops knowledge and thought by way of sustained and focused dialogue. To that end, in this section we offer some advice to help you facilitate or lead a meaningful, thoughtful discussion. It is the fruit of years of experience working with undergraduate students (midshipmen) and with academic and military colleagues.

Rules of Engagement

It is worth taking a few moments for a reminder on rules of engagement (ROE). In the last chapter we went into some detail on how discussion group members should think about their participation. However, in addition to those, facilitators should ensure that everyone in the seminar observes the conventions of civil discourse as part of the ROE. In an ideal world these elements of our discussion of ROE would be commonly understood, neither written nor spoken. Unfortunately, we do not live in such a world, and in the military we tend to use speech that is direct to the point of bluntness, frequently without much tact, and quite often "salty." In the seminar room we need to remember to be respectful, positive, open-minded, and even humble. We need to be sure we avoid ad hominem statements and criticize ideas or arguments but not individuals. That also means no insults and avoiding the snark that has tended to creep into our exchanges from the world of social media. And speaking of social media: no screens. Put all of your phones, laptops, tablets, and devices out of sight. There is no such thing as "multitasking." Emailing, texting, and monitoring one's social media will undermine serious engagement in a conversation.

In reality, these are all instances of the Golden Rule. But they are worth stating and reviewing at the first meeting of the seminar. And feel free to remind everyone whenever it seems appropriate (right after a stressful training evolution, for example).

Preparation

On its surface, most facilitators might think: What could be easier than leading a discussion? It's not a lecture, and the members of the group will carry the thing along by their active participation. All you have to do is read the article, come up with a few questions, and pitch them to the group. They'll do the rest. If the discussion starts to lag, you can throw in another question. When the list of questions or the allotted time runs out—whichever comes first—the discussion is over, and people can go home or on watch or back to their never-ending list of things that have to be done yesterday. Sounds easy, right?

Well, not really. Preparing to lead a stimulating, engaging discussion can be just as challenging as preparing to deliver a stimulating, engaging lecture or brief. The pressure is greater, too, for the first discussion in the seminar. While you may be acquainted with most or all of the discussants, you probably do not yet know the group dynamics for this kind of activity. Then, of course, there is the issue of rank or position, whether one is military or civilian. Junior members of the group will usually feel more pressure to do well with superiors watching, which could mean they rush to speak too much or they say nothing at all. And being the lone whatever in a group can add further stress, even if—maybe even especially if—you are the executive officer or commanding officer.

The first step for the facilitator is the obvious one: do the reading. If you have read the article, chapter, or book already, then reread it, closely. Maybe it was something you skimmed at War College months or years ago. You'll likely discover that you missed a thing or two the first time through. You should seek to be the expert in the room on at least that particular text, so try to have an exceptionally firm grasp of the author's argument and, if possible, its context. It is not necessary to be an expert on all the issues raised, but you should understand as well as you can what the author claims and how he or she establishes that claim. Spend some time thinking about and drawing out the connections between the material to be discussed and other readings in the seminar. This can be challenging to do for the first meeting because you have to read a little bit ahead of the group. Once you're past that first meeting, review your notes from earlier discussions and see how the article relates to continuing threads of conversation, look for key points that others have made, recurring questions, and so on. In other words, bring the reading to be discussed into dialogue with the other readings and discussions.

Next, think of and write down a set of questions to discuss. These should go beyond simply asking content or knowledge-based questions that can be answered readily and factually from the reading. The goal is to initiate and sustain discussion, not to run a quiz show or an oral board. The questions should follow the progress of an argument, focus on one or two central themes, and provoke response. Randomly ordered lists of unrelated questions may be better than nothing at all, but they are not optimal. Questions should refer or relate specifically to the reading. Vague, general questions will usually lead to vague, general answers that are not conducive to a conversation focused on the reading and its central ideas. For example, unhelpful, vague question: "What does Mahan say in the reading?" Better question: "Where is Mahan wrong?" Even better: "Mahan concludes that decisive victory in fleet-on-fleet engagement is the goal of any naval power. Why did he say that, and is he right or wrong?"

It is helpful to prime the discussion by drawing attention to the reading at least one day in advance. Priming helps to get a discussion under way more quickly, eliminating or at least minimizing time-wasting chitchat, stutter-step starts, and awkward silences. Here are three useful techniques:

1. A couple of days before the meeting, pose a question and ask for brief (e.g., 100–250 words) responses to it. Review the responses and then refine the question, toss it out, or develop a substantial follow-up question. You could reserve a particularly perceptive, funny, or provocative response for use as an opener. If there are two opposing responses or groups of similar responses, consider using them to open with a brief debate.

2. Ask each member of the group to share two or three questions about the reading. This may help you build a set of questions for discussion, identify areas of common interest, spot issues to wrestle with, or note sensitive topics that may require tactful handling or deliberate avoidance.

3. Ask everyone to share with the rest of the group one problematic or confusing quotation from the reading and one that is notably insightful or clear. Again, this can help you to identify areas on which to focus, either to clarify or to dig into. This also nudges members of the group to read or review the article more carefully instead of merely skimming it a few minutes before walking into the room.

Earlier we told you to put away your devices for the discussion itself, but in preparation you can use technology to great advantage. But much depends on what tools you and the rest of the group have available: email (cumbersome) or Slack (better); a shared document on Google Drive, Dropbox, or Box; a blog with comments open; an online discussion forum. There are many options, and for the sake of convenience and consistency, the group should agree on which tools to use for communication and collaboration and then stick with them. In this case perfect is definitely the enemy of good enough.

Carefully review any input from the group well ahead of time. This is not a task to leave for the last few minutes before the meeting, hurriedly printing whatever you have received and reading it on the way or, worse, just after you sit down and as the group is gathering. (Yes, we have learned that this is not a recipe for success. It may even do harm.) Budget at least fifteen to twenty minutes to analyze the group's premeeting responses and incorporate them into your own notes and questions.

No matter how senior you are, show up early and make sure the room is staged and ready with sufficient seating, adequate lighting, comfortable air temperature, fresh coffee, and so on. As a group, you may have divided up these responsibilities, but it is wise to follow up. Operations, maintenance, and emergencies large and small have a way of causing diligent professionals to forget small chores. As with so much else in our profession, "trust but verify." (Speaking of small chores, bring extra copies of the article with you. Someone might have brought a copy of the latest squadron instruction or change in uniform regulations instead their marked-up pages of the reading. Could be that new ensign, but it easily could be the CO—it's always good to have a spare to share.) Think about where you will sit as the facilitator. Choose a spot from which you can be easily seen and heard, ideally without making you the focus of attention. Sitting at the front of the room with everyone facing you but not each other is obviously not a good way to get discussion going, but it is also sometimes wise to avoid sitting at the head of the table. Circular arrangements are best.

Execution

Show time. Everyone is at the table. It's time to break into the silence, idle chatter, or that animated conversation about the watch bill or flight schedule. You have to interrupt whatever is going on and get things going. The longer you wait, the harder it will be to begin. Use whatever gimmick you are comfortable with: ring a bell, cough, rap the table, play "Anchors Aweigh." Once you have everyone's attention, bring the group up to speed by offering a quick overview of the reading and how it might relate to previous readings and discussions. If you assigned them, thank the group for their premeeting responses and note any significant trends or patterns that emerged. The discussion could start there, but depending on the subject matter, it might be more appropriate to address that material later.

Open the discussion by sharing the most provocative question, comment, or quotation that you have come up with or received. If no one responds right away, try waiting for a few heartbeats before filling the silence with a response of your own or with another question. In our classrooms, we have often found that counting to ten in your head goes a long way. Most people are uncomfortable with silence and would rather break it than endure it. If you are patient, someone will speak up.

As the discussion leader you need to guide the flow of conversation after you have initiated it. Momentum and focus are essential. Sometimes a discussion will take off and move along on its own, with one topic moving easily and naturally into another and with every member of the group fully engaged and contributing. If that happens, be thankful for your good fortune. You cannot expect to be lucky, however, and you need to be ready for moments when a line of conversation slows down or stops altogether as the group decides by unspoken consensus that a question or subject has been adequately addressed or has simply become uninteresting. This is a tricky moment to judge, and you will get better as you learn how the group interacts. Is the topic done? Or are they just clamming up and need a nudge to keep going?

If the question has run its course, introduce a new question or one of the premeeting responses before a pause grows into a full, stifling halt. Be prepared as well, on the other hand, for the opposite problem—namely, so much momentum in one direction that the conversation is in danger of running out of time before it has covered all or most of the significant points of the reading. In that event you have a choice. Do you follow Stringfellow Barr's advice and let it happen because the conversation is so good? Or do you try to steer the discussion tactfully but assertively onto another element of the reading? This is an opportunity for you as the facilitator to shape what kind of group you are leading. In a professional discussion group like this (without a teaching requirement or formal learning objectives or grades) it is up to you to improvise on the spot and adjust course.

Take notes as the discussion progresses. Although everyone should be scribbling down ideas and thoughts, very few people write down what they themselves say, either while they are speaking or soon after they have finished speaking. Most people also assume that they will clearly remember what they have said. Memory is fallible and malleable, however, so a discussion leader should be the chief recorder, too, paying careful attention not only to what is being said but also to who is saying it. Do not try to write everything down as if taking dictation, which inhibits genuine listening anyway. Brief, accurate notes are sufficient for identifying points of connection, agreement, contradiction, ambiguity, and confusion, especially among remarks separated by some time. Why do you need notes? They are especially useful for returning to the topic of discussion after digressions, changes of subject, or interruptions from outside have caused the group to wander far afield. Furthermore, being able to recall who said what allows you to give credit for an insightful statement, a thought-provoking idea, or a penetrating question. If you need to nudge a waning topic, you have someone specific to turn back to and you can ask them to elaborate on something they said earlier.

It is vital that the discussion leader be a careful listener because the appearance of agreement can often mask disagreement and vice versa. We all know that arriving at real consensus can be difficult, but it can be just as difficult to achieve real disagreement. Really good discussions "drill down," teasing out implications, drawing distinctions, clarifying ambiguity, working through complex logic. Does the group keep circling back to a particular issue? Are members of the group talking past each other, without fully understanding what each one is saying? Is the conversation misunderstanding or ignoring an important argument or point in the reading? Are there assumptions and biases that need to be brought into the open and examined? Is agreement or disagreement based on a clear understanding of premises and sound reasoning? Deep listening with such questions in mind will help you take useful notes and identify what the group may need to work through before it considers another subject.

Don't feel obligated to stick to a script or schedule. Be flexible but keep the discussion on topic. Lively discussions may veer into meandering digressions (e.g., sea stories, which will wreck your discussion on a shoal very quickly), bog down in confusion, or circle around a minor issue. When that happens you should lightly but firmly bring the group back to a relevant line of conversation. Speak up and return the group to where it left off or turn its attention to a different question. This is where humor can be very helpful, but that depends on your wit and level of comfort with the group. If a cooling-off period seems necessary, which is not unusual if you have an hour or more put aside for your discussion, take a two- or three-minute break (but staying in the room), reconvene with a brief recap of the discussion so far, and propose a new question or point to address.

Remember to focus on facilitating discussion. If you are a senior member or an expert on the subject at hand, resist the temptation to do most of the talking or pontificate. Stay off your soapbox. Let the group wrestle with the ideas in play. Don't immediately correct a statement that is wrong in fact or logic. Be patient and wait for someone else to do so. If no one steps in, tactfully ask questions that seek clarification. For example: "What did you mean when you said x, y, and z?"; or "I don't think I understand what you said a couple of moments ago. What I take you to mean is a, b, and c? Is that correct?"; and so on. If long experience has given you a treasure trove of sea or war stories, draw on them only sparingly and appropriately. Be wary of sliding into mere yarning or turning the meeting into a "bull session."

On the other hand, if you are one of the reserved, silent types who tends to let everyone else talk while you listen, leading a discussion may pull you well outside your comfort zone, especially if you are a junior member. You might be in the habit of happily letting everyone else do all the talking, but when you are a discussion facilitator, you do not have that luxury. After you get things going, you will very likely need to speak up and assert yourself in order to keep the discussion moving along and on course. If you have prepared well, listen carefully, and take good notes, you will be fine. Dare to speak up. It's what you are expected to do, and you might even pleasantly surprise yourself with how well you do it.

Facilitating discussion requires paying attention to not only your own level of participation but also that of the other members. You should try to involve as many people and as many perspectives as possible. Two or three people may dominate the room by having their own animated conversation while the rest stay passive. One or two may try to preach from their own soapboxes or may simply be long-winded. Meanwhile, at the far end of the table or in a corner of the room, someone may be frequently raising their hand to speak and putting it down again because others keep jumping in to have their say. It falls to you as the facilitator to rein in the more energetic talkers and pull out the others who are more polite, more timid, or just inclined to be quiet. That can be a challenge among one's peers, especially if one is the sole representative of a minority group, and a real test of courage and tact when dealing with one's seniors. A courteous but firm intervention usually works: for example, "Hang on, Ensign Barry has been trying to say something. Ensign Barry?"; or "Thank you, Commander Mahan, that's a lot to consider. What you've said reminds me of something that Lieutenant Nimitz wrote before the meeting. Lieutenant Nimitz, would you like to say more on this point?" Maybe Ensign Barry or Lieutenant Nimitz will decline, but you will have recognized them, and that can go a long way toward encouraging participation. On the other hand, you will have tactfully reminded Commander Mahan that he isn't the only one with things to say.

Above all, politely and consistently enforce the ROE. It is possible to have a civil conversation that involves strongly held opinions and energetic disputation while adhering to good manners. In fact, those are often the most memorable discussions. But it takes work. Everyone must be on guard against allowing bitterness or rancor to creep in through cutting remarks, sarcasm, and snark. Otherwise all future conversation will likely be poisoned, and there will probably be harmful effects on professional relations and teamwork outside the seminar room. It is wise to keep always in mind that people "may forget what you said, but they will never forget how you made them feel." All that being said, have fun and get everyone going. Set the example and lead the way on this, and you'll be facilitating the development of naval minds.

5

CHEER UP!

DESIGNING YOUR OWN SEMINAR

When we hear the word "syllabus," it tends to pull us back to our time in college, whether we are officers who attended higher education before commissioning or enlisted Sailors and Marines who are working through it piece by piece while serving in the fleet. Unfortunately, it probably makes us think of laundry lists of classroom policies and rules, admonishments to hand in work on time, insistence on attending class, all commonly written in a kind of academic legalistic style. Does anyone even read the syllabus? As professors ourselves, we often wonder that very question. But at a more philosophical level, a syllabus is fundamental to the preparation for a course of study, not only for students but also for teachers themselves.

Part II of this book offers a syllabus for an initial voyage into leading a professional naval seminar on board your ship or in your fleet unit. Rather than a list of graded items, policy statements, or overly prescriptive learning objectives, these chapters are really just a collection of readings. These are twelve essays, articles, or combinations of writings that we have selected in order to begin naval discussions with a broad scope. With a dozen of them to work through, you may elect to conduct your seminar a number of other ways based on your unit's battle rhythm and schedule. Some of the readings are about leadership and ethics. Some are about strategy or tactics. Some are about the Navy and some about the Marine Corps because we are all a part of the naval service and should have some understanding of one another.

Along with each reading assignment, we have constructed an initial group of discussion questions for the seminar's facilitator. We often find it helpful to circulate the initial discussion questions so that seminar participants can think about their answers in advance. Our purpose with this initial list of readings and questions is not to give the readers definitive knowledge or to force the "learning of lessons," whether technical or doctrinal. Instead, the purpose is to broadly consider naval topics and to discuss them in a professional and intellectual way. In so doing, rather than come away with programmed lessons, we hope that your seminar attendees will develop their naval reasoning skills, whether that is ethical reasoning, strategic reasoning, tactical reasoning, or other ways of thinking about naval and military matters.

Once a wardroom, ready room, or group has the opportunity to run through the initial syllabus in Part II, it is time to move on to developing your own seminar. At its heart, the creation of a seminar syllabus is the planning for a sequence of discussions and intellectual engagements with either text or other mediums of communication. When done well, it is a professionally rewarding but also a very creative process. The remainder of this chapter discusses the creation of a course of study, the resources that are available to naval and military professionals from groups like the Naval Institute, and our professional military education institutions. It also discusses some of the things to think about when charting a course into the future development of your own naval mind, and in helping intellectually mentor those who serve with you.

The first thing we should do is throw out that traditional concept of an academic syllabus. The academic jargon, the official-sounding language, the administrative trivia that often inhabit them, all need to be tossed overboard. Instead, as we emphasize in the previous chapters, we should focus on the foundational ideas of what you are looking to study and how you are going to do it while also embracing the idea that a good seminar will grow on its own and sometimes take the discussion and learning in an unexpected but valuable direction.

Formal or Informal?

One of the initial questions that everyone must ask themselves when designing a syllabus is the issue of length. How often your group meets and how long you want to focus on a single topic or a theme give the initial parameters to work within. Our initial syllabus and list of readings in this book is a consciously selected number: twelve. With a dozen readings, the seminar can meet in a flexible number of ways. Meeting every week while on deployment might mean that a ship's wardroom could work through the readings during the middle months while at sea, after settling into the rhythm of deployment but before the rush of end-of-cruise tasking settles in. Likewise, if a ready room at homeguard were to meet only once a month, the discussions we have outlined might be completed over the course of a year. Deciding how often you would like your group to meet and for how long gives you the starting point.

This book has offered a relatively formal approach to developing the naval mind, with set readings known well in advance, discussion questions available for circulation, and a small amount of prepared contextual material. However, that does not mean that all seminars or discussion groups have to be this formal. It could be quite informal instead. For example, the leader of a monthly discussion group might simply select her favorite article or an interesting topic from each month's issue of the Naval Institute's journal *Proceedings* and circulate the selected piece to the group a week or two before they meet. This method could, in a relatively relaxed manner, go on indefinitely. It is also a method that has worked for naval and military leaders for about a century and a half and is part of the very reason that the institute was formed in 1873 and why it began publishing "papers" for the fleet to read. *Proceedings* is not the only source of these kinds of "in the moment" readings; such readings can come from academic journals or online and print magazines as well.

There is also the possibility, however, that you, as a leader, have a specific topic or theme that you think your participants would benefit from considering. This requires a more formal approach, and one with more work up front for the discussion leader. Selecting a contemporary challenge related to current events, like the rise of China or even more specifically events in the South China Sea, would serve a forward-deployed Seventh Fleet discussion group well. But it also requires the discussion leader to stay on top of the literature and plan a sequence of readings to tackle the subject in width and depth while continuously considering the larger context.

Resources and Readings

Selecting the material to consider for discussion around the ready room or wardroom might seem like a challenging task at first. However, there are many resources that can help, either with published and curated works or with opportunities to design your own creative and eclectic mix of subjects. As we've already discussed, an informal discussion group can be created around the monthly issue of *Proceedings*, other journals like *Foreign Affairs* or *The Naval War College Review*, or regular reading of popular defense and national security online publications like *War on the Rocks*, *The Strategy Bridge*, or the Center for International Maritime Security's *Next War*.[1]

The discussion leader can also turn to an edited volume for a book that offers the opportunity to be more formal or focused in the selected readings, a one-stop source. Using an edited book also offers the chance to have an expert editor do the curating and collecting of readings to save time and effort for the discussion leader. The Naval Institute Press often publishes books that would serve this purpose very well, including the following:

The Wheel Books Series. These books are edited collections of old *Proceedings* articles. They are selected and brought together by an expert editor and often include insightful and context-driven introductions to help a discussion leader think about larger, comprehensive themes across the selected articles that serve as the books' chapters. For example, the excellent *The U.S. Naval Institute on Naval Tactics* offers noted naval scholar Wayne Hughes' favorite articles and book excerpts about tactics in war at sea. Other volumes tackle subjects like strategy, leadership, innovation, and several others.

The Chronicles Series. This series of edited books focuses on the relevance of history by exploring topics like significant battles, personalities, and service components. Tapping into the institute's robust archives, these carefully selected volumes help readers dive into nuanced subjects by providing unique and wide perspectives. While they lack contextual descriptions or introductory essays, they include some of the best contributions that have helped shape naval thinking over the many decades since the institute's founding. Subjects cover a wide range of topics including the challenges associated with integrating women in the U.S. Navy, the strategic and international value of the Panama Canal, and Marine Corps aviation, just to name a few.

The 21st Century Foundations Series. Following the reminder from Alfred Thayer Mahan in 1911 that "the study of military history lies at the foundation of all sound military conclusions and practices," the books in this series give a modern perspective to the great strategists and military philosophers of the past. The essays and papers collected in the books of the series are dedicated to an individual writer or thinker. They don't spell out cut-and-dried answers to modern problems but instead help make sure we are asking good questions as we face the future. The books include volumes with the lesser-known writings of Mahan himself and the collected work of other naval and military thinkers and leaders like George Patton, Pete Ellis, and several others.

The American Naval Tradition. A list of eminent naval historians and writers contribute chapters to the three books in this series. Broken up by era, they trace the biographies of key figures across American naval history. These chapter-length biographical sketches allow a discussion group to wrestle with issues of leadership, combat effectiveness, and change within naval and military organizations. Many of the larger themes of preparing a fleet for conflict, as well as the peacetime responsibilities of navies, are illustrated in the individual narratives of leaders' lives in these books, and they offer a chance to use naval biography as a tool for approaching other topics for discussion.

Individual Edited Volumes. There are many collections that would serve well as core texts to develop a seminar syllabus. If the leader or the group is interested in ethics and modern conceptions of the military profession, a book like *Redefining the Modern Military* would serve as an excellent source of a dozen essays on the subject from across a joint and civil–military perspective. Books like *China Goes to Sea* offer chapters that allow a discussion group to wrestle with deep analysis of the rise of the People's Republic of China and its navy and to understand how it fits in a deeper examination of continental power and sea power. There are also creative and fun ways to approach key topics for discussion, including books like *Strategy Strikes Back: How Star Wars Explains Modern Military Conflict.* The choices are almost endless with an Amazon account or a library card.

Besides edited volumes, however, the wardroom seminar or ready room discussion can easily be structured around stand-alone books. Classics of naval history and strategy offer obvious starting points. Like *Rules of the Game,* or *Decision at Sea,* many excellent books by leading naval historians will grip the readers and offer a multitude of areas for discussion. But there are also books from the business and management world with keen insights on leadership, or books that focus on our contemporary world through the lens of foreign affairs or understanding particular geographic regions. The military reading lists of the different services and military organizations are a straightforward source for these kinds of books.

Finally, we don't want to suggest that professional discussion only happens after reading text. There are a lot of other ways to consume professional content. We both commonly use video in our classrooms, whether in the form of short clips to emphasize a point or longer documentaries. These are excellent fodder for professional discussion groups as well. Podcasts, documentaries, and even feature-length movies offer excellent resources. The Stockdale Center for Ethical Leadership at the Naval

Academy has even prepared discussion guides for a number of naval- and military-related movies that focus on leadership and military professionalism, from films like *Crimson Tide* and *Black Hawk Down* to *Saving Private Ryan*, among many others.[2] We would not rely entirely on audio or visual presentations, but they can often liven up a discussion group that seems to have become stale after reading article after article.

Preparing in Advance

Despite our effort to throw overboard the worst parts of a syllabus, effective seminars still require a certain amount of preparation. That effort should include the process of sitting down and writing or typing out your plans for leading the discussion group. Many of us have discovered that, as former dean of Naval Warfare Studies at the Naval War College Robert "Barney" Rubel wrote, we write to think.[3] Taking a moment to write a simple and clear paragraph stating your intent of the seminar and the themes or topics you intend to pursue often pays enormous dividends in helping to maintain clarity throughout your effort. After that starting point, make a list of the meetings you intend to have, whether they are weekly or monthly events or some other periodicity, then start assigning individual readings to those dates and times when you plan to meet. All of this is intended as a draft, and you should plan to iterate repeatedly as you narrow in on what you plan to present to your group.

Working through your list of individual readings while preparing a plan doesn't necessarily require you to do the deeper work of preparing discussion questions yet. If thoughts come to mind, as they often do while we are writing or doing intellectual work, keep a notebook or scratch pad file open to ensure you don't lose the ideas. Once you have constructed your purpose paragraph, set up the expected times and places of your meetings, and constructed the list of readings associated with those meetings, the real work is done. The basics of a syllabus are actually pretty easy.

When discussing resources for discussion, we mentioned using full books, and in particular books on the CNO reading list or, as Will Hunting said, whatever blows your hair back. However, there is a danger that comes with using individual books that you have to consider while formally thinking about a syllabus. Using them regularly can cause the seminar discussion to devolve into a kind of professional book club. We don't want to discourage that generally, but specifically it raises a challenge for a seminar leader. Book clubs can, and often do, result in simplistic discussions of plot or character and in participants simply comparing notes on what they liked or disliked about the text. While these offer starting points for discussion, they lack the depth that will bring real development of our naval minds. That is why, when using a full book, we recommend that a seminar leader spend more time in preparation.

First, the best way to use a full book for seminar discussion is to ensure that you have read it cover to cover yourself before beginning the discussions with your group. Without consuming the entire text, you won't have any idea what the larger themes are or how to draw out the important moments in each chapter or section as the group reads them. There is a temptation to experience the "joy of discovery" alongside your seminar mates, and we admit that the shared moments of epiphany that can come from this style of discussion can give you a real intellectual charge. However, we have found that careful preparation beforehand is a far more effective method for ensuring that the hour or so spent in discussion is fruitful and deep in its analysis. Part of reading the text in full also involves looking for natural breaking points in order to divide up the reading and the discussion. It is possible to read an entire book and then discuss it in an hour. We have both done it. But it tends to leave the discussion broad and focused more on summary than critical analysis. It is not always effective to break things up simply by chapter; sometimes dividing it into parts or thirds might be more relevant for the nature and message of the book itself. Reading and preparing your syllabus—deciding how you will divide it up with specific page assignments and how you will approach the topics via effective discussion questions—takes some time in advance to ensure efficient use of time in discussion.

A Voyage of Discovery

While the majority of this book focuses on the intellectual development that military professionals can find via self-study and engaging in spirited and deep discussion, creating your own seminar syllabus is also a learning process. It is a creative endeavor that will also help you think through your own professional ideas, and leadership and strategic understanding. Teaching something is often the best way to work through your own understanding of the material, and that comes from both the preparation as well as the seminar discussions themselves. The resources and ideas offered in this chapter are truly just the tip of the iceberg. Think of them as navigational markers to get you out of port, but once you are in the open water there's an extensive amount of material to consider and a fantastic voyage of discovery that you can chart for yourself and your shipmates.

« 6 »

READ, THINK, SPEAK...AND WRITE

Reading books, essays, and articles from professional journals is a critical part of the development of a naval mind, and vital to the kind of thinking, adapting Sailor and Marine necessary for a world of constant change and challenge. The previous chapters have made the case that, beyond simply reading the material, servicemembers must think hard about their chosen profession and its complications, and must talk to each other in constructive and intellectual ways to work through how to address contemporary problems. Reading effectively and analyzing the arguments of officers, authors, or scholars is only a starting point. Discussion allows us to test our thoughts and our analysis in the realm of ideas and professional, intellectual engagement. After engaging in reading and thinking about the challenges the Navy and Marine Corps have faced in the past, and face in the present, and testing our thoughts with our fellow professionals across a wardroom table or in a ready room discussion about the future, we can take the development of the naval mind even one step further. We can begin writing our ideas and analysis down and contributing to contemporary professional debates by publishing our own essays and articles on naval subjects.

In June 2016 CNO John Richardson and Lt. Ashley O'Keefe wrote a short opinion essay for the Naval Institute's *Proceedings* entitled "Read. Write. Fight." Lieutenant O'Keefe and the CNO made the case that because "warfare is a violent, *intellectual* contest between thinking and adapting adversaries" (emphasis added), naval professionals must "read and write . . . with that singular purpose: to confound our enemies and make our Navy more powerful."[1] Their call to "break out the books and sharpen our pens" follows a long historical tradition of preparing for conflict through the intellectual preparation of self-study and writing for publication. Adm. James Stavridis wrote a similar clarion call almost a decade earlier in his article "Read, Think, Write, Publish."[2]

The CNO did not discover a new idea but instead lent his voice to a chorus calling for more professional engagement. More than just a naval idea, this is a joint effort. It mirrors not only suggestions from leaders like Stavridis but also calls to contribute that came with the establishment of the Army Press and efforts supported by Army leaders like Lt. Gen. H. R. McMaster, alongside similar propositions by more junior soldiers and veterans.[3]

There has been a long list of professionals throughout naval and military history who participated in the development of military affairs in this way. On the naval side, Sailors from Matthew Perry to Alfred Thayer Mahan, Chester Nimitz to Elmo Zumwalt have published their thoughts. Fleet Adm. Ernest J. King won the General Prize from the Naval Institute for an article he wrote as a lieutenant in 1909.[4] There is also a long history of wider military participation in the arena of ideas, from soldiers in the nineteenth century to leaders like Patton in the twentieth century. Gen. Dwight D. Eisenhower overcame a threat to his career because he had the audacity to publish as a junior officer. However, the repeated calls to arms over time, or perhaps calls to pens, have sometimes missed something: How do you do it?[5]

Our military services tend to be technically oriented, each of them to a greater or lesser degree. Our educational policies focus on engineering, technical, and tactical study and rarely encourage us to learn how to communicate in writing beyond a bare minimum. In our staff positions, we use briefing slides and other communication methods that inspire partial thoughts, quick hits, and incomplete sentences and little practice in understanding the roles of paragraph structure or style in putting together a coherent argument. For cultures raised on procedure and PowerPoint, what is the method for writing a professional article? Some simple steps inspired by the words in the mission of the Naval Institute might help set our course.

R . . . T . . . S . . . W

The mission of the Naval Institute is to "provide an independent forum for *those who dare to read, think, speak, and write* to advance the professional, literary, and scientific understanding of sea power and other issues critical to global security" (emphasis added). The emphasized words are not an original naval construction.

Instead, they are borrowed directly from President John Adams. In his 1765 pamphlet "Dissertation on the Canon and the Feudal Law," Adams examined monarchy and feudalism and compared them to the growing movement for freedom and liberty in the American colonies. The future president called for Americans who valued liberty to develop their knowledge, and their argument, by daring to read, think, speak, and write on the subject.[6] It was a clarion call, but it also hinted at a certain amount of process. Adams was a careful writer. Rather than a lucky turn of phrase, it is more probable that he put these words in a very specific order. Following his counsel can help professionals chart their process for developing an article that contributes to understanding of our profession.

READ

In order to make a contribution to the field of naval, military, or national security knowledge, you have to understand the state of the field. The way to do that is by reading, by moving more broadly across what academics call "the literature," using the foundational knowledge that the readings from this book provide. If you have come up with an interesting analogy for a current debate, the only way to know if someone has made the argument before is by reading the field. If you wonder what counterarguments may be offered against your position, that also comes with reading the field. Articles in journals like *Proceedings*, *Naval War College Review*, journals of the other services like *Military Review*, online publications like *War on the Rocks* and *The Strategy Bridge*, and a wider number of blogs and websites all contribute to the state of the field. Not only will reading them give you new information, and new ideas, but they also tell you what others have said before. It can save you from an embarrassing response: "Yeah, Major Jones said it six months ago and had a better argument." It is not that you have to be completely original; building on the work of others is a great way to expand our understanding, but knowing the field helps you understand where you fit.

It is not just articles and online posts we should be reading. Books have long given us the deep knowledge needed to understand where the profession has been and where it may head in the future. This naturally follows from the saying "if you want new ideas, read old books," often attributed to Ivan Petrovich Pavlov. But there is a common refrain in the modern world that we simply do not have time for books. The watch schedule on board ship keeps us too busy. Digital media has affected our attention span. Military service and deployments are demanding, and we need time with our families. We find time for physical exercise while we discount intellectual exercise. According to some studies, the average college graduate reads around three hundred words a minute. If we read fifteen minutes each evening, it totals up to eighteen to twenty average-length books a year. The excuse there is "no time" would never be accepted when we failed our physical fitness tests. Accept the challenge to read more widely. Maybe this sounds "highbrow" or too "egg headed" but, as President Truman, a World War I Army veteran once said, "Not all readers are leaders, but all leaders are readers."

THINK

Once a servicemember or national security professional has an idea of the subject they want to write about, has done some research and reading about it, and has come up with the initial kernel of an argument, they need to spend some time thinking about it. This advice probably goes against the grain and the incentives of digital media or what social media seems to encourage. It also takes us a step beyond the wardroom table where we should be encouraging engagement in discussion and conversation that sometimes means proposing half-baked ideas or just jumping into the intellectual scrum. However, when looking to write an article, essay, or blog post, the point of the effort is to make a contribution to the field of naval affairs or national security, not to rush into being a "thought leader" in the crashing tide of the blogosphere.

Thinking hard about the subject you intend to tackle includes attempting to employ the skills of critical thinking. Critical thinking gets a lot of attention these days, and there are numerous competing definitions of what it means. Unfortunately, too many people seem to think "critical thinking" means "thinking about important or critical things." That is not the case. Instead, you need to level criticism at yourself and your ideas. You need to examine your ideas with depth and rigor in order to get to the heart of whatever issue you want to write about. In an example from the study of military history, the famed British historian Sir Michael Howard advised military officers examining the past to ensure that they study in width, depth, and context in order to make sure they get the whole picture and challenge their initial ideas.[7] This includes becoming a critic of yourself and your own ideas, as well as the ideas of others. As you develop the concept for your article, be exacting and penetrating with the evidence you have amassed through both research and your own experiences.

SPEAK

Having researched, considered experience, and critically examined the subject in your own mind, it is important to get a sanity check from someone else. In the academic world, this is part of the reason there is peer review before journal articles are published. In the professional and popular press, editors and editorial boards will judge your work with a dispassionate eye and often provide some feedback for revision. The best way to ensure your argument makes sense, and you have developed a sound approach before thinking about publication or contacting an editor, is to talk about it with other people.

Speaking about your idea can take a number of forms. It can happen with a pint in your hand or a cup of coffee at the local base coffee shop with a mentor or group of respected friends. In the lost days of our Officer Clubs this was actually a common way of helping people develop professional ideas. Seek out a mentor whom you trust, whether a senior officer or a former professor or coworker, and see what sticks in your conversation with them. In reality, after working through the methods and readings in this book with a wardroom or ready room group of fellow professionals, you will also have built the skills to conduct an effective workshop for working through ideas and helping each other as well. Speaking also does not have to be taken literally, even if some of us work better in the give and take of live conversation. It can take the form of an email or long social media exchange. The goal is to introduce new criticisms that you, as the writer, have not considered, or to clarify the way to express the ideas.

WRITE

Sit down and write the article. Just do it. Don't allow the blank page on the computer screen to intimidate you. Some people find that pulling out a pad of paper and a pen is actually an easier way to start. That's fine, just get started writing words on a page. One of the benefits of having thought through the idea systematically and then speaking about it with a trusted friend or mentor is that you have already started to develop the words to express the idea. As many successful authors have told us, from Stephen King to Anne Lamott: the first draft is going to be bad. Ernest Hemingway famously advised a young author who was looking for advice that "the first draft of anything is shit."[8] It does not matter. Sit at the keyboard and bang away until you have said everything you want to say.

Once the words are on the page, raw and terrible as they might be, you have crossed a major hurdle. After that, it is a matter of editing, organizing, and rewriting, which should be easier than putting the idea down the first time. As the famed Russo-American novelist and poet Vladimir Nabokov once said, "I have rewritten—often several times—every word I have ever published. My pencils outlast their erasers."[9] The editing does not need to be rushed, and the mentor or friend you spoke with will probably be excited to take a look at the article and help make suggestions to improve it. You have already made them feel like a part of the process. When the draft is something that reads well and you're happy with it, then it is time to start looking for a place to publish it. Good editors, strong editorial boards, and the review process they use will help strengthen the piece even more. Be ready to make more adjustments to help clarify any issues they discover.

The RTSW Loop

One way to look at this "RTSW" process is to think of it as a sort of observe-orient-decide-act loop for professional writing. In some ways it is similar to Col. John Boyd's stratotactical ideal, which said that decision making had to work through an OODA loop. For example, just like in Boyd's OODA, each element can send you back to a previous spot. Speaking with a mentor may send you to a book or article you had not heard of before, which you need to check out, or the process of writing may cause you to return to your thinking and reorganize your approach. But there are also differences with Boyd's OODA sequence—most notably, speed. Boyd's framework was built around working through the loop faster than an opponent in order to outthink and outact them on the battlefield. But speed can be your enemy when writing a good professional article. There is no hurry. Please do not try to beat the rush of modern media. More often than not, this will take time, and multiple rounds of the "RTSW loop." But that only makes the article stronger and a better contribution to our profession.

Once you have an article or essay that you like, that you're happy with, you may decide it is time to publish. Note that we say "like" and "happy with" and not "perfect." There is no such thing as the perfect professional article. But once you are ready to publish, it is time to turn what you have written into a manuscript. That involves a number of further steps, including finding the right publication, conforming to submission guidelines, and working with editors to improve the piece of writing even further so that it is ready to face the world. Practical advice for thinking about those further steps is included in the appendix of this book, with some quick hits on how to approach everything from where to find material and ideas to how to professionally work with editors and publishers.

Writing for publication is a rewarding challenge. It is also something a legion of Sailors, soldiers, Marines, airmen, and security professionals have done throughout history. Many discover that the process of writing clarifies their thinking. It also develops our communication skills, our critical faculties through practice, and by extension our leadership ability. All of these make us better military professionals. Writing for publication is not something we should do because we need another fitness report or evaluation bullet or because we think we can impress our boss. We don't do it simply because a service chief or senior officer says so. It is something we do in order to move our profession forward, to improve our service or our nation's security, and to wrestle with the challenges of the modern world. So, it is time to dare. Dare to read, think, speak . . . and write.

《7》

CONCLUSION
CAST OFF ALL LINES . . .

Don't Delay: The best is the enemy of the good. By this I mean that a good plan violently executed now is better than a perfect plan next week. War is a very simple thing, and the determining characteristics are self-confidence, speed, and audacity.

—George S. Patton Jr.

OK, OK, we know—beat Army and all that. But General Patton's imperative is most appropriate for your endeavor. Education and war are radically different things, of course, but one's approach to doing either activity should be the same. Do not delay and dread nought (pun intended). Be bold, cast off all lines, and get under way. You can adjust your course as circumstances require. This book offers the raw materials you need to get a naval seminar going. Nothing will happen, though, without initiative, courage, and energy, which you already have and no one can give you anyway.

It's alright to start small. There is no need to spend a lot of time and effort on gathering participants. Six to seven is an ideal group size, but don't give up if you can't recruit that many. You need only yourself and one other person to have a discussion, and if that is all you have, then so be it. Two will have to be good enough. Maybe a couple of people will overhear your lively conversation in the wardroom, ready room, or conference room and ask to join you. The momentum can increase slowly, so long as there is momentum to begin with.

Once you have gathered the group, agree to a regular time to meet. Again, perfect is the enemy of good enough. There might not be a time that is ideal for everyone, and the difficulty of finding such a time increases with the size of the group. You will have to accept that not everyone can attend every single discussion. Be realistic and practical, too. Everyone might be available at 1500–1600 on Friday, but do you really want to spend Happy Hour that way? (And no, it's not a great idea to combine the two. Commit to one or the other.) Lunch time is often the best available option, and a "brown bag" seminar can be an enjoyable yet productive break in the middle of the workday.

Remember the related issue of space. Finding a suitable venue might be a challenge, especially in operational units. It might be necessary to wander or to adjust the meeting schedule if there is no single room that can be reserved for every discussion. If you and the rest of the group have the means, consider going online once in a while to work around the constraints of time and space. Online or "virtual" meetings aren't equivalent to in-person meetings—not by a long shot—but they are usually better than nothing. They can be worse than nothing, though, if there is a lot of lag and noise in transmission. The outcome then is frustration at best and misunderstanding at worst.

The great Yogi Berra famously observed, "The future ain't what it used to be." We historians know that this has always been true, but it seems especially fitting now, in the first quarter of the twenty-first century. Black swans are showing up everywhere with dizzying frequency: the attacks of September 11, 2001; the Iraq War; the Great Recession; the ubiquity and dominance of Facebook, Twitter, and other social media; the meteoric rise of China (at least to most of the West); Brexit; the development of cyber threats; and now a global pandemic that has so far eluded diminishment, let alone a cure. No one but perhaps a tiny few saw any of it coming, and not even the prophets who did could have foreseen the effects.

This present era is like those areas on ancient and early modern maps that the cartographers labeled "terra incognita"—unknown land. To some that implied danger to be avoided. To others it signified opportunity to be explored. We are inclined to the latter, and we think that you probably are too. No one knows what the future holds, but naval leaders should still think about it. We strongly believe that it is a matter of duty for the naval mind to wonder "what if?" or "what next?" or "what should I/we do if?" Undertaking to answer those questions requires critical thinking and an informed, disciplined imagination. It requires a willingness to grapple with ambiguity, to deal with uncertainty, to ask questions relentlessly, and to search for one's own answers. It does not always require more time in a school-house, but it does involve active engagement with other minds in reading and dialogue.

Good luck to you and your group as you wrestle with the exigencies of the present and explore the terra incognita of the future. We wish you joy of discovery.

[Part II]
THE READINGS

8

THE STRENGTH OF NELSON

Alfred Thayer Mahan

(From *Naval Administration and Warfare: Some General Principles, with Other Essays* [Boston: Little, Brown, 1908])

With a temperament versatile as that of Nelson, illustrated in a career full of varied action, it is not easy to know how to regard its subject, in brief, so as to receive a clear and accurate impression; one which shall preserve justice of proportion, while at the same time giving due emphasis and predominance to the decisive characteristics. Multiplicity of traits, lending itself to multiplicity of expression, increases the difficulty of selection, and of reproducing that combination which really constitutes the effective force and portrait of the man. The problem is that of the artist, dealing with a physical exterior. We can all recall instances of persons, celebrated historically or socially, in whom the prominence of a particular feature, or a certain pervading expression, causes all portraits to possess a recognizable stamp of likeness. As soon as the pictured face is seen we identify the original without hesitation. There are others in whom the mobility of countenance, the variations depending upon feeling and expression, quite overpower in impression the essential sameness presented by features in repose.

Great indeed must be the difficulties of the artist, or the writer, who has to portray the man capable, within a half-hour, of such diverse moods as Wellington witnessed in his one only interview with Nelson. The anecdote is too familiar for reproduction here. Less well known, probably, or less remembered, is a similar testimony borne by two officers, Captains Layman and Sir Alexander Ball, who served with him under varying circumstances.

One day, after tea in the drawing-room at Merton, Lord Nelson was earnestly engaged in conversation with Sir Samuel Hood. Mr. Layman observed to Sir Alexander that Lord Nelson was at work, by his countenance and mouth; that he was a most extraordinary man, possessing opposite points of character—little in little things, but by far the greatest man in great things he ever saw; that he had seen him petulant in trifles, and as cool and collected as a philosopher when surrounded by dangers in which men of common minds with clouded countenance would say, "Ah! what is to be done?" It was a treat to see his animated and collected countenance in the heat of action. Sir Alexander remarked this seeming inconsistency, and mentioned that after the Battle of the Nile the captains of the squadron were desirous to have a good likeness of their heroic chief taken, and for that purpose employed one of the most eminent painters in Italy. The plan was to ask the painter to breakfast, and get him to begin immediately after. Breakfast being over, and no preparation being made by the painter, Sir Alexander was selected by the other captains to ask him when he intended to begin; to which the answer was, "Never." Sir Alexander said he stared, and they all stared, but the artist continued: "There is such a mixture of humility with ambition in Lord Nelson's countenance that I dare not risk the attempt!"

Contrast with such a one the usual equable composure of Washington or Wellington, and the difficulty of a truthful rendering is seen; but reflection reveals therein likewise the intensely natural, spontaneous, impulsive character, which takes hold of our loves, and abides in affectionate remembrance.

In such cases how can there but be marked diversities of appearance in the attempted reproductions by this or that man, painter or writer? Not only will the truthfulness of the figured face depend upon the fleeting mood of the sitter; the aptitude of the artist to receive, and to penetrate through the mask of the instant, is an even greater factor. Both the one and the other will enter into the composition of the resultant portrait; for as, on the one hand, the man shows himself as he for the moment is, so, on the other, the power to see and to express that which is shown depends upon the revelation to the artist; a revelation due as much to his own insight as to the visible thing before him. The miracle of Pentecost lay not only in the gifts of speech bestowed upon the Apostles, but in the power of every man to hear in that tongue, and in that tongue only, to which he is born; to see with the spiritual vision which he has received, or to which he may have grown.

In this respect portrayal by pen will not differ from portrayal by pencil or by brush. The man who attempts to depict in words a character so diverse in manifestation as that of Nelson will reflect from what he sees before him that aspect of the man with which he himself is most in touch. The writer of military sympathies will—must—give predominance to the military qualities. Despite his efforts to the contrary, they will make the deepest impress, and will be most certainly and conspicuously reproduced. And to a degree this will accord with the truth; for above all, undoubtedly, Nelson was a warrior. But he was also much more, and in virtue of that something else he survives, and is transmitted to us as—what shall I say?—as Nelson; there is no other word. He is not a type; still less does he belong to a class. He is simply himself—the man Nelson; a man so distinct in his individuality, that he has thus imposed himself on the consciousness and recollection of a great nation. He rests there, simply himself, and no other; and no other is he, nor stands near him. I say not that he is higher or lower, greater or less, than any other. I do not, at least now, analyze his qualities, nor seek to present such an assembly of them as shall show why the impress of individuality is thus unique. I only draw attention to the fact that this is so; that Nelson now lives, and is immortal in the memory of his kind, not chiefly because of what he did, but because in the doing and in the telling, then and now, first and last, men have felt themselves in the presence of a personality so strong that it has broken through the barriers of convention and reserve which separate us one from another, and has placed itself in direct contact with the inner selves, not of contemporaries only, but of us who never saw him in the body. We have not only heard of him and his deeds. We know him as we do one with whom we are in constant intercourse.

This is of itself an extraordinary trait. Thus to make a man known, to reveal a personality, is what Boswell did for Johnson; but he accomplished this literary marvel of portraiture by the most careful and minute record of doings and sayings. His is a built-up literary prodigy, resembling some of those striking Flemish portraits, which not only impress by their ensemble, but stand inspection under a magnifying glass. But what Boswell did for Johnson, Nelson has done for himself, and in quite other fashion. He is revealed to us, not by such accumulation of detail, but by some quality, elusive, perhaps not to be detected, by reason of which the man himself insensibly transpires to our knowledge in his strength and in his weakness. We know him, not by what his deeds or his words signify; but through his deeds and words the inner spirit of the man continually pierces, and, while we read, envelops us in an atmosphere which may be called Nelsonic. Such certainly seemed to me the effect upon myself in a year given to his letters, to his deeds, and to his recorded words. I found myself in a special environment, stimulating, exalting, touching; and while we confess that there are morbid symptoms attendant upon the writing of biography, tending to distort vision, and to confuse the sense of proportion, faults which the reader must appreciate—the writer cannot—there can be no mistake about the moral effect produced, and the outburst of this Trafalgar Day proves it to be not limited to the biographer. The reserve which for the most of us cloaks each man's secret being from the knowledge of those nearest him among his contemporaries, casts no such impenetrable veil over the personality of this man whom we never saw—who died just one hundred years ago this day. We have with him an acquaintance, we feel from him an influence, which we have not with, nor from, one in a score of those whom we meet daily.

Many Lives of Nelson have been written, but no one of them marked with the artistic skill and untiring diligence which Boswell brought to his task. A singular proof of the latter's combined genius and care, which I do not think is always appreciated, is to be found in the fact that the portrait of Johnson is surrounded by a gallery of minor portraits, as real and living as his own, though duly subordinated in impression to the central figure of the group. This is indeed the triumph of the great artist. He has, so to say, succeeded beyond himself, and beyond his intentions, simply because he *is* great. In the way of portraiture he touches nothing that he does not quicken and adorn. The same certainly cannot be said for those who have transmitted to us the companions of Nelson, in their relations to their chief. Yet we know Nelson as well as we know Johnson, and more usefully, despite every disadvantage in his limners. The spell of his personality has compelled them to reproduce him; and its power—its magic, I might say—is to be found in that influence exerted upon them. In Boswell's Johnson we have the vivid reproduction of a man of the past; a study complete, interesting, instructive, but not to a reader of to-day influential beyond the common teachings of biography. In Nelson, who died but twenty years later, we have a living inspiration. He presents a great heroic standard, a pattern. We set ourselves at once to copy him; not because, in the record of his acts, we have received an ordinary suggestion or warning, but because heart answers to heart. The innate nobility of the man's ideals, which transpired even through, and in, the lamentable episode which sullied his career, uplifts us in spite of ourselves, and of all that was amiss in him. The jewel shines, even amid defilement. It certainly cannot be claimed that Nelson's unflinching professional tenacity is nobler than Johnson's brave struggle against his mental depression and numerous bodily infirmities; his life unstained, though without Puritanic affectation. But, as a present force, Johnson is dead, Nelson is alive. Nelson is no mere man of the past. Not his name only, but he himself lives to us; still speaks, because there was in him that to which man can never die, while he remains partaker of the Divine nature. It is but a few days since that I received a letter from a junior officer of the British Navy, expressing the wish that all young officers might be ordered to master the career of Nelson, because of the uplifting power which he himself had found in the ideals and actions of the hero.

What is the secret of this strange fascination, which has given Nelson his peculiar place, by which it may be said of him, as of some few other worthies of the past: "He being dead yet speaketh." It certainly is not merely in the standards which he professed, even although his devotion to them continually was manifested, not in word only, but in deed; yea, and in the hour of death. The noblest of all, the dying words, "Thank God I have done my duty," is no monopoly of Nelson's. You may count by scores the men of English-speaking tradition, in Great Britain and America, who have brought as single-minded a purpose to the service of the "stern daughter of the voice of God," and have followed her as unflinchingly through good and ill. But how many of them who have departed exercise a conscious influence upon the minds of the men of to-day? Their deeds and examples doubtless have gone to swell that sum total of things, by which the world of our generation is the better for the lives of the myriads who have lived unknown and are forgotten; but their influence, their present, direct, personal, uplifting force on men now alive, in how many instances can you point to it? And to what one other, among the heroes of Great Britain, from whom it is so generally distributed that it may fitly be called national? Despite the Nile and Trafalgar, there may be several who have more radically and permanently affected the destinies of the Empire. We are not here concerned with such analytic computations, or with estimates of indirect consequences which the doer of the deeds could by no possibility have foreseen. If such there be, what one among them evokes to-day the emulative affection and admiration which is the prerogative of Nelson? Whence comes this? Grant even the cumulative dramatic force, the immense effectiveness of the double utterances, so closely following each other, "England expects every man to do his duty," and "Thank God, I have done my duty," you have advanced but a step towards the solution of the question. Why is Nelson still alive, while so many other sons of duty are dead? What prophetic power, power to speak for God and for man, was in this man, that such enduring speech should come forth from his life; that he, being dead, is still speaking?

It is not permitted to man so to search the heart of his fellow as to give a conclusive reply to such a question; yet it is allowable and appropriate to seek so far to appreciate one like Nelson as at least to approach somewhat nearer towards understanding the secret of his character and of its power. The homage to duty as the supreme motive in life, and the strong conviction that there are objects worthier of effort than money getting and ease, were characteristics possessed in common with many others by Nelson. But, while I speak with diffidence, I feel strongly that the mode of tenure was somewhat different in him and in them. The recognition of duty, and of its high obligation, is impressed upon most of us from without. We have been taught it, have received it by the hearing of the ear, from others to whom in like manner it has been imparted by those who went before them. It is, so to say, a transmitted inheritance—"in the air"; perhaps not to quite such an extent as might be desired. We render it a tribute which is perfectly sincere, but still somewhat conventional. This condition is not to be despised. The compelling power of accepted conventions is enormous; but, like much religious faith, such attention to duty is not founded on the individual bottom, but depends largely on association, for which reason it will be found more highly developed in some professions, because it is the tone of the profession. Unquestionably, in many individuals the thought is so thoroughly assimilated as to become the man's very own, as hard to depart from as any ingrained acquired habit; and to this we owe the frequency of its manifestations in nations where the word itself has received a dignity of recognition which sets it apart from the common vocabulary—deifies it, so to say.

All this is very fine. It is superb to see human nature, in man or in people, lifting itself up above itself by sheer force of adhesion to a great ideal; to mark those who have received the conception elevated, not through their own efforts, but by force of association, like the tonic effect of an invigorating atmosphere. But our hard-won victories over ourselves cannot by themselves alone make us that which by nature we are not. Nature has been suppressed in its evil, and upon its restless revolt good enthroned; but the evil lives still and rebels. The palace is kept and held by a strong man armed; but ever in danger that a stronger than he, whom we call Nature, shall return in force and retrieve his past defeat. It was finely said of Washington, by one who knew him intimately—Gouverneur Morris—"Control his passions! Yes; and few men have had stronger to control. But many men have controlled their passions, so as not to do that to which they were impelled. But where have you known one who, like him, always, under whatever conditions, could do, and did, what the duty of the moment required, despite fatigue, or distaste, or natural repulsion." The writer who made this comparison had moved amid all the scenes of dire distress and anxiety that marked the American War of Independence, and had personal acquaintance with the chief actors. This is the innate positive quality, not the acquired negative self-control, battling with self. I doubt if most of us stop to realize the full force of the word "innate," which slips glibly enough from our tongues without appreciation of its significance. Inborn; this is not nature controlled, but nature controlling; not the tiger, or the ape, or the sloth, held by the throat, but the man himself in the fulness of his powers exercising his natural supremacy over himself. Such was duty to Nelson; a mistress, not that compelled obedience, but that attracted the devotion of a nature which intuitively recognised her loveliness, and worshipped. Like the hearers at Pentecost, he recognized in her voice the tongue to which he was born; he saw her—yes, despite his one great fall, we may say it—he saw her fairer than the daughters of men.

> Stern Lawgiver! Thou dost wear
> The Godhead's most benignant grace;
> Nor know we anything so fair
> As is the smile upon thy face.

A natural character, we have all felt the attractiveness of such, the attractiveness of truth and beauty; but when, to such a nature, is added nobility as well, we have one of the rare combinations which compels homage. Nelson was eminently natural, affectionate, impulsive, expansive; but it is this singular gift, this peculiar recognition of duty, with another I shall mention, which has set him upon his pedestal, given him the niche which only he can fill. In the spirits of his people he has found a nobler Westminster Abbey than that of which he dreamed. But, you may ask, how do you demonstrate that he had this gift? Alas, I am not a Boswell; I wish I were, and that there survived the records of conversations with which I, or another, could reconstruct his image, as Boswell drew Johnson. Yet when a career opens and closes upon the same keynote, we may be sure of the harmonious whole—of which, indeed, traces enough remain to confirm our assurances. You know the two stories of childhood handed down to us. The brothers starting for school after Christmas holidays, driven back by the weather, and started again with the father's mandate, "You may return if it is necessary; but I leave it to your honor not to do so unless it is really dangerous to proceed." It seemed dangerous, and one was for returning; but [then] Nelson said, "No, it was left to our honor." Not the word "duty," no; but the essence of duty, the look out from self, the recognition of the something external and higher than the calls of the body. In one so young—he was but twelve when he went to sea some time after this—it is Nature which speaks, not an acquired standard. In later years, in terms somewhat fantastic, he said he beheld ever a radiant orb beckoning him onward. Honor he called it, the twin sister—rather let us say the express image—in which duty, regarding as in a glass, sees herself reflected. Then, again, there is the story of stealing the fruit from the schoolmaster's pear-tree—a trivial enough schoolboy prank, risking the penalties of detection which his comrades dared not face. Neither duty nor honor goes to such a feat in its nakedness; but the refusal to eat the fruit, the proud avowal that he went only because the others feared, bears witness to the same disregard of personal advantage, the same determination of action by considerations external to self, the same eye to the approval of the consciousness—of the conscience—which spoke in the signal at Trafalgar, and soothed the dying moments by the high testimony within: not, "I have won renown"; not "I have achieved success"; but, "I have done my duty." He was not indifferent to success; he was far from indifferent to renown. "If it be a sin to covet glory," he once quoted, "then am I the most offending soul alive." But the solemn hour which gives the validity of an oath to the statement of the dying, assuredly avouches to us that then the man, as once the child, spoke out the true secret of his being—the tongue into which he was born.

And in this also is the secret, not only of his own devotion to duty, but of the influence of his personality upon others; both in the infancy of his professional career, and now in the maturity of his immortal renown. What he thus possessed he possessed naturally, positively, aggressively, and therefore contagiously. He had root in himself, to use a familiar expression; and the life which was thus no mere offshoot of convention, but his very own, gave itself out abundantly to others, mul-tiplying himself. He gave out by example; he gave out by words, uttered, indeed, expressly, yet so casually that the impression resembles the fleeting glimpse of an interior, caught through the momentary tossing aside of a curtain; he gave out through the heroic atmosphere of self-devotion which he bore about him; he gave out by cordial recognition of excellence in others. Any other man who did his duty, whether comrade or subordinate, was to him a fellow worshipper at the shrine; his heart went out to him, whether in failure or in success, if only the will was there.

No testimony is clearer or more universal than that to his generosity in appreciation of others; and it was seen, not only in recognition of achievement already accomplished, but in the confident expectation of achievement yet to be effected. The original form of the Trafalgar signal, spoken by himself, "Nelson *confides* that every man will do his duty," was no mere casual utterance. It summed up the conviction and habit of a lifetime. As the words, "Thank God, I have done my duty," were his dying words personally, so those just quoted may be said to have been his last words professionally. Indeed, he himself said as much, for when they had been communicated to the fleet he remarked, "Now I can do no more. We must trust (confide) to the great Disposer of all events." His great career ended when that signal had been read and acknowledged.

Because in himself so trustworthy, he trusted abundantly; and all of us know the stimulus of feeling ourselves trusted, of looking forward with certainty to just appreciation of good work done. "I am well aware," wrote one of his younger captains, "of the good construction which your Lordship has ever been in the habit of putting on circumstances, although wearing the most unfavorable appearances. Your Lordship's good opinion constitutes the summit of my ambition and the most effective spur to my endeavors." "I am pleased," writes another, "that an opportunity is offered for showing my gratitude in a small degree for his almost fatherly kindness." In a letter of instructions to a captain about to encounter some perplexing and critical conditions, after prescribing for several circumstances that may arise, he concludes, in the case of the unforeseen, "You must then act as your judgment may direct you, and *I am sure* that will be very proper." If delinquency actually occurred, as he conceived it had in the case of Sir Sidney Smith, his wrath had all the fierceness of trust betrayed, for he was a man impatient and of strong passions; but otherwise doubts of another's doing his duty did not occur to him. His confidence in himself, in his own self-devotion and capacity, made him trustful of others, and inspired them with devotion to the service and to the country, for his sake, and because they saw it in him. A captain who met him for the first time just before Trafalgar, and who fell in the battle, wrote home, "I have been very lucky with most of my admirals, but I really think the present the pleasantest I have met with. He is so good and pleasant that we all wish to do what he likes, without any kind of orders."

This was the clear reflection of his own spirit, begot of his own confidence in others, because he met them and trusted them as himself. Dutiful, probably, in any event, as imitators of him they were more so. He expected in others what he felt in himself, and diffused around him the atmosphere of energy, zeal, and happiness in endeavor, which was native to himself. "He had in a great degree," wrote a contemporary who had known him from boyhood, "the valuable but rare quality of conciliating the most opposite tempers, and forwarding the public service with unanimity, among men not of themselves disposed to accord." Yes; but the unanimity was not that of accordant opinion, but of a common devotion to a common object, before which differences subsided; to duty, seeing in others a like devotion, a like purpose to do their best. This spirit Nelson shed about him; with this he inspired others in his day, and still does in our own. It was the contagion of his personality, continuous in action, and ever watchful against offence, and even against misunderstanding. "My dear Keats," he wrote to a captain whose worn-out ship was incorrigibly slow when speed was most desirable, "I am fearful you may think that the *Superb* does not go as fast as I could wish. I would have you to be assured that I know and feel that the *Superb* does all which is possible for a ship to accomplish; and I desire that you will not fret." "My dear Collingwood, I shall come out and make you a visit; not, my dear friend, to take your command from you, but to consult how we may best serve our country by detaching a part of this large force." St. Vincent's testimony here is invaluable: "The delicacy you have always shown to senior officers is a sure presage of your avoiding by every means in your power to give umbrage." He wrote himself, "If ever I feel great, it is in never having, in thought, word, or deed, robbed any man of his fair fame."

Instances of this delicate consideration for the feelings of others, dictated often by appreciation of their temperaments as well as of their circumstances, could be multiplied. But we read them imperfectly, missing their significance, if we see in them mere kindliness of temper; for, though kindly, Nelson was irritable, nervously sensitive to exasperating incidents, at times impatient to petulance, often unreasonable in complaint. Open expression of these feelings, evidences of temperament, flit often across his countenance, traversing the unity of the artist's vision and embarrassing his conception. Nelson was not faultless; but he was great. It is not, indeed, unprecedented to find such foibles in connection with much kindliness; they are easy concomitants in a warm temper. But this appreciation and consideration were with him no mere kindliness of temper, though that entered into them. They were the reflection outward of that which he knew and experienced within. In his followers he saw himself. To use the quaint expression of Swedenborg, he projected around him his own sphere. Because duty, zeal, energy inspired him, he saw them quickening others also; and the homage he intuitively paid to those qualities them-selves he gave to their possessors whom he saw around him. Each man, unless proved recreant, thus stood transfigured in the light which came from Nelson's self. This spontaneous recognition took form in an avowed scheme of life and action, which rested, consciously or unconsciously, upon the presumption in others of that same devotion to duty, that same zeal to perform it, and, in proportion to the individual's capacity, the same certainty of achievement which he found in himself. "Choose them yourself," he replied to the First Lord of the Admiralty, when asked to name his officers. "You cannot go amiss. The same spirit actuates the whole profession; you cannot choose wrong." The man to whose lips such words rise spontaneous simply attributes to others what he finds within, and what by experience he has found himself able to transfer. Out of the abundance of the heart he speaks, and by his words he is justified.

Closely connected with this characteristic, as is warp with woof, interwoven manifestation indeed of a quality essentially one and the same, is a trait in Nelson upon which I myself have been inclined to lay an emphasis which I do not find in other writers. So far as analysis can draw lines between the essential features of a particular character, the one to which I now allude is peculiarly military in its effec-tiveness; whereas devotion to duty, and confidence in others, may rather be called personal. At least they are not to be attributed exclusively to the military profes-sions, much as these undoubtedly have gained from the insistence, approaching monopoly, with which in them the idea of duty has been enforced, as supreme among the incentives of the soldier. To the Happy Warrior, Duty does not bar devo-tion to other virtues, except in rivalry with herself. Courage, obedience, fortitude, Duty recognizes them all and admits them; but not as equals. They are but parts of herself; the children, not the mother. Differing one from another, in her they find that which unites and consecrates them all. But while from all Duty exacts much, there are gifts which she cannot confer; and among them is one found in few, but conspicuous in Nelson.

In my own attempt to deal with his career, I spoke of this as Faith; and the word was criticized as inadequate and misleading, apparently because I was thought to use it in a narrowly religious sense. Now, I do not think that Nelson would have rejected religious trust in God as a prime motive in his professional action; but certainly, to my mind, if Jesus Christ spoke with only the authority of a man, he expressed a profound philosophy when He placed faith at the foundation of all lofty and successful action, religious or other. But while faith has a recognized technical meaning in theology, it has a much wider practical application; and when called confidence, or conviction, it is more easy to understand its value in the perplexities, the doubtful circumstances, which go to make all life, but especially the life of the military leader, responsible for great issues, such as fell to Nelson's determination. Then conviction, when possessed, becomes indeed the solid substance of things which the man cannot see with his eyes, nor know by ordinary knowledge. It is the bedrock upon which action rears its building, and stands four square against all the winds that blow. It is not so much a possession as that the man is possessed by it, and goes forward; not knowing whither he goes, but sure that, wherever the path leads, he does right to follow. As Nelson trusted his fellows, so he trusted the voice within, and for the same reason; in both he recognized the speech to which he was born.

Most of us know what it is to be tossed to and fro by hesitations, and thereby too often deterred from action, or weakened in it. Can anyone who has felt this inward anguish, and the feebleness of suspense, and at last has arrived at a working certainty, doubt the value and power of a faculty which reaches such certainty, reaches conviction, by processes which, indeed, are not irrational, but yet in their influence transcend reason? How clearly does reason sometimes lead us step by step to a conclusion so probable as to be worthy of being called a practical certainty, and there leave to our unaided selves the one further step to acceptance; the step across the chasm which yawns between conviction and knowledge, between faith and sight. This we have not the nerve to take because of the remaining doubt. Here reason, the goddess of to-day, halts and fails. The leap to acceptance, which faith takes, and wins, reason cannot make, nor is it within her gift to man. The consequent weakness and failure are more conspicuous in military life than in any other, because of the greatness of the hazards, the instancy and gravity of the result, should acceptance bring disaster. The track of military history is strewn with the dead reputations and the shattered schemes which have failed to receive the quickening element of conviction.

Of all inborn qualities, this is one of the strongest, as it is the rarest; for, let it be marked, such conviction consists, not in the particular conclusion reached, but in the dominating power with which it is held. This puts out of court all other considerations before entertained,—but now cast aside,—and acts; acts as though no other conclusion were possible, or ever had been. This to me has always invested with the force of a most profound allegory the celebrated incident of Nelson putting the glass to his blind eye, when looking at the signal which contravened his conviction. The time for hesitations had passed; there had been a time for discussion, but there remained now but one road to success. Conviction shuts its eyes to all else; the man who admits doubts at such an instant is lost. It is again single-mindedness, the single eye, the undoubting, revealed amid new surroundings. Conviction is one; doubts many. At the moment of this sublime exhibition, the words of the bystander depict Nelson as one breathing inspiration: "Though the fire of the enemy had slackened, the result had certainly not declared in favor on either side. Nelson was sometimes animated, and at others heroically fine in his observations. 'It is warm work, and this day may be the last for any of us at a moment; but mark you, I would not be elsewhere for thousands.'" "Leave off action! D------ me if I do." The man was possessed, in the noble sense of the word.

With less dramatic force, but no less telling and decisive effect, the same power of conviction manifested itself in a peculiarly critical moment of his career, near the close of his life. In May, 1805, he left his station in the Mediterranean to pursue an allied fleet to the West Indies. He had done this without other authority than his own inferences from the data before him; yielding, to quote a French admirer, to one of the finest inspirations of his genius. The West Indies reached, he failed to get touch of the enemy, owing to misinformation given him; and they started back to Europe, leaving no certain trace of where they were gone. Opinions and rumors clamored and clattered around him; certainty could not be had. He has recorded the situation himself in words which convey, more forcibly than my pen can, what is the power of conviction. "So far from being infallible, like the Pope, I believe my opinions to be very fallible, and therefore I may be mistaken that the enemy's fleet has gone to Europe; *but I cannot bring myself to think otherwise*, notwithstanding the variety of opinions which different people of *good judgment* form." "My opinion is *firm as a rock*, that some cause has made them resolve to proceed direct for Europe." Can conviction use stronger words?

And what is conviction but trust; trust in the unseen? Trust not irrational, not causeless, not unable to give some account of itself; but still short of knowledge, ignorant in part, deriving its power, not from what it sees, but from an unseen source within. To deny the existence and strength of such a faculty in some favored men is to shut one's eyes to the experience of history, and of daily life around us; a blindness, or a perversity, quite as real as it would be to ignore the shilly-shally vacillations of the multitude of clever men, who never find in themselves the power to act upon their opinions, if action involves risk, because opinion receives not that inward light which we called conviction, confidence, trust, faith. In Nelson this confidence, like his devotion to duty, and his trust in others, envelops his record, like an atmosphere which one insensibly feels, but the power of which is realized only by stopping to reflect. Lord Minto, who had known him intimately from the very beginnings of his greatness, and who knew the navy too, wrote after his death: "The navy is certainly full of the bravest men; but there was a sort of heroic cast about Nelson that I never saw in any other man, and which seems wanting to the achievement of *impossible things*, which became easy to him." Not that he had not to encounter perplexities and doubts in plenty. There is little singularity in conviction where there is nothing to shake it. None of us have trouble in admitting that two and two make four. But as Nelson's actions are followed, whatever the obscurity of the conditions, one finds oneself always in presence of a spirit as settled in its course, when once decided, as though doubt were not possible.

Our quest has been the strength of Nelson. I find it in the inborn natural power to trust; to trust himself and others; to confide, to use his own word. Whether it is the assurance within, which we call conviction, or the assurance without, which we call confidence, in others or in one's own action, this is the basic principle and motive force of his career, as Duty was its guiding light and controlling standard. I make less of his clear perceptions, his sound judgment, of the general rational processes which illuminated his course, as I also do of the courage, fortitude, zeal, which illustrated his deeds. All these things, valuable as they are, he shared with others. He possessed them, possibly, in an unusual degree, but still in common with many to whom they could never bring success, because unassociated with that indefinable something, which, like a yet undiscovered element in nature, or an undetected planet, we recognize by its workings, and may to it even attribute a name, though unable as yet adequately to describe. Genius, we not infrequently say; a word which, not yet defined, stands a mute confession of our ignorance wherein it consists. As I conceive it, there is no genius greater than faith; though it may well be that in so saying we have but given another name with no nearer approach to a definition.

In a celebrated funeral oration, which we all know, the speaker says: "I come to bury Caesar, not to praise him." It is for no such purpose that men observe this day; for the man, the memory of whom now moves his people, is not one to be buried, but to be praised and kept in everlasting remembrance. True, he needs not our praises, but we need to praise him for our own sakes. The Majesty on high is exalted far above all praise, yet it is good to praise Him; for the essence of praise is not the homage of the lips, but the recognition of excellence; and recognition, when real, elevates, ennobles. It fosters an ideal which tends to induce imitation, and to uplift by sheer force of appreciation and association. And as with the Creator, so with the excellent among his creatures. We need not ignore their failings, or their sins, although an occasion like the present is not one for dwelling upon these; but as we recognize in them men of like frailties with ourselves, we yet perceive that, despite all, they have not only done the great works, but have been the great men whom we may justly reverence. That they in their weakness have had so much in common with us gives hope that we may yet have something in common with them in their strength. It is the high grace and privilege of a man like Nelson that he provokes emulation rather than rivalry, imitation rather than competition. To extol him uplifts ourselves. As it was when he lived on earth, so it is now. His life is an inheritance to children's children; of his own people first, but after them of all the nations of the earth.

Discussion Questions

1. What does Mahan say is Admiral Nelson's most important trait, which made him a great leader? Why was this the key trait?

2. Mahan mentions George Washington a number of times. How does Washington compare to Nelson, and what does that suggest to you about leadership?

3. From what you can tell from Mahan's writing, does the culture of the Navy or Marine Corps treat the concept of trust the same way today that the Royal Navy did in the late eighteenth and nineteenth centuries? If it does, why do you think that is the case? If it does not, why?

4. What does Mahan mean when he talks of a dual nature of Nelson's ability to trust? Does good leadership require both? Or just one of them? How does that apply to your role in your unit?

5. Which of the quotes or anecdotes that Mahan includes in this writing was the most memorable to you? What do the ones that demonstrate Nelson's weaknesses mean to your understanding of leadership?

9

MILITARY CONSERVATISM

William S. Sims

(U.S. Naval Institute *Proceedings* 48, no. 3, March 1922)

19 November 1921
To the Graduating Class of 1921

In bidding good-bye to the members of the class of 1921, at the termination of their course of one year at the Naval War College, it has occurred to me that it may be of some interest to invite their consideration of a subject to which too little attention has heretofore been paid, namely, that type and degree of military conservatism which has so often been responsible for defeat in battle, and sometimes for national disaster.

Ever since men first began to use weapons to fight each other, military men have been reproached for excessive conservatism, a polite term often intended to imply a dangerous class reluctance to accept new ideas.

All men are naturally more or less conservative; certainly all civil professions are decidedly so; but they can afford to be without much danger to the country, whereas, in the case of the military profession, national disaster might easily result from a lack of the vision necessary to recognize the superiority of a new weapon or a new method of warfare.

That military men are conservative admits of no doubt. Whether they are more so than civilians is beside the question. The important point is that their conservatism may be so dangerous that it is highly important that they should so train their minds in logical thinking as to eliminate, or at least minimize, this danger.

We hope that the training at the Naval War College will have this effect; and I believe that it will, provided our understanding of the influence of conservatism in the past is such as to convince us that we must avoid its danger in future. With this end in view it will be useful to invite attention to certain instances of this defect that are recorded in the history of warfare, and also to certain recent instances that will show the influence it has exerted, and perhaps is still exerting, upon the minds of our contemporaries. These latter illustrations will include a number of instances that are within my own experience, and doubtless some of these are within your recollection; and from them we may be able to determine the cause of the state of mind in question, and possibly to indicate the remedy.

So strong has been the resistance to the general introduction of any new weapons or methods of warfare that one is almost forced to conclude that the military classes of all ages were all recruited from the Missouri of their respective countries. However this may be, it may be stated in general terms that most arguments in favor of fundamentally new weapons have failed except those that resulted in shedding the blood of the unbelievers; that defeat alone has been accepted as a final demonstration. The following are a few examples of the nature of the resistance in question, beginning with ancient times in order to show that this influence has been continuous, and that such conservatism as we retain at present is a legitimate inheritance from our naval forebears.

Considering, first, the most primitive weapons, there is no doubt but that the bow was a vastly more efficient instrument of warfare than the sword, the mace, or the pike; but almost without exception it was never accepted as a proper arm for the knight or warrior. The ancient wars were mainly fought with the sword and javelin, and both Greeks and Romans looked upon the bow as plebeian. It was not until the decline of the Roman Empire that the bow was used to any large degree by the Romans, the victory over the Franks at Casilinum (A.D. 554) being won by the horse-archers.

The warriors of medieval Europe viewed the bow in the same way. Thus Charlemagne endeavored to dignify and extend its use by edicts and the establishment of schools of archery, but to little avail, for the bow remained, until supplanted by firearms, the arm of the inferior classes and the yeomanry.

The crossbow was an advance over the bow in power and efficiency but it never became the predominant arm, although it was extensively used during the Crusades. In A.D. 1139, the Lateran Council condemned its use as a murderous weapon. This resulted in a partial abandonment of it as a mode of warfare. The attitude of the nobleman respecting the cross-bow is indicated by the action of Philip of France at the battle of Crecy (August 26, 1346), who rode down his Genoese cross-bowmen with the words, "Forward and strike down this useless rabble, who are thus blocking up the way in our front." But Crecy was won by bowmen, the English archers, who, unlike the Genoese, had kept their bow-strings dry, devastating the chivalry of France.

"A first-class English archer," said Prince Louis Napoleon, "who in a single minute was able to draw and discharge his bow twelve times with a range of 240 yards, and who in these twelve shots only once missed his man, was very lightly esteemed."

It would seem that there was for many centuries a settled prejudice against projectiles, or perhaps rather against the men who launched the projectiles, because it was considered that these men required less courage than the wielders of short-arm weapons. This prejudice persisted for a considerable period even after the introduction of firearms.

Although gunpowder is said to have been discovered in Europe by Roger Bacon during the early years of the 13th century, it was not until 1338 that we have any account of the use of artillery. This was at the battle of Cambrai. Cannon are again mentioned as used in the battle of Quesnoy (1339). At this time, however, they were looked upon as curiosities more than anything else, and it was the general opinion of military experts that artillery would not supplant the sword and the pike.

In fact the pike or the lance was considered superior to the gun as late as the 18th century. We know that the Emperor of Germany changed his pikemen to musketeers in 1689, which led Louvois, the French minister, to propose a similar change in the armies of France. Louis XIV, however, while he confessed that he was impressed by the minister's arguments, said that he did not consider them strong enough to warrant such a great change. Pikes were not abolished in France until 1703. Incidentally, they were still supplied to our ships 180 years later.

Nor was our cloth less conservative as regards the introduction either of weapons or of methods of propelling war vessels. For example, it is apparent that oars were used more than sails in the sea battles of the ancients. The sail was mainly an auxiliary. The Egyptians, the Romans and the Greeks all trusted to the oar on account of its freedom from weather conditions. This attitude persisted quite to modern times; the battle of Lepanto (1499) was fought with galleys, and the Spanish Armada (1588) contained a great number of galleys. Artillery did more to do away with the oar than anything else, for the guns occupied the positions of the oarsmen.

Also Mahan states in *From Sail to Steam*, that: "The parting with sails as the motive reliance of a ship of war was characterized by an extreme conservatism.

Steam was accepted first as an auxiliary, for towing, etc. A man of unusual intelligence maintained that steam would never prevail over sail; the steamer 'broke down,' and owing to the fuel question could never be as self-contained as a sailing ship. Admiral Baudin, a Napoleonic veteran, was very sarcastic over the uncertainty of steamers."

And Wilmot, in his book *The Development of Navies*, states that: "In England we were disposed to rely on what had in former years admirably answered the purpose, and given us supremacy on the sea by which the security of the country was ensured. Had our fleet suffered defeat, we might have been more ready to adopt new inventions, indeed, to initiate them, rather than wait until their utility was proven by others."

Barnaby, in his *Naval Developments of the Century*, shows the extreme reluctance of those in authority even to consider the adoption of new weapons. He states that: "This demand of the fighting man for the most perfect weapons throughout the entire armory, however often the change may be necessary, has a curious effect upon the good Admiralty and War Office official. He does not hesitate to take up an attitude of hostility to all innovation and to do his best to suppress it. Sad experience as to what advancing tides will do is perhaps working changes in the official mind, but the author well remembers the authority and seriousness with which the doctrine was held fifty years ago."

Wilmot again states that: "The discovery that steam could be profitably utilized for the propulsion of ships, and the tardy adoption of the screw, did not for many years materially affect the construction of war vessels. There was a strong prejudice to overcome in the minds of those who retained a vivid recollection of the glories accomplished in the past under sail, and who had a natural love for the art in which we excelled. Rear Admiral Sir William Symonds (director of naval construction), to whom I have alluded as effecting considerable improvement in the qualities of our sailing ships, had, as his biographer states, no love for steamers in any shape. . . . In a letter to Lord Auckland he states: 'I consider steamers of every description in the greatest peril when it is necessary to use broadside guns in close action; not alone from their liability to be disabled from shot striking their steam-chest, steam-pipe, machinery, etc., but great probability of explosion owing to sparks from funnel.'"

His opposition was so great that he was forced to resign in favor of a committee of naval architects, under Sir Baldwin Walker, "a naval officer distinguished for his seamanship"; but this officer's distinction in this respect was such that progress under his control is described as follows by a British historian:

"The naval members of the Board of Admiralty were men who had long looked upon the noble line-of-battle-ships of the navy as not to be surpassed, and they could not apparently make up their minds to desecrate them, as they seemed to consider it, by the introduction of steam power. The result of this somewhat romantic feeling was, that early in Sir Baldwin Walker's administration a number of sailing three-deckers were laid down, in opposition to the expressed opinion of the leading civil professional officers attached to the Admiralty. Not one of these vessels, as had been predicted, was ever launched as a sailing vessel. They were converted into screw ships by being lengthened in midships, at the bows, and also at the sterns. The greater proportion of the other sailing three-deckers were also cut down and converted into two-decked screw ships, their sterns only being altered."

Inventors have always had a hard time in convincing high naval officials of the merits of their inventions. It usually required the pressure of war necessity or strong political influence, or both, to insure even a hearing. Fulton and Ericsson are cases in point.

Fulton's *Demologos*, a steam-propelled floating battery, contained all the elements essential for a battleship today—positive and well-protected motive power, heavy battery, and impregnable armor, the latter five feet of solid wood; but naval officers insisted upon masts and sails and heavy bulwarks to protect those handling them, "Thus, on the first possible occasion, did steam and sail power come into conflict, and steam had to take the inferior position."

In 1837–38 Ericsson was unable to gain recognition from the Admiralty, and in 1839 he returned to America and, under the patronage of Captain Stockton, one of the few officers who favored the use of steam, superintended in 1842 the building of the sloop-of-war *Princeton*, the first screw steam vessel of war built in any country.

In the fifties Congress ordered the building of "six first-class steam frigates." They were full-rigged ships but with steam power so ridiculously small as to call forth the following comment from the late Rear Admiral Edward Simpson:

"There were those at that time who, wise beyond their generation, recognized the full meaning of the advent of steam, and saw that it must supplant sails altogether as a motive power for ships. These advocated that new construction should be provided with full steam power, with sails as an auxiliary; but the old pride in the sailing-ship, with her taut and graceful spars, could not be made to yield at once to the innovation; old traditions pointing to the necessity of full sail power could not be dispelled; it was considered a sufficient concession to admit steam on any terms, and thus the conservative and temporizing course was adopted of retaining full sail power, and utilizing steam as an auxiliary."

Barnaby states that: "There was the same prejudice against the adoption of iron for vessels as for the adoption of steam propulsion. Furthermore the opponents of armor were sufficiently entrenched to delay the adoption of these new ideas for years. Iron was first used in vessels in 1812, but it was not until 1834 that the British Admiralty began to make experiments in this field, and not until 1845 that an armored ship was produced by Laird."

The introduction of armor was opposed very strenuously for many years. Barnaby further states that: "In 1876 Admiral Sir George Elliott circulated a pamphlet designed 'to stop the useless expenditure by the Admiralty of vast sums of money on the ships ordered by them not because the ships were partially unarmoured, but because they were armoured at all.' In that pamphlet he declared armour-clad ship-building to be the result of want of foresight. . . . But he contended that the evidence of the superiority of the gun, and the developments of the efficacy of the ram and the torpedo had deprived us of sufficient excuse of late years to continue to fight the losing game of armour against guns."

"The great naval tactician, Sir Howard Douglas, in 1858, published a book entitled *Naval Warfare with Steam* in which he said that the *Renown* was the best type of war vessel in the British navy. This vessel was unarmoured."

In comparatively recent times we have seen wide fluctuations of opinion as to the relative importance of armor and volume of gun-fire, including Farragut's unfortunate phrase, "The best protection against the enemy's fire is a well-directed fire from our own guns."

This phrase had a profound influence upon the design of ships in certain navies. The Russian cruisers of the *Gromoboi* class were equipped with a battery so heavy for their displacement and speed that not only were many guns left without armor but the personnel of her ammunition supply was so exposed that she fell an easy prey to a Japanese vessel of the *Asama* class, with half the number of guns all adequately protected.

The long and costly controversy over the adoption of breech-loading guns is too well known to require reference to more than the very significant fact that purely mechanical difficulties were constantly allowed to overshadow in importance the fundamental principle involved. Breech-loaders were installed in the British navy, replaced by muzzle-loaders, and reinstalled until their final adoption in the latter part of the 19th century. Thus Barnaby states:

"In 1875, owing to accidents to breech-loaders, the muzzleloader was reinstated in the service. The great munitions firm of Armstrong fought the breech-loader for years and was instrumental in deferring its adoption. The firm, of course, was supported by many naval officers."

"The breech-loading guns might have been retained for all they were worth, and in course of time men would have become familiarized with them. Defects and weaknesses would have been soberly valued and gradually removed. . . . We had to pay heavily for that and we are called upon now to reverse the process and get rid of all ships having a muzzle-loading armament."

But while ordnance experts were vigorously discussing the question as to the end of the gun into which the projectile would best be inserted, and were still blind to the profound influence the breech-loader necessarily would exercise upon the design of war vessels, they were no less strenuously resisting any improvements in the projectiles themselves. Some of their arguments are curious, and some amusing, particularly those concerning the great cost of the shell of that day. Thus Wilmot states that:

"The old prejudice in favor of solid shot was not easily overcome. The latter were said to be more accurate, and to have greater range and penetration than hollow shell. Objections were also raised to putting too many shell guns in ships on account of the danger of accidental explosions.

"Another argument used against the introduction of projectiles was their cost. Sir Howard Douglas, in his work on Naval Gunnery says, 'the expense of shell equipment is enormous. The cost of every 8-inch shell in box is 11 s. 6 d., or $2.78, and each one fired costs 17 s. 4 ¾ d., or $4.17. (1838).'"

Having in the above account convicted the officers who were before our time of a degree of conservatism that was at least very dangerous to the success of their navies, the question arises as to whether the record of our contemporaries is any better. It is to a certain extent, because during the last fifty years we have become so accustomed to great advances in all mechanical appliances and scientific processes that it is hard to surprise us by anything new in these lines.

During the lifetime of officers still living it may be said that navies have advanced from wood and sails to steel and steam. Some of our senior admirals began their careers on full rigged wooden vessels with feeble auxiliary steam power and smooth bore guns.

During a visit I made to the Portsmouth dockyard in 1905, the first dreadnought was anchored in the harbor alongside Nelson's *Victory*, and the admiral in command of the yard invited attention to the enormous progress that had been made since he began his career as a middy when vessels of the *Victory* type were still standard capital ships.

This rapid progress has of course tended to diminish conservatism as much in foreign navies as in ours; but the important question now is as to whether the training we are actually giving our officers in systematic and logical thinking will enable our navy, not simply to adopt improvements after their value has been proved in foreign navies, but so to utilize our undoubted inventive ability, and so promptly to recognize demonstrated facts, that we may keep safely in the van of progress, and thus eliminate the danger of being outclassed through the superior vision and alertness of possible enemies.

In this connection it may be useful to invite attention to two very significant facts:

First, that America has been distinctly in the lead in originating many important features of naval design, and in the invention of types and weapons of fundamental importance I need cite as examples only the monitor, the submarine and the airplane. There are many others.

Second, that, generally speaking, our navy has lagged behind in the adoption and general application even of our own American improvements and inventions. Many of our inventors have had to go abroad for recognition.

This indisposition on the part of our navy at once to utilize new ideas, weapons and methods of demonstrated value is a fact of supreme importance. In fact it is the gist of this whole subject. It is due to a habit of mind that could be indulged in the past with comparative safety, but which is manifestly a danger to a country that has become involved in international politics, and whose policies are likely to be disputed by other powers.

This habit of mind was not the result of a lack of intelligence or patriotic interest, but was due chiefly to the long period during which our country was relatively free from foreign entanglements, and, consequently, when we so lacked the pressure of the probability of war that is continuously felt by European nations, that we naturally thought we could afford to let other navies experiment with, and demonstrate the usefulness of, new designs and weapons before we adopted them. We can no longer safely do so. In order fully to realize the extent to which at times we have been unprogressive it will be necessary briefly to review our attitude in the immediate past, and thus show why we must, and perhaps how we can, avoid this danger in future.

Almost all controversies over questions of the adoption of new methods or weapons have had one perfectly natural feature in common: they have been contests between the younger men with their naturally more progressive minds and the more conservative seniors at the top of the list who had the power of decision. This has been as true in former times as it has been in our time; and moreover, it goes without saying that while in general such controversies have been based upon honest differences of opinion, sometimes strongly influenced by natural conservatism, still they were not free from the influences of our fallible human nature.

Criticisms from juniors fall with great severity upon the responsible seniors, especially in a military service; and questions of personal ambition, and the assumed necessity of defending established reputations, both of men and of organizations, do not create a condition of mind that is favorable to the reception of new ideas. The consequence too often has been successful resistance on the part of responsible naval officials, sometimes continued until overcome by the civil authorities or by the force of public opinion.

It is doubtless well known to all of you that in the past our navy vigorously resisted the introduction of steam propulsion, then reluctantly consented to auxiliary steam with full sail power, then to full steam with auxiliary, sail power, and finally, but very tardily, gave up sails altogether. There was the same opposition to the introduction of armor, breech-loading guns, and other improvements of minor importance; and nothing but the extreme pressure of war necessity overcame the opposition to Ericsson's monitor. It is not necessary to review all of these phases of our navy's resistance, as they were similar in all respects to those already noted in the experience of the British and other navies but it should be recorded that these controversies were fought out in some instances not only with extreme bitterness but with an apparent inability or indisposition to accept the plainest possible evidence.

This was not simply conservatism, it was conservatism complicated not only by national conceit, but by personal interests and human passions, and too often, by a certain degree of dishonesty exhibited in the defense of reputations.

In order to accentuate the military necessity of logical ability and intellectual honesty in reaching decisions that may be vital to the efficiency of military forces, I will review briefly the kind and degree of opposition that had to be overcome in order to accomplish the general adoption only of the most important of all modern improvements, namely, the new methods of gunnery training, the all-big-gun capital ship, and the submarine.

These improvements are probably within the experience of all officers present, but I think it is doubtful whether many of you are aware that there was much opposition to their adoption, and still more doubtful that you are informed of its nature or intensity. The extent of this opposition is hereinafter described for the sole purpose of inviting attention to the errors in this respect that we seek to avoid in future. That such errors must hereafter be avoided is apparent from the fact that in all three of the cases just cited—gunnery training, the dreadnought type of design, and the submarine—our resistance left us so far behind other navies that if war had been declared before we had adopted such fundamental improvements we would, in all probability, have suffered defeat in consequence.

As regards efficiency in gunnery it would seem that the naval mind has always been particularly self-satisfied. Even an officer of such vision as Nelson, when asked to grant an interview to an inventor of an improved method of aiming the guns of a ship of the line, consented to receive him but said he did not expect to live to see the day when it would be necessary accurately to aim these guns, as he always expected to engage the enemy within pistol range.

The risk that the British navy ran becomes apparent when we consider that the effective range of the guns of the period was about 3,000 yards, particularly against the enemy's rigging; that simple mechanism for pointing the guns was easily realizable and the slow approach, for example, at Trafalgar, would have permitted the enemy to fire ten or twelve broadsides before the British ships closed to the range at which they could hit without aiming.

In 1895, while serving as intelligence officer of a vessel on the China Station, I made reports upon some sixty odd foreign men-of-war. These included a description of a new cruiser of the *Edgar* class, and of the British so-called "H" sight, and an account of the, at that time, quite extraordinary number of hits-per-gun-per-minute made by the *Edgar*'s 6-inch guns fitted with these sights. These results were so far in advance of ours that the reports were probably not believed. At all events not only was no attention paid to them at the Navy Department, but they were considered of so little value that they were all destroyed.

During the four years from the beginning of 1897 until the latter part of 1900, I made from France and Russia extensive reports on the gunnery training of the French and Russian navies. France was at that time firing at relatively long ranges; the Russian training, though largely mistaken in principle, was probably the most complete and extensive of that of any navy, and her expenditure of ammunition was by far the greatest. Reports on ordnance, construction, and so forth, during this period showed a great superiority of design over the astonishing inefficiency of our contemporary ships. In all, these reports comprised over eleven thousand pages. They produced no appreciable effect at the time, and were not only destroyed but the letter-press copies in Paris were burned by order of the Navy Department.

In 1901 and 1902 many reports were submitted from China on the design of foreign ships, their systems of protection, ordnance mechanism, methods of gunnery training, and so forth. These included a comparison showing that notwithstanding the relative weight of armor carried by the *Kentucky* class, then just commissioned and the pride of our navy, their turret and broadside guns were greatly exposed, and even their magazines were so open as to render it very dangerous to fire the guns. This report attracted some attention at the Navy Department. It promptly disappeared and was never thereafter located; and the defects to which it invited attention were defended up to, and even after, the fearful turret accidents that caused the death of so many officers and men in the turret explosions in the *Missouri, Kearsarge, Georgia* and other vessels.

During the same period extensive reports were made upon Captain Sir Percy Scott's method of training gun-pointers by means of the dotter. Not only were the records made at Scott's target practices disputed, but the most fundamentally important improvement recorded in the history of naval artillery, that is, the continuous aim that enables us to hit at long ranges, and which has consequently profoundly modified the design of war vessels, was not only ridiculed as absurd, but it was officially "proved" to be so by an elaborate paper prepared by the Bureau of Ordnance to show that it was mathematically impossible for a pointer to keep a six-inch gun on a target throughout a roll of even a few degrees.

All the reports just mentioned that were submitted from China were destroyed. The effort to secure the adoption by the Navy Department of the improvements in question was at the time a flat failure, notwithstanding the fact that the commander-in-chief of the China Station, Admiral Remey, brought them to the attention of the Navy Department in special communications, in which he stated that the situation was extremely critical as regarded the design of our vessels, the mechanism of our ordnance, and the training of our gunnery personnel.

The new system of gunnery training and fire-control was at that time opposed by the great majority of our senior officers, many of whom expressed their disapproval in letters to the Department advocating the retention of our former practice of requiring each gun-pointer to estimate the range and control the fire of his own gun. This opposition produced an order requiring that all men, including mess attendants, should frequently be exercised at estimating distances.

Subsequently, our inefficiency in gunnery was brought directly to the attention of President Roosevelt, who issued peremptory orders that the new methods of training should at once be put in practice and that all guns should be fitted with efficient sights. Under this order, our marksmanship developed with great rapidity, though the system of training was still opposed by practically all of the senior officers concerned, including, for example, all but one of the captains of the North Atlantic fleet.

When in 1903 and 1904, this development had demonstrated the accuracy of heavy turret guns at distances beyond the effective range of the secondary battery, and when, in consequence, a number of our junior officers opposed the building of any more mixed caliber ships and recommended the all big-gun ship, or dreadnought type, the recommendation was successfully opposed by most of our senior officers, including Admiral Mahan, until its adoption was forced by President Roosevelt. But for this conservative attitude we would have launched the first dreadnought. A painting in my possession of the design recommended is dated 1904.

Many of you may remember that this opposition was based chiefly upon the Department's official opinion that the greater the calibre of the gun the less its ability to hit; also upon the singular opinion implied by the phrase "the smothering effect of the fire of the small secondary battery guns"—a phrase without meaning when applied to the fire of such small guns against battleship armor, but, nevertheless, tenaciously believed in for many years by some of our leading authorities—a striking example of the peculiar power of a picturesque phrase when substituted for the careful reasoning that is of such vital importance in military matters.

In the case of all the vitally important improvements indicated, we have followed instead of leading. Sometimes we have not even followed though outclassed by new types in all important navies. All competent students of naval warfare have long since recognized the necessity for battle cruisers, particularly if our possible enemies possess them; but until recently our navy has failed to recommend them to the Congress, though for a great many years their value has been conclusively demonstrated on the game board.

The case of the submarine need be hardly more than mentioned. Though American designers of this type of vessel are responsible for most of the principles upon which its success depends, they received so little encouragement from our navy that not only was the first practical development in foreign navies, but even as late as our entry into the Great War, the capabilities of this type of vessel were seriously misunderstood.

The same is true to an even greater degree as regards the development of the airplane as a weapon. Even while foreign countries were appropriating large sums of money and were making every effort to develop it, our naval authorities were actually resisting its introduction.

These are only a few of the instances of the deadly effect of unreasoning conservatism. Many others could be cited in connection with practically every more or less radical departure in design, weapons, methods or appliances. Generally speaking, all such improvements have met with more or less effective resistance from those in authority; and the examples cited show that this resistance has been in certain important cases so very determined as to cause juniors to think twice before placing themselves definitely in opposition to their seniors; and it should be specially noted that the more important or fundamental the improvement advocated, the more strenuous and prolonged is likely to be the opposition, and consequently, the greater the danger of delay in giving it impartial and unprejudiced consideration.

It is by reason of this attitude that our navy found itself so absurdly deficient in marksmanship during the Spanish war; so deficient in destroyers, submarines and airplanes when we entered the Great War; and it is for this reason that we are still without battle cruisers.

The rapid development of the submarine and the airplane during the war, and the continuous development of both, and especially the latter, since the war, have shown that these powerful weapons are still in their infancy; that great possibilities of development are clearly in sight; and that it will require the most careful, devoted, and logical consideration upon our part even to keep abreast of the developments in foreign navies, much less to anticipate these developments.

Are we approaching the consideration of the influence of these revolutionary weapons in a judicial frame of mind? I am afraid not, in view of recent examples of minds absolutely closed to the plainest facts. In spite of adequate experiments clearly showing that airplanes could make a certain percentage of hits upon ship targets, a secretary of the navy expressed his disbelief in the ability of bombing planes to injure a vessel by affirming his willingness to stand upon the bridge of the *Ostfriesland* during the proposed bombing experiments. It is of course not remarkable that a civilian should have made such a statement; but it is very significant that this statement was based upon similar statements by naval officers and upon the assurance of naval advisers who were suffering the blighting influence of conservatism to an extent not exceeded by that of any of the examples just cited from history and from recent experiences.

So great indeed was the unwillingness to admit anything at all to the disadvantage of the battleship that many of our senior officers solved the difficulty for themselves by simply denying all the claims made by the airmen. For example, a captain on duty at the Navy Department expressed the opinion that a battleship can shoot down planes as fast as they attempt to get into bombing position; that even unopposed bombers could not hit a vessel underway; and in any case that bombs would not do much damage; that a bomb exploding on the protective deck would not penetrate below if it contained less than three thousand pounds of T.N.T.

Manifestly, our mental attitude in these matters must be radically changed unless we are to repeat the errors of the past, and cause our navy to follow instead of leading.

Verily, we must be on our guard against the dangers of a lack of vision and of a lack of confidence in the conclusions derived from a candid and logical examination of the significance of established military facts.

Our objective must not be "safety first" in the sense of adherence to already tested practices and implements, but safety first in being the first to recognize, the first to experiment with, and the first to adopt improvements of distinct military value.

Doubtless many of us have suffered from pain of a new idea, and some have recorded their suffering in writing. I remember ridiculing many years ago an imaginative article, describing a naval battle of the future, because the author had ships destroying each other by gunfire at 12,000 yards; and I am consoled only by the fact that many of my seniors inveighed at the time against the absurd idea that naval actions would ever be fought at "the enormous range of 7,000 yards."

Our navy has in our own time passed through periods of great danger. At the battle of Santiago we made but three per cent of hits at ranges shorter than are ever likely to occur again; and so inefficient was our gunnery up to 1900 that an equal force of ships of any efficient navy could have inflicted upon us a most humiliating defeat.

In my opinion we are now entering a period that may become still more dangerous if we fail correctly to interpret the significance of the rapid development of fundamentally new weapons of enormous destructive power and of relative immunity to effective resistance by any means except a decisive superiority of similar weapons.

We may escape this danger in future, as has so often been the case in the past, through the superior vision of a Roosevelt, or through the pressure of public opinion, overcoming the excessive conservatism of military minds.

From the above examination of this important subject, I think it is apparent that the remedy we seek is comprised in a combination of logical ability and military character—the ability to reach sound conclusions from established facts, and the character to accept, adopt, and fight for these conclusions against any material or spiritual forces.

A navy to be successful must be guided not only by men of ability but by men of an intellectual honesty that is proof against personal ambition or any other influences whatsoever.

Which of us will be quoted in future as examples of dangerous conservatism? Of which of us will it be said that we were of:

> The many who follow the beaten track,
> With guideposts on the way
> They live and have lived for ages back
> With a chart for every day.
> Someone has told them it is safe to go
> On the road he has travelled o'er,
> And all that they ever strive to know
> Are the things that were known before.

Discussion Questions

1. What examples does Sims use to illustrate what he means by "military conservatism"? Which ones do you think best illustrate his point, and why?

2. Why does Sims think that military officers are conservative? Do these reasons still apply today?

3. According to Sims, how does seniority in the service (or age) contribute to the ability to innovate or to embrace new ideas? Is he right? Why or why not?

4. Sims ends by saying, "A navy to be successful must be guided not only by men of ability but by men of an intellectual honesty that is proof against personal ambition or any other influences whatsoever." Does this describe the Navy and Marine Corps today? How do our personnel policies today fit into the ideas Sims spoke about?

5. How should we apply the ideas in Sims' essay to our understanding of naval "innovation" in the twenty-first century?

10

WHY A SAILOR
THINKS LIKE A SAILOR

J. C. Wylie

(U.S. Naval Institute *Proceedings* 83, no. 8, August 1957)

Every autumn there is a series of internal crises in the Navy Department, growing in intensity until finally the annual budget requests take shape. During the winter the Department of Defense and the Congress work over the budgets of all three services to try to get them into some kind of acceptable meshing. Then finally in the spring, before the Congress goes home for the summer, there is usually some sort of an eruption into public debate related to authorizations or appropriations or changes to laws governing the services.

A couple of years ago it was Reorganization Plan 6. Last year it was the Symington Hearings. No one knows exactly what the subject may be in the months just ahead—budget allocations, or a common supply system, or efficiency, or economy, or civilian control, or an earlier spring, or a combination of any or all of them.

The only thing we can be fairly sure of is that the services will, somehow, find themselves in some sort of public opposition. And, whatever may be the point at issue, each of the services will have strong ideas and clear ones on its own side of the discussion.

The basic problem is why they do not agree. Why does the soldier think like a soldier, the sailor like a sailor, and the airman like neither of these but like an airman?

Let there be no delusion. Even though they all serve the same common purpose and do so in all the honesty and sincerity of able and dedicated men, they do not think alike. There are areas of agreement and coincidence, to be sure, and these are by far the most numerous and inclusive. But there are areas of differences, important differences, even though they may be subtle and hard to isolate and hold up for examination.

Before going further, it would be well to inject a caution: Asking why they do not agree is quite a different matter from asserting that they should agree. On the contrary, these differences of judgment, these clashes of ideas, these almost constant pullings and haulings among the services, are the greatest source of military strength that the nation has. We do differ, within and among the services, and may Heaven help us if we ever enter into a period of prevailing sweetness and light and unanimity. Nothing would be more dangerous to our nation than the comfortable and placid acceptance of a single idea, a single and exclusively dominant military pattern of thought. The political parallel is almost too obvious to mention.

Let us only recognize that the unique advantage we have over the monolithic organizations which may oppose us is built into our system politically and militarily—the capacity to detect and expose our own weaknesses. As a concomitant of that we have always at hand an intellectual reserve, a reserve of strategic concept, the capacity to put to practice an alternate plan of action.

Strangely enough, the one aspect of the situation that has never really been publicly aired, nor even examined with enough perception and depth to make it worth the effort, is the underlying basis of the disagreement. Why do the soldiers think one way, and the sailors another, and the airmen still a third?

There will be no attempt in this discussion to speak for the soldier and the airman. The aim here will be to try to sketch out some foundations of the sailor's thought pattern—why he thinks the way he does. To do this, we shall take up a few war-planning assumptions, and then take up briefly the maritime concept of warfare. Then, after that, perhaps the package can be related to the general tasks of war and to one or two specific current problems to demonstrate the effect of these basic patterns of thought on the sailor's attitude toward the matters of the times.

As for the matter of war-planning assumptions, they are brought into this discussion for two reasons. First, because the planning phase of strategy is the link between the ideas of war and the conduct of war. And second, because recognition of these basic planning assumptions (and most sailors adhere to them whether they have ever consciously phrased them or not) may give some clues to the sailor's behavior even in situations only remotely related to planning for war. In no sense are they formal or official. They are just an attempt to condense some fairly general tacit understandings.

The first assumption is that the aim of war is some measure of control over the enemy. By control, in this broadest sense, we mean in effect the creation of conditions more favorable to us than would have existed had we not gone to war, a control over the enemy sufficient to resettle him, after the fighting, into some acceptable status in whatever may be the postwar scheme of the world. The key in this rather loose statement is the idea that control, in one fashion or another, is the distant strategic aim. Our war aim is not necessarily met with defeat of the enemy's armed forces. It may not even be met by his governmental collapse or surrender. And it is certainly not met if all the enemy citizens (and most of our own) are the victims of a thermonuclear double-suicide. A primary and central problem in warfare is the sensing of what kinds and degrees of control may result from this or that action in this or that situation. And one can reasonably doubt that we can be very specific about it before an actual situation is at hand to be weighed in judgment. A type and intensity of control, direct or indirect, that may be excellent for one situation may be quite inapplicable in another. But the idea of control, as an aim, does markedly widen the horizons open to us in our thoughts and planning for war.

There are several methods by which control may be sought, either at sea or on the land. Some degree of military control may be achieved by destruction, the direct destruction of enemy strength, the men, the weapons, and the component parts of the physical supporting structure leading from the weapons all the way back through the communications to the basic raw materials. This is an area with which most of the world by now is thoroughly familiar.

A sort of corollary or offshoot of this might be called control by immobilization or paralysis . . . and it is mentioned here because it may be an area worth considerably more thought than has been given it in the recent past.

A more positive degree of control and a more viable one, though a more difficult one to attain, may be had by occupation, i.e., the physical occupation of an area or of selected governing focal points.

A control of sorts may be exercised by the announced or tacit threat of destruction, or perhaps by the threat of occupation. While control-by-threat is variable and sometimes uncertain both in its degree and its durability, it is often politically and militarily the most advisable method of applying force.

There are, of course, the more indirect forms of control by economic, political, social, and psychological pressures, all of which, by the way, have consistently played an important role in the application of maritime strategies.

The second basic assumption for war planning is that we cannot with certainty predict the complete pattern of the war for which we prepare ourselves. The time, the place, the scope, the intensity, the course, and the general tenor of a next war are all dim and uncertain matters. Aggressors can fix the initial time and place, and we may not see it until late in its making. Who saw well ahead to Guadalcanal, or Korea, or the Suez? It is the possibility of these situations that we must keep in mind, and the more astute and inclusive is our planning the better can we manage them when they do appear.

When we accept this admittedly oversimplified premise that we cannot with certainty forecast the pattern of war, nor its time, nor its place, nor its characteristics, then we arrive at the conclusion that the primary requisite in peacetime planning is more than a single rigid plan for war. Our first requirement is for a planning concept that covers a spectrum of possibilities, for the broadest possible conceptual span embracing in both time and character any military-force situation which might arise. Then, after we have in mind a full span of concept, we can take up specific situations for one of two reasons. The first is for the derivation of logistic and material needs; and the second is to meet circumstances in which the probability or the hazard (either or both of them) is so clearly marked that specific and realistic plans can in fact be drawn on such a basis. We have one such specific situation now in Europe, and it is met by the NATO arrangement. We have another of a different sort in the Middle East, and the nation's response to that one is not yet clear at this writing.

Recent game theories have sharpened one aspect of this. The player who employs only one rigid strategy runs a great risk simply because his opponent soon detects the single strategy and counters it. The requirement is for strategies of depth and breadth, flexible and adaptable, which by intent and by design can be applied to unforeseen situations. Planning for this kind of relative uncertainty is not as dangerous as it might seem; there is, after all, some order in military affairs. But planning for certitude is the greatest of all military mistakes, as military history demonstrates all too vividly. This point is noted here to indicate that we need not remain always within whatever may be the prevalent opinion of the moment.

The field is wide open.

Leaving this slippery business of assumptions, we come to the maritime concept of strategy, which is a much more inclusive matter than the specific subject of naval warfare. The sailor's view of strategy presupposes a situation in which maritime communications can have an effect on warfare. The United States, connected to the rest of the world by all its oceans, is in a situation where maritime communications do in fact have great influence on the national conduct and the national policy. It is not necessary here to go into our dependence on ocean transportation as a critical feature of our economy. And hardly more so to comment that our worldwide commitments and our foreign policies themselves, all around the world, are founded on two and only two common factors. One of these is a sort of loose harmony of political aims (individualism as opposed to statism in the broadest sense), and the other is the common link of maritime communications. The most important of our current political alignments actually takes its name from the common linkage of the North Atlantic maritime communications system.

This should be enough, on behalf of the sailor, to establish that the United States is legitimately concerned with matters maritime in its strategy. He does not claim that our national interest is exclusively maritime by any means, but he does insist that maritime interests and the maritime elements be considered among the fundamental factors in any total assessment.

In the maritime pattern of thought, the sailor sees his tasks falling into two major fields, and while they are separated here simply for convenience in this discussion, one should recognize that in practice they are so closely interwoven that it is hard to tell where one stops and the other starts.

One half of the task is the establishment of control of the sea which, of course, includes the depths of its waters and the air above it. The other half is the exploitation of that control of the sea toward extension of control from the sea on to the land.

Control of the sea is a very terse phrase for a very fluid and dynamic and many-faceted series of situations. It is seldom absolute and it seldom need be. In a great many situations, a potential control of the sea is all that need be exercised. We are doing that today, all around the world. Without potential control, the NATO and the SEATO and all our other formal and informal organizations would at once collapse. Limited degrees of control may suffice, or local controls. We need not go further than to indicate that control of the sea is a situational problem that we adapt to whatever may be the requirements of the moment.

The business of setting up and holding and enjoying control of the sea is an early and potent step in establishing control over the enemy. It sets the scene of war closer to his territory, not ours, and it gives us the strategic choice of the next move. It makes it more readily a case of "what shall we do?" instead of "what do we think he will do?" When we own the world's maritime communication system, the strategic freedom of choice is ours more than his.

Then there is the extension of control from the sea onto the land—control sought in part by destruction, in part perhaps by paralysis, in part by injection of soldiery when and where it serves our needs. In general, our control of the seas imposes on the enemy a very real limitation on his freedom of action and this pervasive stifling operates quietly but continuously to project our control onto the land. The seas are to him a barrier rather than an avenue. The restrictions that bind him, militarily, economically, politically, psychologically, are not less real because they are subtle and elusive. Every U.S. soldier in Europe or in the Far East today is an extension of this nation's maritime power. Every one of our air bases outside our continent is an extension of our nation's control at sea toward the establishment of control over the enemy.

From these two, control of the sea and its exploitation, come the missions of the Navy. They are clear and direct. These are the sailor's reason for his being:

The Navy will defend the United States from attack across the seas.

The Navy will seek out and destroy enemy naval forces, shipping, bases, and supporting activities.

The Navy will deny to the enemy his use of the seas.

The Navy will control the vital sea areas, the narrow seas, the ocean approaches, the Mediterranean, the China seas, and our own adjacent waters.

And the Navy will exploit our general sea supremacy to project, protect, and sustain the combined military and civilian powers of the United States across the seas.

Against this background, then, we approach the full span of war contingencies and the part the Navy must play in any war, large or small, limited or unlimited, local or general, nuclear or non-nuclear.

It should be amply clear by now that the United States has no intention of starting any wars. So that leaves two alternatives. First, a war could be deliberately initiated against the United States by an enemy. If he did start a war, he would hardly do so in expectation of his own early defeat. It might be by a sudden blow (which is the way wars often start), or it might be at the culmination of a period of heightened tension with attendant warning of his preparation. In either event, he would have some sort of plan which would give, as he saw it, promise of a fairly sure victory over us.

The other way it might start would be from a gradual and unwanted expansion of a local conflict because of increasing friction and expanding tension in some local area. A good melee in the Middle East, for instance, might very well be expanded by growing intransigeance to include Europe, and then we would probably be well into it.

No matter how it might start, the operational stages of almost any kind of war might be classified by the sailor in this fashion:

Defense of the United States
Maintenance of our worldwide communications
Stabilization of the war
Taking control of the pattern of war
Establishment of control over the enemy.

This is not quite the orthodox method of breaking down a war for analysis, and so a little explanation here may be in order.

The first of these, defense of the United States, is fairly clearcut. As far as the sailor is concerned, it is the indisputable task of the Navy to defend the United States from attack across the seas, be it by submarine, or by missile, or by aircraft, or by ship. By standing ready between the United States and any enemy, it is the duty of the Navy to ensure that a war is fought overseas instead of over Chicago.

The second, the maintenance of worldwide communications, means control and use of the seas. The sailor feels that this is critical. Unless we do this, the ground forces have had it, and the deployed Air Forces have had it, and our allies are all done, and we are all in a truly serious situation. If we do not have a control of the sea adequate to deliver food to Europe and fuel to the overseas pipelines and ammunition to the troops abroad, then things will be black indeed.

The third item listed was stabilization of the war. This is worth a moment of comment. We noted earlier that the United States has no intention of starting the war. If an enemy starts it, he will, of course do so in terms that are favorable to him. No one is so silly as to start a war any other way, therefore we can expect a fair measure of initial success by whoever may be the enemy. We are, one way or another, probably going to get our ears pinned back in the beginning. Our early task, then, is to bring into being some sort of a stabilized situation where we can get our breath and flex our own muscles. We will have to reinforce and shuffle our forces to accommodate to his initial moves, hold what we can, and whittle down his forces until we get some kind of dynamic balance in this total sum of the fighting.

Then, unless we are willing to fight the war through on his terms (as we did, for instance, in World War I), we will have to take control of the pattern of the war and shift it to a character or locale of our own choosing, some type of war in which we are strong and in which, preferably, he is weak.

The process of deliberately changing the character or the scene of the war is a matter that has not been consciously thought through as thoroughly as it deserves. It requires a far more searching study than can be covered in so short a space as this. In World War I, the entire war was fought by the Allies along the pattern initially set by the Germans. Once World War II was more or less stabilized, the Allies changed the character of the war both in Europe and in the Pacific. In Europe, once the Western forces were driven off the continent, the centers of pressure were moved in succession to North Africa, to Italy, and then back to France. The center of air interest was moved from the channel to Germany itself.

In the Pacific, the Japanese had their initial interest in the southern islands. The war there was finally stabilized by actions at Midway and in the South Pacific, and then we took charge and shifted the main scene of that war at our will to the Central Pacific and eventually to the Empire itself. It made a far easier problem than it would have been had we kept to the Japanese plan and tried to work back over their chosen routes from, let us say, Singapore and New Guinea through Indonesia and Southeast Asia.

In Korea, we were having the devil's own job in the south until the scene and the entire character of the war were shifted by the move to Inchon and Seoul. Later in that war, incidentally, the intense desire of a goodly number of the participants to shift the scene and character of the air war was not granted for reasons outside our interest in this discussion. There is no need to speculate on what the effect might have been; there are strong opinions on both sides of that matter.

These are cited to illustrate a concept that is a little difficult to describe in precise terms. The contestant who controls the pattern of the war has an inestimable advantage. He can, in great measure, call the tune and make the opponent dance to it.

Let us assume for illustration that the main feature of the war, as an enemy might start it, is a drive to conquer Western Europe. If he wants this, he will of course have to attempt many other tasks, such as denial to us of our sea communications and destruction of the United States industrial and military support, but these latter would be means to his end of conquering Western Europe.

Then let us assume that somehow or other we have managed to stabilize the war, holding somewhere in Europe, keeping our sea lanes sufficiently clear for use, keeping the United States militarily and economically functioning under whatever may be the damage from the air. Then how do we go on, how do we aim to take control over the enemy?

One school of thought feels that a sufficient degree of control can be had by destruction, massive and near-total destruction of the enemy war-machine. Since we have postulated that this war does, somehow, start, then we must recognize that an enemy will have figured either that he can absorb our punishment, fend it off, or deliver more than he gets. The point to be made is that there is a possibility that destruction alone will not force him to quit. Knowing what he would of his own strength and of ours, we cannot assume that he would start a war in the face of certain defeat. This means hard fighting ahead. Even after a nuclear exchange, tough men will fight on. Once we have stabilized the war, we may have to do something more than try to impose our control by destruction alone. We may well need to inject troops—the classical man on the scene with a gun—to exercise the durable and continuing control that can rarely be had in any other way.

There are three ways to do this. One is to push the enemy armies all the way back where they came from, another is to fly the troops in, and the third is to sail them in. It is a long and dreary walk across an entire continent, and one can only hope that the soldiers don't choose to try that one. The other two ways offer considerable promise. Flying them in in limited numbers might be quicker, and it offers more choice of destination, but it is far more demanding and difficult in terms of continued support. The logistic problems for a force of any appreciable size are enormous. Injection from the sea offers less latitude in terms of initial destination, but it is a far more manageable proposition both in the strengths of the forces which can be injected and in the continuing support after they get there.

Fortunately, since we have the maritime strength, we can use whatever waters may lead most conveniently to some of the more sensitive areas. That ability we should exploit. Keep in mind, in this respect, that of all the techniques and methods of warfare, there is only one in which any nation holds a monopoly. This is the attack from the sea. No other nation in the world has this great potential to any significant degree. We should exploit it to the fullest. And further, we should combine it with other types of pressures leading toward control, some of them only remotely military and which appear as political, social or economic measures.

All of these are directly involved in the business of waging war to gain some measure of control over an enemy. The peculiar versatility of naval power, in peace or war, serves to keep the sailor constantly aware of the wide range of pressures available in the national power structure.

So, one base of the sailor's planning process is a tacit appreciation that the aim of war is not limited to any particular military or naval accomplishment, rather, that all our military actions, and our non-military actions as well, must contribute to eventual control over the enemy.

This, to go back to the beginning, is really the aim of war. The other of the two basic assumptions noted that the full shape and course of war were not predictable with certainty.

In this connection, it is interesting to note that our present national attitude toward war seems to lean rather heavily on the expectation of control by destruction and the resultant immobilization. Indeed, the newly appointed Supreme Allied Commander in Europe made this quite clear in one of his first public announcements.

But along with this we have also at hand the not irrational supposition that no enemy would let himself get into a war unless he thought he could win it. So there does appear some possibility, through some combination of defense or mutual air exhaustion or mutual recognition of radiological hazard or something not now foreseen, that we might not attain an adequate control through our nuclear destruction effort alone.

In whatever case may be taken under study, it is the nation with the maritime strength that has the freedom of action. The maritime power need not irrevocably commit itself to any single course of action. Once the war is stabilized, it can pick and choose its opportunities. It is the nation with the maritime strength which is in the best position to control the course of war, to select the strategic pattern of the war, to fit its strength to whatever may be the requirements as the war progresses, and to impose on any enemy whatever kind and degree of control may be needed to meet the nation's aims.

Perhaps this indicates a little of why sailors think the way they do. Why, for instance, they design and plan the Navy as a versatile and multi-purpose instrument of power, designed to defend the United States and to respond to the needs of national policy in whatever situation may develop.

The conclusion that the sailor has not always been able to explain too clearly is that, no matter what single situation is taken up for discussion be it great or small, nuclear or non-nuclear, it is not adequate to assess the usefulness of naval power only in terms of that one situation. The collateral values in other situations must be brought into the equation to arrive at a valid judgment.

In closing, though, one point should be made quite clear. Although the sailor is no less, and one can hope no more, partisan than any other military man, no sailor is so naive as to suppose that the Navy alone is going to sail out and win all our wars. But what he can do is fix it so the soldier's strength and the airman's strength and the sailor's strength as well as the political, economic, and social strengths of this country can be applied in combinations as needed to defend the United States and to establish whatever kind and degree of control the United States may need.

That is why the sailor asks, when his nation considers these matters, that the nation keep in mind that the maritime strategies are the one field in which the United States has an inherent advantage over any enemy. The sailor hopes the nation, if it is ever forced to war, will take advantage of that, use it, and exploit it for all it is worth. It will save time, and it will save effort, and when all the figures are totaled up, it will probably save a good many lives.

Discussion Questions

1. Does Wylie believe that interservice disagreement or rivalry is bad? He gave his answer in the 1950s, in the immediate wake of the creation of the Department of Defense and new restrictions on the services. Does that historical context matter? Is his position still valid today, with our modern joint concepts and doctrine?

2. What are Wylie's two key assumptions for developing war plans? He wrote this essay within the context of the beginning of the Cold War. Are his assumptions still valid in our current world, with our contemporary challenges? Why or why not?

3. What are the key elements of what Wylie calls "the maritime concept of strategy"? How do these apply to the twenty-first century and its global competition or friction?

4. How does Wylie apply his ideas about strategy and, in particular, the issue of control to specific examples? How might those ideas apply today?

5. Do today's culture and doctrine of the Joint Force negate the differences between services? Does Wylie's maritime concept of strategy differ from how we see war and military operations today?

« 11 »

NATIONAL POLICY AND THE TRANSOCEANIC NAVY

Samuel Huntington

(U.S. Naval Institute *Proceedings* 80, no. 5, May 1954)

I. THE ELEMENTS OF A MILITARY SERVICE

The fundamental element of a military service is its purpose or role in implementing national policy. The statement of this role may be called the *strategic concept* of the service. Basically, this concept is a description of how, when, and where the military service expects to protect the nation against some threat to its security. If a military service does not possess such a concept, it becomes purposeless, it wallows about amid a variety of conflicting and confusing goals, and ultimately it suffers both physical and moral degeneration. A military service may at times, of course, perform functions unrelated to external security, such as internal policing, disaster relief, and citizenship training. These are, however, subordinate and collateral responsibilities. A military service does not exist to perform these functions; rather it performs these functions because it has already been called into existence to meet some threat to the national security. A service is many things: it is men, weapons, bases, equipment, traditions, organization. But none of these have meaning or usefulness unless there is a unifying purpose which shapes and directs their relations and activities towards the achievement of some goal of national policy.

A second element of a military service is the resources, human and material, which are required to implement its strategic concept. To secure these resources it is necessary for society to forego the alternative uses to which these resources might be put and to acquiesce in their allocation to the military service. Thus, the resources which a service is able to obtain in a democratic society are a function of the *public support* of that service. The service has the responsibility to develop this necessary support, and it can only do this if it possesses a strategic concept which clearly formulates its relationship to the national security. Hence this second element of public support is, in the long run, dependent upon the strategic concept of the service. If a service does not possess a well-defined strategic concept, the public and the political leaders will be confused as to the role of the service, uncertain as to the necessity of its existence, and apathetic or hostile to the claims made by the service upon the resources of society.

Organizational structure is the third element of a military service. For given these first two elements, it becomes necessary to group the resources allocated by society in such a manner as most effectively to implement the strategic concept. Thus the nature of the organization likewise is dependent upon the nature of the strategic concept. Hence there is no such thing as the ideal form of military organization. The type of organization which may be appropriate for one military service carrying out one particular strategic concept may be quite inappropriate for another service with a different concept. This is true not only in the lower realms of tactical organization but also in the higher reaches of administrative and departmental structure.

In summary, then, a military service may be viewed as consisting of a strategic concept which defines the role of the service in national policy, public support which furnishes it with the resources to perform this role, and organizational structure which groups the resources so as to implement most effectively the strategic concept.

Shifts in the international balance of power will inevitably bring about changes in the principal threats to the security of any given nation. These must be met by shifts in national policy and corresponding changes in service strategic concepts. A military service capable of meeting one threat to the national security loses its reason for existence when that threat weakens or disappears. If the service is to continue to exist, it must develop a new strategic concept related to some other security threat. As its strategic role changes, it may likewise be necessary for the service to expand, contract, or alter its sources of public support and also to revamp its organizational structure in the light of this changing mission.

II. THE CRISIS OF THE NAVY

That the United States Navy was faced with a major crisis at the end of World War II is a proposition which will hardly be denied. It is not as certain, however, that the real nature and extent of this crisis has been so generally understood. For this was not basically a crisis of personnel, leadership, organization, material, technology, or weapons. It was instead of a much more profound nature. It went to the depths of the Navy's being and involved its fundamental strategic concept. It was thus a crisis which confronted the Navy with the ultimate question: What function do you perform which obligates society to assume responsibility for your maintenance? The crisis existed because the Navy's accustomed answer to this question—the strategic concept which the Navy had been expressing and the public had been accepting for well over half a century—was no longer meaningful to the Navy nor convincing to the public.

The existence of this crisis was dramatically symbolized by the paradoxical situation in which the Navy found itself in 1945: It possessed the largest fleet in its history and superficially it had less reason to maintain such a fleet than ever before. The fifteen battleships, one hundred aircraft carriers, seventy cruisers, three hundred and fifty destroyers, and two hundred submarines of the United States Navy floated in virtually solitary splendor upon the waters of the earth. It appeared impossible, if not ridiculous, for the Navy still to claim the title of the Nation's "first line of defense" when there was nothing for the Navy to defend the nation against.

Critics of the Navy were not slow in undermining the latter's public support by pointing out these paradoxes. As one high ranking Air Force officer put it:

Why should we have a Navy at all? The Russians have little or no Navy, the Japanese Navy has been sunk, the navies of the rest of the world are negligible, the Germans never did have much of a Navy. The point I am getting at is, who is this big Navy being planned to fight? There are no enemies for it to fight except apparently the Army Air Force. In this day and age to talk of fighting the next war on the oceans is a ridiculous assumption. The only reason for us to have a Navy is just because someone else has a Navy and we certainly do not need to waste money on that.

The public appeal of this simple logic was enhanced by the widespread postwar reaction against the military, the popular desire to reduce the defense budget, and the fact that one of the Navy's sister services possessed in intercontinental atomic bombing a strategic concept which seemed to promise a maximum of security at a minimum of cost and troublesome intervention in world politics. It is hardly surprising that as a result a 1949 Gallup Poll revealed that 76% of the American people thought that the Air Force would play the most important role in winning any future war whereas only 4% assigned this role to the Navy.

This lack of purpose had its organizational implications also. Most important among these was the tendency to increase naval opposition to unification of the armed forces. Without an accepted strategic concept the Navy had to rely upon organizational autonomy rather than uniqueness of mission to maintain its identity and integrity. This had additional unfortunate implications for naval public support, however, since it enabled its critics to paint the picture of a willful group of die-hard admirals opposing unification for purely selfish purposes.

The causes of this crisis of purpose and its unfortunate political and organizational implications were to be found, of course, in the redistribution of international power which occurred during World War II, the new threats to American national security which emerged after the War, and the consequent shifts in American foreign policy to meet these threats. The critics of the Navy argued in effect that these changes left the Navy without a strategic concept relevant to the postwar world. If they were to be proved wrong and if the Navy were not to be reduced to a secondary service concerned exclusively with protection of supply lines, the Navy must find a new role for itself in national policy. It is the principal thesis of this article that out of the postwar uncertainty, demoralization, and confusion, there has developed a new naval doctrine which realistically relates the Navy to national goals. The substance of this concept has already been described and formulated by a number of naval writers and leaders, and the development of this doctrine must eventually have a significant effect on the public support and organization of the Navy. This doctrine, however, will require a fundamental revolution in naval thinking. Consequently before describing it in detail, it will be appropriate to consider briefly the nature of the relation between the Navy and national policy in the past.

III. THE NAVY AND NATIONAL POLICY: CONTINENTAL PHASE

The first stage of American national security policy may best be described as the Continental Phase. This lasted approximately from the founding of the Republic down to the 1890s. During this period the threats to the national security arose primarily upon this continent and were met and disposed of on this continent. The limited capabilities of the United States during these years did not permit it to project its power beyond the Western Hemisphere. And, indeed, the history of this period may also be interpreted as the history of the gradual struggle by the United States for supremacy within the American continent. This policy manifested itself in our refusal to enter into entangling alliances with non-American powers, in our promulgation and defense of the principles of the Monroe Doctrine, and in our gradual expansion westward to the Pacific.

During these years those threats which arose to the national security were generally dealt with on land, and sea power consequently played a subordinate role in the implementation of national policy. The most persistent security threat, of course, came from the Indian tribes along the western and southern frontiers. These could only be met by the army and the militia. Similarly during the War of 1812 the American Navy was unable to prevent the British from reinforcing Canada, seizing and burning the national capitol, and landing an army at New Orleans. Instead, each of these threats had to be countered by what land forces there were available. The Mexican War was likewise primarily an army affair, although the Navy in the closing campaign of the war performed yeoman service in landing Scott's army at Vera Cruz. Still later in the century when the activities of the French in Mexico violated the Monroe Doctrine, the threat was met not by cutting the maritime communications between France and Mexico, but rather by massing Sherman's veterans along the Rio Grande. American power was thus virtually never utilized outside the American continents during this period and was confined to the gradual elimination of all potential threats to American security which might originate within that Hemisphere. This phase may be said to have come to an end with the final pacification of the Indians in the 1890s and its termination is symbolized in Olney's bold statement to the British government during the 1895 Venezuela boundary dispute, "Today the United States is practically sovereign on this continent, and its fiat is law upon the subjects to which it confines its interposition."

The Navy's subordinate role during this Continental Phase of policy is well indicated by the miscellaneous nature of its military functions. These were basically threefold. First, there were the Navy's responsibilities for coastal defense. From the time of Jefferson's administration down through the 1880s this resulted in the construction of a whole series of gunboats and monitors designed solely for this purpose. Secondly, the Navy was responsible for protecting American commerce overseas and, in the event of war, raiding the commerce of the enemy. For this purpose the Navy was deployed in half a dozen squadrons scattered about the world from the Mediterranean to the East Indies and was largely equipped with fast frigate-cruiser type vessels. Thirdly, during the Mexican War and the Civil War, when the United States was fighting two nations powerless at sea, the Navy performed valuable functions in blockading the enemy and assisting in amphibious operations. These miscellaneous military functions did not, however, exhaust the activities of the Navy during this period. Since these military functions were of a general secondary nature, the Navy tended to acquire a wide variety of essentially civilian functions not directly related to any security threat. These included the support of general scientific research, the organization of a number of exploring expeditions, the frequent performance by naval officers of diplomatic functions, and the utilization of members of the naval service to administer civilian departments of government. In general, during this period the Navy had no clearly essential role to play in meeting any major security threats and consequently tended to dissipate its energies over this wide variety of civilian and military functions.

The subordinate role of the Navy in implementing national policy was reflected in the weak public support which it received during this period. The continuous expansion of the nation westward tended steadily to decrease the political power of those sections most sympathetic to the Navy, and after the Federalists were swept out of office in 1800 it is not inaccurate to say that the government was generally dominated by political groups either indifferent to or actively hostile towards the Navy. The farmers of the interior tended to view the naval establishment as an unnecessary if not dangerous burden on the national economy. Consequently the Navy was frequently allowed to fall into fairly serious states of disrepair, reaching its lowest point in the post Civil War years.

Since the Navy had no definite role to play in implementing national policy, it was unnecessary for it to have a type of organization which emphasized a distinction between its military and civilian functions. Consequently, although there was a major change in naval organization in 1842, when the bureau system was introduced, nonetheless the basic pattern of naval organization remained the same throughout this entire period. Neither under the Board of Naval Commissioners nor under the bureaus was there any clear differentiation between the military and the civilian functions of the naval department under the supervision of the Secretary. When during the Civil War the Navy was called upon to perform a significant military function, a special officer had to be designated to direct the military activities of the fleet. With this exception, however, naval organization reflected the inability of the Navy to develop a strategic concept relating it to the goals of national security policy.

IV. THE NAVY AND NATIONAL POLICY: OCEANIC PHASE

All this changed in the 1890s when the United States began to project its interests and power across the oceans. The acquisition of overseas territorial possessions and the involvement of the United States in the maintenance of the balance of power in Europe and Asia necessarily changed the nature of the security threats with which it was concerned. The threats to the United States during this period arose not from this continent but rather from the Atlantic and Pacific oceanic areas and the nations bordering on those oceans. Hence it became essential for the security of the United States that it achieve supremacy on those oceans just as previously it had been necessary for it to achieve supremacy within the American continent. This change in our security policy was dramatically illustrated by the war with Spain. What began as an effort to dislodge a secondary European power from its precarious foothold on the American continent ended with the extension of American interests and responsibilities to the far side of the Pacific Ocean.

This new position of the United States made it one of several major powers each of which was attempting to protect its security through the development of naval forces. This meant dramatic changes in the position of the Navy, and the role of the Army in implementing national policy became secondary to that of the Navy. Instead of performing an assortment of miscellaneous duties none of them particularly crucial to the national security, the Navy was now the Nation's "First line of defense." In a little over twenty years, from 1886 down to 1907, the United States Navy moved from twelfth place to second place among the navies of the world. This dramatic change required a revolution in the thinking of the Navy, the operations of the Navy, and the composition of the Navy.

The revolution in naval thinking and the development of a new strategic concept for the Navy reached its climax, of course, in the work of Alfred Thayer Mahan. The writings of this naval officer accurately portrayed the new role of the Navy. Attacking the old idea that the functions of the Navy were related to coastal defense and commerce destruction, Mahan argued that the true mission of a navy was acquiring command of the sea through the destruction of the enemy fleet. Mahan vented his scorn upon the "police" functions to which the Navy had been relegated during this previous period of national strategy. Writing at a time when national strategy was undergoing a profound change, he failed to realize that these "police" functions had been just as well adapted to the achievement of national aims in this period as his "command of the sea" doctrine was in the new age which was just beginning. To secure command of the sea it was necessary to have a stronger battle-fleet than the enemy. This could only be secured by building more ships than other nations, insuring that the ships which one did build were larger and had more fire power than those of other nations, and keeping those ships grouped together in a single fleet instead of deployed all over the world in separate squadrons. The net results were naval races, big-gun battleships, and the theory of concentration as the chief aim of naval strategy.

As generalized in the preceding paragraph, the Mahan doctrine was accepted by virtually all the world's naval powers. Each country, however, also had to apply the doctrine to the threats peculiar to it. Down until World War I the United States was about equally concerned with the threats presented by the Japanese and German navies. The fleet was kept concentrated on the Atlantic coast—this was the location of most of the shipyards and the Navy's most consistent public support—and the Isthmus canal was rushed to completion. With the destruction of German surface power the fleet was shifted to the Pacific, and throughout the following two decades American naval thought was oriented almost exclusively towards the possibility of a war with Japan. This was responsible not only for the location of the fleet but also for the development of weapons and techniques which could be effectively employed in the broad reaches of the Pacific. In the 1941–1945 naval war with Japan, the Navy in effect realized the strategic concept which dominated its planning for twenty years.

The increased importance of the Navy to national security towards the end of the nineteenth century was paralleled by the increased prestige of the Navy throughout the country. Public opinion came to view the Navy as the symbol of America's new role in world affairs. Business groups which were now playing an increasingly important role in government were generally more favorably inclined towards the Navy than the agrarian groups which had previously been dominant. The Navy League of the United States was organized and played a major role in interpreting the Navy to the public. Presidents—particularly the two Roosevelts—and congressional leaders turned a more sympathetic ear to the Navy's requests for funds. Thus the Navy was able to get that public support which was necessary for it to implement its strategic concept.

The emergence of a well-defined military function for the Navy meant that the old organization of the Navy Department had to be altered also. The formation of the fleet and the development of its purely military role permitted the business of the Department to be roughly divided into the two categories of military functions and civilian functions. The reformers within the Navy hence campaigned for an organizational structure which reflected this duality of function. This campaign resulted in the creation of the General Board in 1900, the institution of the naval aids in 1909, and eventually the creation of the Office of Naval Operations in 1915. In time, the Chief of this latter office assumed the responsibility for the military aspects of the Navy while the bureau chiefs continued to report directly to the Secretary on the performance of their civilian duties.

V. NATIONAL POLICY IN THE EURASIAN PHASE

The close of World War II marked a change in the nature of American security policy comparable to that which occurred in the 1890s. The threats which originated around the borders of the Atlantic and Pacific Oceans had been eliminated. But they had only disappeared to be replaced by a more serious threat originating in the heart of the Eurasian continent. Hence American policy moved into a third stage which involved the projection, or the possible projection in the event of war, of American power into that continental heartland. The most obvious and easiest way by which this could be achieved was by long-range strategic bombing and consequently American military policy in the immediate postwar period tended to center on the atomic bomb and the intercontinental bomber. Subsequently the emphasis shifted to the development of a system of alliances and the continuing application of American power through the maintenance of United States forces on that continent. These two approaches furnished the Air Force and the Army with strategic roles to play in the implementation of national policy. What, however, was to be the mission of the Navy? How could the Navy play a role in applying American power to the Eurasian continent? This was the challenge which the new dimension of American foreign policy placed before the Navy, which temporarily caused the Navy to falter and hesitate, and which finally was met by the development of a New Naval Doctrine defining the role of the Navy in the Cold War.

VI. THE NEW NAVAL DOCTRINE: THE TRANSOCEANIC NAVY

This new doctrine as it emerges from the writings of postwar naval writers and leaders basically involves what may be termed the theory of the transoceanic navy, that is, a navy oriented away from the oceans and towards the land masses on their far side. The basic elements of this new doctrine and the differences between it and the naval concept of the Oceanic phase may be summarized under the headings that follow.

1. *The Distribution of International Power*

The basis of the new doctrine is recognition of the obvious fact that international power is now distributed not among a number of basically naval powers but rather between one nation and its allies which dominate the land masses of the globe and another nation and its allies which monopolize the world's oceans. This bipolarity of power around a land-sea dichotomy is the fundamental fact which makes the Mahanite concept inapplicable today. For the implicit and generally unwritten assumption as to the existence of a multi-sea power world was the foundation stone for Mahan's strategic doctrine. Like any writer Mahan grasped for the eternal verities and attempted to formulate what seemed to him the permanent elements of naval strategy. But also like every other writer his theory and outlook were conditioned by the age in which he lived. That age was one in which the decisive wars were between competing naval powers. This multi-sea power world had its origins in the rise of the European nation-state system, the discovery of the New World, and the resulting competition between the European nations for overseas colonies and trade. This period of sea power competition lasted roughly from the middle of the seventeenth century to the middle of the twentieth and is divisible into two sub-periods. The first sub-period lasting to 1815 was characterized by intense naval competition and warfare between Spain, the Netherlands, France, and Great Britain. In the end, after the series of exhausting conflicts culminating in the Napoleonic Wars and Trafalgar, Great Britain emerged as the dominant sea power. From 1815 down to the 1890s she maintained this position without serious challenge. By the end of the century, however, a new round of competition developed as Germany, the United States, and Japan arose to challenge British naval supremacy. This second period witnessed the defeat of the German and Japanese navies in World War I and World War II respectively, and ended with Anglo-American, or, more specifically, American naval power dominant throughout the world.

In the light of this naval history it is important to recognize that Mahan's entire thought was geared to this sea power stage in world history. Basically what he did was to study intensively the first sub-period in this stage and then apply the principles gained from such study to the second sub-period in which he lived. This technique gave a superficial air of lasting permanence to his doctrine: for if the principles underlying seventeenth century naval warfare and sea power were applicable at the end of the nineteenth century, then surely these must be universal principles valid throughout history. In actuality, these two sub-periods were, however, unique in their similarity. The first coincided with the initial surge of European colonialism into the New World, and the second coincided with the later surge of that colonialism into Africa and Asia. These are not situations which will be repeated again.

It should also be noted that it was not just chance which led Mahan to concentrate his historical studies on the period from 1660 to 1815. For, although he admitted in a letter to Rear Admiral Stephen A. Luce that "there are a good many phases of naval history," he nonetheless believed that he had been "happily led to take up that period succeeding the peace of Westphalia, 1648, when the nations of Europe began clearly to enter on and occupy their modern positions, struggling for existence and predominance." And it was also generally characteristic of this period that, as Mahan said, except for Russia and possibly Austria, the force of every European state could "be exerted only through a navy."

All the other facets of Mahan's thought rest upon his assumption of the existence of two or more competing naval powers. The idea that the purpose of a navy is to secure command of the sea, that to achieve this end concentration of force in a battlefleet is necessary, and that victory will go to that fleet with the biggest ships, the biggest guns, and the thickest armor, all rest logically on this premise. For obviously the concentration of force in a battlefleet is necessary only if the enemy is capable of doing the same. And, as Bernard Brodie has pointed out, the idea of developing a battlefleet to secure command of the sea originated in the Anglo-Dutch Wars of the middle seventeenth century, at the beginning of this sea power phase of history.

To deny the permanent validity of Mahan's theory is not to deny the brilliance of Mahan's insight. To describe and formulate the principles underlying the major developments in world history over a period of three hundred years is no mean achievement. But we must not permit the impressiveness of Mahan's accomplishment to blind us to the inapplicability of his strategic concept at the present time. A world divided into one major land power and one major sea power is different from a world divided among a number of rival sea powers. The strategy of monopolistic sea power is different from that of competitive sea power. The great oceans are no longer the no man's land between the competing powers. The locale of the struggle has shifted elsewhere, to the narrow lands and the narrow seas which lie between those great oceans on the one hand and the equally immense spaces of the Eurasian heartland on the other. This leads us to the second element which distinguishes the new strategic doctrine from the old.

2. *The Site of Decisive Action*

The Mahan theory justly emphasized not only the influence of sea power but also the decisiveness of naval battle. The sea was a battleground, "a wide common," and the only avenue through which every power could strike at the interests of every other power. Major fleet actions were the decisive events in most of the principal wars of this period from the defeat of the Spanish Armada in 1588 to the dispersion of the remnants of the Japanese Fleet in the Battle of the Philippine Sea in 1944. Between these encounters there were a whole series of naval battles which significantly influenced the course of history: Lowestoft, The Texel, Beachy Head, Ushant, Trafalgar, Manila Bay and Santiago, Tsushima Straits, Jutland, Coral Sea, Midway. Mahan demonstrated the decisive character of the naval engagements in the first round of naval competition; and his teachings and his successors have illuminated the decisiveness of the subsequent ones. While not denying the importance of land battles, nor the significance of such techniques as naval blockade, the strategic concept of this previous age nonetheless emphasized the significance of naval engagements fought solely at sea.

In a world in which a continental power confronts a maritime power, this is no longer possible. As most recent naval writers have recognized, major fleet actions are a thing of the past. The locale of decisive action has switched from the sea to the land: not the inner heart of the land mass, to be sure, but rather to the coastal area, to what various writers have described variously as the Rimland, the Periphery, or the Littoral. It is here rather than on the high seas that the decisive battles of the cold war and of any future hot war will be fought. Consequently, naval writers in the period since 1945 have not hesitated to admit and, indeed, to proclaim the importance of ground force. The reduction of enemy targets on land, Admiral Nimitz stated, "is the basic objective of warfare." Criticizing the Mahan doctrine for tending to erect sea power into an independent thing-in-itself (a view which was not far wrong when the conflict of sea power against sea power was the decisive event in war), Walter Millis argues that:

"Korea is one long lesson in the double fact that all military power is 'land power'; and that it can be effectively exercised, under the conditions created by modern technology, only by the most skillful combination and concentration of all available weapons, whether airborne, seaborne, or earthborne to achieve the desired political ends under the particular circumstances which may arise."

3. *The Mission of the Navy*

This fact that decisive actions will now take place on land means a drastic change in the mission of the Navy. During the previous period, this mission was to secure command of the sea. "[In] war," Mahan said, "the proper objective of the navy is the enemy's navy," and as he further remarked in another classic passage:

> It is not the taking of individual ships or convoys, be they few or many, that strikes down the money power of a nation; it is the possession of that overbearing power on the sea which drives the enemy's flag from it, or allows it to appear only as a fugitive, and which, by controlling the great common, closes the highways by which commerce moves to and from the enemy's shores. This overbearing power can only be exercised by great navies . . .

Since the American navy now possesses command of the sea, however, and since the Soviet surface navy is in no position to challenge this except in struggles for local supremacy in the Baltic and Black Seas, the Navy can no longer accept this Mahanite definition of its mission. Its purpose now is not to acquire command of the sea but rather to utilize its command of the sea to achieve supremacy on the land. More specifically, it is to apply naval power to that decisive strip of littoral encircling the Eurasian continent. This means a real revolution in naval thought and operations. For decades the eyes of the Navy have been turned outward to the ocean and the blue water; now the Navy must reverse itself and look inland where its new objectives lie. This has, however, been the historical outlook of navies which have secured uncontested control of the seas, and as Admiral Nimitz has pointed out, during the period of British domination, "it is safe to say that the Royal Navy fought as many engagements against shore objectives as it did on the high seas." It is a sign of the vigor and flexibility of the Navy that this difficult change in orientation has been generally recognized and accepted by naval writers and the leaders of the naval profession.

The application of naval power against the land requires of course an entirely different sort of Navy from that which existed during the struggles for sea supremacy. The basic weapons of the new Navy are those which make it possible to project naval power far inland. These appear to take primarily three forms:

(1) carrier-based naval air power, which will in the near future be capable of striking a thousand miles inland with atomic weapons;

(2) fleet-based amphibious power, which can attack and seize shore targets, and which may, with the development of carrier-based air lifts, make it possible to land ground combat troops far inland; and

(3) naval artillery, which with the development of guided missiles will be able to bombard land objectives far removed from the coast.

The navy of the future will have to be organized around these basic weapons, and it is not utopian to envision naval task forces with the primary mission of attacking, or seizing, objectives far inland through the application of these techniques.

4. *The Base of the Navy*

In the old theory the sea was the scene of operations and navies consequently had to be based on land. In the ultimate sense that is still true since man must still draw his sustenance and materials from land. But it is also possible to argue that the base of the Navy has been extended far beyond the limits of the continental United States and its overseas territorial bases. For in a very real sense the sea is now the base from which the Navy operates in carrying out its offensive activities against the land. Carrier aviation is sea based aviation; the Fleet Marine Force is a sea based ground force; the guns and guided missiles of the fleet are sea based artillery. With its command of the sea it is now possible for the United States Navy to develop the base-characteristics of the world's oceans to a much greater degree than it has in the past, and to extend significantly the "floating base" system which it originated in World War II. The objective should be to perform as far as practical the functions now performed on land at sea bases closer to the scene of operations. The base of the United States Navy should be conceived of as including all those land areas under our control and the seas of the world right up to within a few miles of the enemy's shores. This gives American power a flexibility and a breadth impossible of achievement by land-locked powers.

The most obvious utilization of this concept involves its application to carrier aviation. In the words of Admiral Nimitz:

The net result is that naval forces are able, without resorting to diplomatic channels, to establish off-shore, anywhere in the world, airfields completely equipped with machine shops, ammunition dumps, tank farms, warehouses, together with quarters and all types of accommodations for personnel. Such task forces are virtually as complete as any air base ever established. They constitute the only air bases that can be made available near enemy territory without assault and conquest, and furthermore, they are mobile offensive bases that can be employed with the unique attribute of secrecy and surprise, which contributes equally to their defensive as well as offensive effectiveness.

From this viewpoint it is possible to define the relation of the Navy's important antisubmarine responsibilities to these newer functions. Submarine warfare is fundamentally a raiding operation directed at the Navy's base. If not effectively countered, it can of course have serious results. But A.S.W., although vitally important, can never become the primary mission of the Navy. For it is a defensive operation designed to protect the Navy's base, i.e., its control and utilization of the sea, and this base is maintained so that the Navy can perform its important offensive operations against shore targets. Antisubmarine warfare has the same relation to the Navy as guarding of depots has for the Army or the protection of its airfields and plane factories has for the Air Force. It is a secondary mission, the effective performance of which, however, is essential to the performance of its primary mission. And, indeed, the successful accomplishment of the primary mission of the Navy—the maintenance of American power along the littoral—will in itself be the most important factor in protecting the Navy's base. For holding the littoral will drastically limit the avenues of access of Soviet submarines to the high seas.

5. The Geographical Focus of Naval Operations

This new theory of the transoceanic navy differs from the old Mahanite doctrine in that its principles are applicable to only one Navy instead of several. We have seen how each nation had to adopt the old Mahanite theory to its own specific circumstances, and for the United States this eventually meant focusing its attention upon the Pacific Ocean. Is there any such specific geographical area which assumes special importance in the application of the new theory? Obviously this theory applies in general to the entire littoral of the Eurasian continent from Kamchatka to the North Cape (and especially to peninsulas such as Korea). Even a superficial glance at the map of Eurasia, however, will reveal that there is one area which specially lends itself to offensive naval operations against the land. This, is, of course, the Mediterranean Basin. For, in effect, the Mediterranean extends the base of American power 2500 miles inland into the Eurasian continent. From this basin naval power can be projected over most of Western Europe, the Balkan peninsula, Turkey, and the Middle East. In the event of a major war with Russia, the Mediterranean would be the base from which the knock-out punch could be launched into the heart of Russia: the industrial-agricultural Ukraine and the Caucasus oil fields. It is consequently hardly surprising to find that the Mediterranean has now replaced the Pacific as the geographical focus of attention for the American Navy.

The recognition of the crucial role of the Mediterranean Basin in the implementation of American foreign policy can be dated from the historic announcement by Secretary Forrestal on September 30, 1946, that American naval forces would be maintained in that area for the support of our national policy. The increase in the strength of these forces and the creation of the Sixth Task Fleet on June 1, 1948, were further steps in the implementation of this policy. The carrier aviation, surface power, and amphibious forces of this fleet have been recognized as being of crucial importance in supporting American policy in this area. This key role of the Mediterranean has been reflected in the attention devoted to it in naval writings, and it has even been described as the "sea of destiny"—a term previously reserved for the Pacific Ocean. This concentration of attention upon the Mediterranean does not, of course, mean that the application of naval power will not be important at other points along the littoral. But it does mean that at least for the foreseeable future the Mediterranean offers the most fruitful area for the Navy's performance of its new function.

6. *The Aim of Naval Tactics*

Under the old theory it was necessary to concentrate naval forces in order to win control of the sea. Consequently the battle fleet emerged as the main instrument of sea power. Now, however, concentration is necessary at or over the target on land, and hence for defensive purposes dispersion and deception are essential for the fleet at sea. Planes from a number of widely separated carriers can, for instance, be concentrated over their target and secure local air supremacy there. Only in amphibious landings would any large-scale concentration of naval vessels be necessary and even there new techniques may avoid the massing of a large number of ships in a small area. Since these new functions permit the Navy to avoid concentrating its ships afloat, there is consequently little basis for the argument that the effectiveness of atomic bombs against a concentrated fleet has ended the usefulness of the Navy. Dispersion, flexibility, and mobility—not concentration—are the basic tactical doctrines of the new Navy.

VII. PUBLIC SUPPORT AND NAVAL ORGANIZATION

Inevitably a new strategic concept must have significant implications for the Navy's public support and its organizational structure. So far as the latter is concerned the implications of this concept are as yet difficult to identify. Certainly once there is general acceptance of the new role of the Navy, the Navy will be able to afford to take a more favorable attitude to further unification of the armed services. Certainly also a recognition of this new function should eventually find its way into law since the National Security Act still defines the primary mission of the Navy as "prompt and sustained combat incident to operations at sea." In general, it is probable that the dual basis of naval organization developed during the Oceanic phase can continue to be the basis of naval organization. In any case, it is likely that the most important implications of the new doctrine involve public support rather than organization.

Perhaps the first necessity of the Navy with respect to this is for it to recognize that it is no longer the premier service but is one of three equal services all of which are essential to the implementation of American Cold War policy. The second necessity is for the Navy to insist, however, upon this equal role. To maintain its position the Navy must develop public understanding of its transoceanic mission. As it is now, the experts on military affairs—columnists such as Hanson Baldwin and Walter Millis—thoroughly appreciate the Navy's role, but too often one still hears from the average American the question: "What do we need a navy for? The Russians don't have one." This attitude can only be overcome by a systematic, detailed elaboration and presentation of the theory of the transoceanic Navy against the broad background of naval history and naval technology. Only when this is done will the Navy have the public confidence commensurate with its important role in national defense.

Discussion Questions

1. Where is Huntington's argument not applicable to today's Navy?
2. What is the role of historical analysis in this essay? Does it succeed or fail, and why?
3. What assumptions underlie Huntington's analysis? (Note how he analyzes Mahan's claims.)
4. What is the Navy's strategic concept now? Does it have all the requisite pieces?
5. Is Huntington's essay relevant to today's world? Why or why not?

12

"PROFESSIONALISM"

A WARDROOM DEBATE

James T. Strong

(U.S. Naval Institute *Proceedings* 92, no. 5, May 1966)

xecutive Officer: All of us in this nuclear-powered, missile-firing submarine have been impressed with the rapid material changes that new technology has brought to our Navy. Some of you are convinced that these technological changes and other factors call for significant changes to our professional standards, the way we think about and prepare for our profession. I have asked two of our more experienced officers, Lieutenant Commanders Patina and Gloss to debate this issue informally for the benefit of our wardroom officers today. Lieutenant Commander Patina represents the view that traditional and long proven standards and values should be maintained; Lieutenant Commander Gloss will argue that new professional standards and values should be identified and accepted.

Lieutenant Commander Gloss: The most significant break that we must make with tradition is an upgrading of the importance of education, of study, or analytical abilities.

As Captain Carl Amme said in his U.S. Naval Institute Prize Essay for 1964, "Crisis of Confidence," we must "develop naval officer scientists and scholars who can insure that new doctrines of sea power will be injected fairly in the momentous debates and studies on national strategy." We will not develop scientists and scholars as long as our professional atmosphere inhibits scholarly pursuits by an overemphasis on non-scholarly qualities.

We can clearly see a major factor in the need for this change by reviewing the acceleration that has occurred in the development of military equipment. Nelson's flagship, HMS *Victory*, was built when he was a boy, and she was still perfectly sound 40 years later when she led the fleet at Trafalgar. Gunpowder had been in use for more than a generation before its employment was significant enough to be recorded in the account of a battle. It took 50 years of development and use to produce an effective submarine, an effective torpedo.

Today, knowledge doubles every ten years. Only seven years of effort brought the nuclear attack submarine from an idea to a very effective ship of war. Merely five more years were required to develop the ballistic missile submarine, a weapon entirely new to warfare. No longer can a naval officer expect to serve an apprenticeship with weapons that resemble closely those weapons he may later command as an admiral. Where change is so rapid with respect to the length of an officer's career, emphasis must be shifted from training to education. Seagoing experience is no longer the primary professional qualification; it has been replaced by knowledge and certain habits of study and objective thought which are scholarly in origin.

Many other factors call for a more scholarly basis for our profession. Missiles, computers, nuclear power, and the sure expectation of even more fantastic devices impose a requirement for a great deal of knowledge of the natural sciences and mathematics.

A revolution in strategic thought forces new stresses on aspects of many other fields of knowledge. There is a growing emphasis on strategy at the expense of a previous preoccupation with tactics. This is partly due to the nature of the technological revolution already mentioned. It is partly due to the recognition that the winning of wars is not enough, that objectives separate from simple military victory are necessary for a proper strategy. Strategy has become more important since the acceptance of the idea that military effort must be closely associated with political, economic, and psychological effort. Strategy in relation to tactics has been accentuated by the Communist challenge with its new and unconventional means of violence.

While the science [of] tactics lends itself both to experience and personal experiment, the development of strategy is a more abstract task requiring more knowledge and certain mental disciplines.

The cost and high yield of our new weapons makes it difficult to experiment and train with them by old trial-and-error methods. This places a premium on gaming and planning methods that require scientific and mathematical discipline.

Our very complex organization for national security imposes new and increased leadership demands on the profession. We must produce large numbers of senior officers for positions in an integrated defense department and a world-wide system of alliances. As an officer advances in rank he is increasingly required to perform duties outside the realm of his formal training and service experience. Where, heretofore, we could afford to select men who displayed a natural bent for those few tasks which required more than experience, now the requirements are such that the number of officers with natural genius is insufficient. We must learn to mold more exceptional strategists, scientists, and experts in scholarly fields than ever before.

I submit that the only way to accomplish this is by recognizing that selected aspects of science, economics, geopolitics, and a host of other fields are as important to the military officer as seamanship is to the sailor. This recognition must be accompanied by an emphasis which will fundamentally change the nature of the profession into a scholarly undertaking. This reform must proceed even at the expense of long cherished but specious beliefs concerning the supreme importance of some other traditional professional values.

Lieutenant Commander Patina: I am glad that my opponent has at last discovered what others have known for so long, namely, that knowledge and thought are vital to a successful military career. We need look no further than the motto of the Naval Academy for evidence of this: Ex Scientia Tridens, "from knowledge, seapower." Our great Admiral Sims expressed the personal significance of this in an address to the Naval War College as long ago as 1920; he said, "It lies with you to determine whether . . . you will find yourselves simply 'practical men'—'beefeaters' or really educated military naval officers." Where sufficient candidates have been available, the services have long striven to obtain well-educated officers initially and then have enhanced this background in selected officers through postgraduate education and military colleges. For those officers not attending advanced schools the services encourage self-study. Both the Bureau of Naval Personnel and the Secretary of the Navy have professional study programs.

It is not at all strange that my opponent, at mid-career, has at last looked up from the equipment manuals, tactical procedures, navigational almanacs that he has been studying for so long and discovered that the duties ahead require much more study and much different study than that which he has already mastered. But this revelation is nothing new except, perhaps, as to degree, to anyone but the conscientious young officer who may personally be making the discovery for the first time.

Although knowledge has always been important, I must challenge the idea that it is the most important professional quality. I question whether the plea for officer scientists and scholars is to be satisfied at the expense of the traditional role that our officers fulfill. The service that our profession provides to society is not a scholarly service. As Bernard Brodie has said, " . . . The military profession is not a scholarly calling . . . it requires in its leaders . . . character traits such as loyalty, physical courage, boldness, decisiveness, and above all, leadership. There are also important technical skills to be absorbed. These are not incompatible with scholarly values, but they do not permit much accent upon the latter, nor will the pursuit of normal duties leave much time for them."

If we in this wardroom tried to take on the scholarly task that has just been proposed, the administration of this ship would suffer and we would not be building up the kind of experience we need. We should be about the ship with our men or in congenial debate with our colleagues, not in some corner with a book.

In the world's frantic effort to find means to avoid the use of military force, the ferment has produced a spate of ideas and theories involving economics, politics, and psychology. While the military profession should be knowledgeable in aspects of those fields that relate to military force, it is important that we do not overstep our traditional bounds and find ourselves where military leaders would attempt to be prime movers in these fields. To do so would violate important restraints on the exercise of military control and might endanger the very form of government we seek to protect. Our task in the management of military force is sufficiently great to demand our full attention. The proposal of my opponent to invest already scarce talent and effort into academic spheres at the expense of our primary task is not only uncalled for but it could even decoy us into an unfortunate rivalry with our civilian mentors.

Officers in high positions of responsibility have experts in the academic fields to call upon. It is absurd to think that a military officer could develop any but a passing acquaintance with science, economics, geopolitics, and so forth. Senior military officers must provide informed leadership and military experience and with these qualifications they should be recognized as pre-eminent in military matters just as we recognize the preeminence of scholars in their own fields.

Lieutenant Commander Gloss: My opponent has just expressed the paradox that is at the root of this debate. He insists that military men must be expert in "military matters" just as scholars are experts in their fields. Yet, the field of military matters can no longer be confined to a narrow, practical endeavor where scholarship is unimportant and leadership and experience are supreme. Whether we like it or not, the management of military power now requires well-educated leaders. If the military profession cannot produce the type of leader who combines knowledge with practical skills, it will now prove incapable of the tasks it has traditionally fulfilled.

My opponent argues that the profession is already committed deeply to education, knowledge, self-study, and so forth. While the ideal that he traces out sounds very good, actual accomplishment is far short of the ideal and what is necessary. As we go along making small improvements here and there, we tend to congratulate ourselves on great progress. Yet, when viewed in the context of the revolution all about us, it is clear that our profession is actually falling further behind the educational demands made upon it.

First, I invite you all to check the military science shelf at any base library. Most of the earlier volumes are written by military authors. There is also a tremendous aggregation of new works on military strategy, but rarely is there a serious new book by a military officer. Could it be that changing requirements have made our professional competence inadequate for the task of contributing to military strategy? You can also see this tendency in the articles of professional publications like the U.S. Naval Institute *Proceedings*, where civilians are gradually overtaking military officers in the writing of thoughtful studies of military strategy.

William R. Kintner, Professor of International Relations at the University of Pennsylvania, and former assistant to President Dwight D. Eisenhower, recently explained the situation this way: "Another aspect of the Problem, however, is the advent of the distinguished civilian analysts . . . who have gained tremendous influence for one simple reason. They have done their homework on the complicated and difficult issues of defense far better than many of the professional military have. I doubt if you could find in certain areas the competence at the staff or senior command level on the intricacies of these problems which are now being decided by default in the upper echelons of the Defense Department."

It is not only that officers cannot write current books on strategy, but also they do not even read what others have written. Here we are in this magnificent ship, at the core of the world's technology. This is no average military group. This is a superior selection of ambitious, serious professionals with far more training, education, and motivation than the average. How much are we committed to even the advertised ideals of knowledge of our profession? Milestone volumes with challenging new ideas concerning our own military mission in our base library like Kahn's *On Thermonuclear War*, Kissinger's *The Necessity for Choice*, or even Marshal Sokolovsky's compendium of Soviet thought, *Soviet Military Strategy*, are gathering dust, undisturbed on their shelves. In a recent questionnaire to more than a hundred of this select group of promising officers, 29 per cent admitted to ever having read a book that was on the recommended reading list long published by BuPers. In the same questionnaire only 8 per cent admitted to ever having completed a Naval War College or academic correspondence course. We have based at our home port the largest collection in the Navy of young officers intimately connected with the employment of Polaris. From this group could come many of the senior officers who will have command of a strategic deterrent force composed of complicated nuclear-powered, missile-equipped, computerized ships and weapons of the future. If these promising young officers do not later correct their present ignorance by massive doses of concentrated schooling, they will come to positions of responsibility where they could be making decisions concerning matters about which they are essentially ignorant.

Will a quick year's injection of concentrated study at a senior military college later make up for years of neglect for even those few officers who are lucky enough to attend war college? I think not. Do you feel that the "experience" and "leadership" you are now absorbing will qualify you well for senior positions in the Navy of today, ignoring the certainty that the situation 20 years hence will be much more complex?

If experience and leadership are not enough and we fail to prepare ourselves otherwise, we face a decline in function. Military officers will become ship and regiment "drivers," contributing little to major military decisions and developments.

We need not all become expert strategists, economists, and historians at the same time, but we can become knowledgeable in the military aspects of all and can even become experts in one by proper application. Scholars have certain mental qualities that our profession must copy. As long as we continue to stress experience in relation to knowledge we will be guilty of parochialism which even the profession itself recognizes as a widespread handicap. If scholars can study military aspects sufficiently to make significant contributions to military strategy, should not the military officer study scholarly matters sufficiently to make even greater contributions to this same military strategy?

The professional attitude toward leadership stems from a tradition that morale is the primary factor in winning wars.

The morale of the fighter pilots defending Britain in the Battle of Britain was superb and important; however, the key to victory was the crash program to develop and deploy radar for that battle. Without this radar all the valor in the world would not have saved Britain. The Japanese, with their Bushido code, had a tremendous military man fighting for them during World War II. Japanese soldiers, sailors, and airmen never hesitated to sacrifice themselves deliberately, even in futile causes. But this tremendous morale did not prevent their total defeat by our own superior material, tactics, and strategy. Had they used their minds more and their tradition less they would not have assigned their engineers and scientists to the foxholes, and they might have had radar for their submarines, a workable convoy and routing system, an effective antiair warfare defense, and many other critical means which their "unprofessional" system forbade them. These are but two examples from the hundreds available to demonstrate that material and ingenuity and knowledge are far more important than before.

Leadership is still very important but not the quality of leadership that can be measured by how many VIPs an officer knows, or how many years at sea he has had, or how well he can prepare a division or ship for an administrative inspection. The leadership that we need today is a leadership founded on knowledge and mental discipline which can only be built into the profession by radically increased dedication to education and study.

Lieutenant Commander Patina: While it may be theoretically desirable to commit all young officers to a career-long reading and study program which practically carries them into the realms of high strategy and scholarly fields, we can accomplish this only if we eliminate something from their already packed routine. Would you prefer that the officers on this submarine read Kahn and Sokolovsky rather than attend to the technology that keeps this complicated weapon operating and ready for combat? While they are not now gaining an intellectual background by their more practical hard work, they are indeed gaining unique experience in the management of technology and men. This experience can well be the best foundation for future contributions while in positions of greater responsibility.

The records of naval selection boards have indicated no need for a more scholarly officer body. An intellectual background has never been recognized by selection boards as an especially significant background for even high command. On the contrary, a recent survey of selectees for flag rank revealed that the main common characteristic of this select group was wide operational and command experience. Morris Janowitz in his statistical study of the military profession titled *The Professional Soldier* describes a survey of 204 admirals made in 1950 which revealed that the career lines and major assignments of these men marked three-fifths of them as command specialists and only about one-fifth each as technical specialists and staff specialists. What is perhaps more revealing is that through this and other surveys Janowitz could document the increasing importance of inter-personal skills over substantive knowledge at each higher level of military administration. While his evidence demonstrated the need of a small percentage of military scientists, the major challenge to the profession was clearly the requirement for a large number of leaders having the fused capacity of the military manager and the combat leader. Neither task is inherently scholarly.

A growing enthusiasm for intellectual achievement is good because it underscores one of the long-standing challenges of our profession. But the proposal that it would be wise to emphasize this at the expense of traditional values is misleading and pernicious.

The prime arbiters of this debate are not outside civilian observers but must always remain those men in uniform who have risen to the top of our profession, who now bear the heavy responsibilities there and who speak of the nature of their task. While these officers continue to stress the relative importance of over-all technical competence, some political, and economic and other scholarly knowledge, they have not yet indicated any lesser role to the traditional functions of practical training, wide professional experience and leadership development.

The general alarm sounded and the officers moved quickly to their battle stations. The navigator checked the latest position obtained by fixing on an artificial earth satellite. The chief engineer checked his nuclear reactor ready for full power. The weapons officer trained his missiles on unseen targets half a continent away. It was only a test; the ship quickly demonstrated that she was ready for the strange new role she had been assigned in an unfamiliar form of conflict.

It was clear that change had created new professional challenges. Each young man reached both to the past and the future for clues to guide him along the uncertain way.

Discussion Questions

1. How is this debate relevant to today's Navy?
2. How is the selection board argument inadequate?
3. Should officers be specialists or generalists, or should there be a mix?
4. Is the objection that "There's no time" really convincing? What is it really saying?
5. Are there voices missing from this debate? If so, which ones?

« 13 »
MISSIONS OF THE U.S. NAVY

Stansfield Turner

(U.S. Naval Institute *Proceedings* 100, no. 12, December 1974)

One of the important challenges facing naval officers today is to define, then articulate, why we need a navy and what it should be able to accomplish for the country. The changes in national attitudes and military technology and the relationship of nations today are such that we cannot accept as sacrosanct the traditional rationale for a navy. We must reexamine and be willing to change the well established missions of our Navy. In 1970 the Chief of Naval Operations defined the current missions of the U.S. Navy as being Strategic Deterrence, Sea Control, Projection of Power Ashore, and Naval Presence. By "missions" he meant the outputs or objectives of having a navy. As a starting point, we should examine how these four missions evolved. We can then ask what they specifically mean today and whether they are an adequate rationale for a navy.

The first mission of the earliest navies was being able to move military forces by sea. As time went on, there were many technological milestones, new tactical concepts, and maritime initiatives, but the basic naval mission to ensure the safe movement of ground forces and their supplies across the sea endured for centuries.

By the 18th century, however, sea trade routes were flourishing, exploration was becoming more far ranging, the horizons of imperialism were widening, commerce was growing, and with it, piracy. As nations began to depend on the seas for their economic well being, they needed security of movement by sea. Control of the sea became the sine qua non of economic growth. The Sea Control mission expanded to include the protection of shipping for the nation's economy as well. At the end of the 19th century, Alfred Thayer Mahan defined maritime power to include merchant marine and naval forces plus all of the bases and coaling stations needed to support each. He popularized the "control of the seas" concept as a key to expanding national power and prestige. To Mahan the term "control of the seas" meant both denying the enemy use of the seas and asserting one's own use, both with a battle fleet superior to that of the enemy.

British and German naval strategy in World War I reflected this heritage. Both navies believed that a decisive battle fleet encounter would determine control of the seas. Hence, tactical caution dominated the Battle of Jutland. After that failure to defeat the British battle fleet, the Germans challenged British seapower indirectly, first with surface commerce raiders, and later with unrestricted submarine warfare. The British reacted by attempting to blockade the German U-boats with mines laid across the exits from the North Sea. This failed, and the World War I struggle for control of the Atlantic evolved into a grueling war of attrition. Large numbers of allied antisubmarine ships and aircraft were pitted against a much smaller number of German submarines. Despite the difference between this kind of warfare and the classic concept that battle fleet engagements would determine control of the seas, few strategists understood how radically the concept of "control of the seas" had been altered by the advent of the submarine. British, German, Japanese, and American preparations for World War II all concentrated on potential battle fleet actions. Only a few voices pointed out that an additional submarine might be more useful than another battleship.

Equally few strategists forecast the dominant role that control of the air over a surface fleet would have. However, in March 1941, off Cape Matapan in Greece, the first engagement of major surface forces since Jutland demonstrated that it was the presence of a British aircraft carrier that allowed an otherwise weaker force to prevail. Throughout World War II the primary use of naval carrier-based air power was in the sea control role of defeating enemy carriers and battleships, with a secondary role of providing close air support for amphibious assaults. By the end of World War II the idea of totally denying the seas to one's enemy while asserting one's own exclusive use had been overtaken by technology. On the one hand it was nearly impossible to deny an enemy submarine fleet access to the seas; on the other, there were likely to be areas of the sea where enemy air power would make the assertion of one's presence prohibitively costly. Yet, for the first several decades after the second World War, the U.S. Navy had such a monopoly on seapower that the term "control of the seas" understandably continued to carry its long-established connotation.

The new term "Sea Control" is intended to acknowledge the limitations on control of the oceans brought about by the advent of the airplane and the submarine. It connotes a more realistic concept of control in limited areas and for limited periods of time. It is conceivable for a navy today to temporarily exert air, surface, and subsurface control in a limited area while moving ships into position to project power ashore or to resupply overseas forces. But it is not conceivable, except in the most restricted sense, to totally control the seas for one's own use, or to totally deny them to an enemy.

This may change with evolving technology and tactics but, in the meantime, we must approach the use of the term "Sea Control" from two directions: denying an enemy the right to use some seas at some times; and, asserting our own right to use some seas at some times. Any seapower may both assert its own use of the seas and deny that right to the enemy at any given time. Its efforts will usually be divided between the two objectives. For instance, if the United States were attempting in wartime to use the North Atlantic to reinforce Europe, it would put the greater percentage of its effort on asserting sea control. In a situation like the war in Vietnam, where our use of the seas was not challenged, we made a substantial effort to deny the other side any seaborne infiltration into South Vietnam.

There are four different tactical approaches for achieving these Sea Control objectives:

Sortie Control. Bottling up an opponent in his ports or his bases is a most economical means of cutting off a nation's use of the seas or ability to interfere. Nevertheless, no blockade is 100% successful. Some units may be beyond the blockade when hostilities commence and will remain to haunt opposition forces. Against the enemy's aircraft there is no static defense. Planes must be bombed at their bases. If we assume an opponent will be in control of the air near his ports, sortie control tactics must primarily depend on submarines and mines. Thus we must conclude that blockades are weapons of attrition requiring time to be effective. But the lesson of history is perhaps the most instructive of all—ingenious man has usually found ways to circumvent blockades.

Chokepoint Control. Sometimes the best place to engage the enemy is in a geographical bottleneck through which he must pass. In so doing, platforms like ASW aircraft that probably could not survive in the area of the enemy's sortie point can be used.

Open Area Operations. Once enemy ships, submarines, or aircraft are loose in, or above, the open ocean, we have the option of instituting search procedures. Open area search is a third form of attrition operations. In short, these operations are not part of defending specific merchant or naval shipping. They are intended to seek out the enemy and reduce the threat before it makes contact with forces to be protected.

Local Defense. In contrast to searching out a large area with the intent of locating, tracking and possibly prosecuting and destroying enemy forces, in local defense we assert our use of the seas. If our attrition forces have not been 100% successful, the enemy may be able to close our forces to within range of attack. If so we must defend ourselves by (1) engaging his attack platforms directly, (2) defeating his attack weapons by direct kill, or (3) decoying or deceiving his weapons. This objective may include contributions, as a preliminary, of sortie control, choke point control and open area operations. Depending upon our purpose in asserting use of the seas we may select (1) to try to evade and deceive, (2) to close in and attack, and (3) to attack enemy forces when they close to within their weapon range, and to defend actively or passively against these weapons.

In executing Sea Control, our relative emphasis on these four tactics will vary with the particular circumstance, especially the enemy threat and our own objectives. For instance, if our objective is to ensure an early flow of supplies to some theater of war, attrition type tactics may not be adequate. Or, if in the early days of a conflict, the enemy has dense defenses near his ports and bases, sortie control may be difficult.

Additionally, in executing Sea Control tactics, two passive techniques deserve particular mention:

Deception. Assertive Sea Control objectives do not necessarily demand destruction of the enemy's force. If the enemy can be sufficiently deceived to frustrate his ability to press an attack, we will have achieved our Sea Control objective. Force routing, deceptive/imitative devices, and other anti-search techniques can be employed, often in combination with other tactics.

Intimidation. The perceptions of other nations of our Sea Control capability relative to that of other major powers can influence military decisions. What a nation says about its capabilities can influence the challenges that are offered or accepted. A Sea Control force that is recognized by the enemy may inhibit the enemy's willingness to commit his sea denial forces.

By the early 19th century, another important naval mission had evolved—the projection of ground forces from the sea onto the land. Modern amphibious warfare began during the wars of the French Revolution. A new dimension in tactics was given to commanders in the Projection of Power Ashore through amphibious assault. During World War I the first major amphibious assault of the 20th century was attempted at Gallipoli. The failure of the assault as a result of poor execution nearly killed the amphibious assault concept. In World War II, however, amphibious assault played a major role in both theaters, and the Inchon assault in Korea in 1950 constituted a stunning tactical maneuver.

Amphibious assault tactics are largely a function of the size of the operation.*

The war in Korea and later the war in Vietnam brought into play two new ways of projecting power ashore: naval bombardment and naval tactical air. Naval bombardment was undoubtedly used on occasions as far back as the 18th century to interfere with enemy coastal communications and installations. But, by 1950, it was employed primarily as a part of amphibious assault. Both Korea and Vietnam have long, exposed coastlines with significant road and rail lines.

Here naval bombardment came into its own as an independent way of projecting power ashore.

Naval bombardment is presently available from naval guns in destroyers utilizing two tactics: direct fire and indirect fire. If the target is visually observable from the firing ship, direct fire is the simplest and most accurate method. If it is not, fire directed by a spotter on the beach, from an aircraft or by pre-arrangement based on geographical coordinates, must be employed.

During World War II, naval tactical air began moving into the projection of power role. Tactical air projection evolved fully as a mission in the post–World War II period. The marriage of the jet aircraft and improved, lesser drag munitions gave the aircraft carrier a capability of extending its reach far past the shoreline. During the Korean War, naval tactical air came to play a major role in support of the land campaign: air attacks on enemy networks; transportation; air superiority over the battlefield; and close air support of ground forces.

The four basic tactical air tactics are: deep interdiction; battlefield interdiction; close air support; and counter-air/anti-air warfare.

Deep Interdiction is usually more strategic than tactical. That is, the impact on the ground campaign is more remote and less immediately felt than in the other tactical air tactics. Attacks can be either directed at the enemy's war making potential, that is against civilian morale, economy, or command structure; or they can be militarily disruptive, that is against military bases, logistics sources, depots, or supply routes. Generally these are fixed targets that are pre-planned. Thus such attacks

---

* The original *Proceedings* article includes a figure illustrating amphibious assault, which the editors have removed from the text for simplicity.

may include advance preparations of target lists, strike group tactics, approach pro-files, defense suppression techniques, and planned staging of attacks. For instance, attack aircraft if threatened by enemy fighters, have three options: continue to tar-get, jettison ordnance and attempt to escape or, in some circumstances, jettison and attempt to engage the fighters. The actual choice will depend on the type of aircraft and the nature of the mission flown. One or another of these tactics may be preferred, but it generally will be determined in advance.

In addition to the primary attack aircraft, a typical operation may also involve special EW, anti-ground defense, or air-to-air configured fighters (see counter-air tactic below), which may be preceded by photo electronic reconnaissance missions. Because deep interdiction operations are remote from the fluid conditions in battle areas, enemy air defenses generally tend to be well integrated. Reasonable radar warning, good air control facilities, airborne patrol or ground alert fighters, and both surface-to-air missiles (SAMs) and antiaircraft fire (AAA) can be anticipated.

Battlefield Interdiction is generally carried out in the enemy's division to corps area, about 5 to 50 kilometers into enemy-held territory from the forward edge of the battle area (FEBA). It is directed primarily against military targets, both static, such as bridges, gun emplacements, and bunkers, and fleeting, such as troop con-centrations or vehicular traffic. The measure of effectiveness of this tactic may not be so much in targets destroyed as in the denial to the enemy of ground force mobil-ity behind the front lines or of increased difficulty in resupplying key items such as POL and ammunition.

Flights and areas of coverage are usually pre-planned but include targets of opportunity with target acquisition being the mission-limiting feature, especially in bad weather, at night, or in jungle terrain. Real-time intelligence may be provided by various types of sensors. In most circumstances, attacking aircraft will penetrate enemy-held territory over short distances only. Because of this, they may well oper-ate at low levels with or without fighter cover. Mobile SAMs, although perhaps not well netted and with only short radar warning time available, plus AAA, can be anticipated. There must be good air space control and coordination because of the close proximity to front line close air support operations.

Close Air Support operations are "call fire" in response to direct requests from ground units or through Forward Air Controllers (FACs). As these same sources may be calling simultaneously for artillery, good liaison procedures between the controllers and the close support aircraft are essential. Aircraft, capable of heavy ordnance loads and low level operations, must be able to scramble quickly from nearby bases or be able to loiter in the area on call. The zone of operations tends to be no deeper than five kilometers from friendly forces, hence accuracy of weapon delivery is extremely important. While large, mobile SAMs are possible in this zone, they are less a threat than AAA and hand held, short-range SAMs. Fighter escort is usually not assigned, though there may be general front coverage against raiding aircraft.

Counter-air/Anti-air. There are two distinct air superiority operations:

- Counter-air to neutralize an enemy's anti-air capabilities sufficiently to minimize attrition to our attacking forces.
- Anti-air operations to deny an enemy the capability of operating attack aircraft in our areas of interest and control.

Escorting fighter aircraft provide counter-air defense against enemy fighters; armed suppression fighters or attack aircraft are directed against ground defenses such as SAMs and their control facilities; and a variety of EW aircraft techniques defend against SAMs and AAA. Escort fighter aircraft tactics can be divided into:

- Long range intercept utilizing sophisticated radar and fire control techniques and air-to-air missiles.
- Dog-fight maneuvering and close in missiles or guns.

In the long range case, positive identification is a critical problem. In either case, air intercept control can be valuable.

For anti-air operations, airborne CAP, ground alert fighters, SAMs, AAA and deceptive electronic measures can be employed.

This type of mission tactic categorization can be valuable in assessing own and enemy capabilities, whereas the usefulness of a simple summary of weapon/aircraft performance characteristics is limited. When we thereupon superimpose weapons and aircraft, we can then better evaluate our capabilities for achieving some part of the tactical air projection mission. By superimposing enemy defensive capabilities, we can move into a dynamic evaluation of our systems in combat. By superimposing enemy offensive weapons and aircraft and our defensive systems we can estimate our vulnerabilities.

Beyond this, we can also use this categorization to identify the weapons and aircraft characteristics that we need for each tactic.*

There will be specific scenarios where some of the judgmental evaluations in these comparisons will be incorrect. It would be desirable to be infinitely flexible and have maximum characteristics in all aircraft and weapons. Unfortunately, the laws of both physics and economics prevent that. Hence, some evaluation of probable use and likely need can be valuable.

Only a fine distinction separates some aspects of the Sea Control and Projection of Power Ashore missions. Many weapons and platforms are used in both missions. Amphibious assaults on choke points or tactical air strikes on enemy air bases can be employed as a part of the Sea Control mission. Sea-based tactical aircraft are used in Sea Control missions for anti-air warfare and against enemy surface combatants. The distinction in these cases is not in the type of forces nor the tactics which are employed, but in the purpose of the operation. Is the objective to ensure/ prevent use of the seas or is it to directly support the land campaign? For instance, much of the layman's confusion over aircraft carriers stems from the impression that they are employed exclusively in the Projection of Power Ashore role. Actually, from the Battle of Cape Matapan through World War II, aircraft carriers were used almost exclusively to establish control of the ocean's surface. Today they clearly have a vital role to play in both the Sea Control and Projection of Power missions.

Both Sea Control and Projection of Power Ashore can be termed "war fighting" missions. We buy forces capable of executing these missions in combat. The Navy's two other missions are "deterrent." We buy forces to ensure against having to engage in combat.

During the 19th century, the term "gunboat diplomacy" came into the naval vocabulary. In the quest for colonies, powerful nations paraded their naval forces to intimidate and serve warning. In time, the range of this activity extended from warnings and coercion to demonstrations of good will and humanitarian assistance. Today, the Naval Presence mission is the use of naval forces, short of war, to achieve political objectives.

We attempt to accomplish these objectives with two tactics: *preventive deployments* and *reactive deployments*. A preventive deployment is a show of presence in peacetime whereas a reactive deployment is a response to a crisis. In a preventive deployment, force capabilities should be relevant to the problem, clearly not inferior

---

* The original *Proceedings* article includes a figure illustrating weapons and aircraft details, which the editors have removed from the text for simplicity.

to some other naval force in the neighborhood, and in capability we should have a reasonable hope that reinforcements can be made available if necessary. On the other hand, a reactive deployment may or may not actually involve a movement or deployment of forces. There will be instances when the threat of doing so, perhaps communicated through an alert or mobilization order, will produce a desired reaction in itself. When a force is deployed, however, it needs to possess an immediately credible threat and be prepared for any contingency. A comparison with other naval forces in the area will be inevitable.

In deciding to insert a presence force, the size and composition of force must be appropriate to the situation. There are five basic actions which a Naval Presence force can threaten: *amphibious assault, air attack, bombardment, blockade,* and *exposure through reconnaissance.*

Almost any size and type of presence force can also imply that the United States is concerned with the situation and may decide to bring other military forces or non-military pressures to bear. All too often, especially in reactive deployments, we tend to send the largest and most powerful force that can move to the scene rapidly. The image created may not be appropriate to the specific problem.

When selecting a *Naval Presence* force, we must also take into account how the countries that we want to influence will perceive the situation. There are three distinctly different categories of national perceivers:

The Soviet Union. When contemplating a U.S. presence force, the Soviets must assess their comparative naval strength available over time, and the expected degree of U.S. resolve. As the United States is not likely to threaten the U.S.S.R. directly, except in a world-wide crisis of the most serious proportions, the principal strength comparison would probably be on which country could actually exercise sea control in the area in question.

Nations Allied to the Soviets. Nations with close ties to the Soviets must assess relative U.S.-U.S.S.R. capabilities. These powers will ask, "Can the United States project its assembled power onto my shores?" and "Can the U.S.S.R. deny them that capability?" Thus, third nation appraisal of relative sea control strengths may be the most critical factor and their assessment may not correspond to either U.S. or Soviet assessments of identical military factors.

Unaligned Third Nations. There will be cases where a nation is not able to invoke major power support in a dispute with the United States. The perceptions of such a country would likely focus on U.S. capability and will to project its power ashore to influence events in that country itself.

Thus, the Naval Presence mission is sophisticated and sensitive and, because of the subtleties involved, probably the least understood of all Navy missions. A well orchestrated Naval Presence can be enormously useful in complementing diplomatic actions. Applied deftly but firmly, in precisely the proper force, Naval Presence can be a persuasive deterrent to war. Used ineptly, it could be disastrous. In determining presence objectives, scaling forces, and appraising perceptions, the human intellect must take precedence over ships and weapons systems.

The second naval deterrent mission came with the introduction of Strategic Deterrence as a national military requirement. Again, the combination of improved aircraft performance and smaller packaging of nuclear weapons made the aircraft carrier capable of contributing to this new mission. With the Navy struggling to readjust its missions to peacetime needs and with the U.S. Air Force at that time establishing its own place in the military family, it is understandable that there was a sense of competition for this new role. However, by the mid-1960s the development of the Polaris submarine eliminated any question of appropriateness of this mission for the Navy.

Our Strategic Deterrence objectives are:

- to deter all-out attack on the United States or its allies;
- to face any potential aggressor contemplating less than all-out attack with unacceptable costs; and to maintain a stable political environment within which the threat of aggression or coercion against the United States or its allies is minimized.

In support of these national objectives, we have three principal military "tactics" or force preparedness objectives. The first is to maintain an *assured second strike* capability in the hope of deterring an all-out strategic nuclear attack on the United States. Today that means dissuading the Soviets from starting a nuclear war. We hope to achieve this by maintaining a strategic attack force capable of inflicting unacceptable damage on any enemy even after he has attacked us. The Navy's Polaris/Poseidon/Trident forces are fundamental to this deterrence because of their high nuclear survival probability.

A second tactic is to design our forces to ensure that the United States is not placed in an unacceptable position by a partial nuclear attack. If the Soviets attacked only a portion of our strategic forces, would it then make sense for the United States to retaliate by striking Soviet cities, knowing that the Soviets still possessed adequate forces to strike our cities? This means making our strategic strike forces quickly responsive to change in targeting and capable of accurate delivery. SSBN forces can be well tailored to these requirements.

A third objective is to *deter third powers* from attacking the United States with nuclear weapons. Because of the great disparity between any third country's nuclear arsenal and ours, the same forces deterring the Soviet Union should deter others.

Finally, we maintain sufficient strategic forces so that we do not appear to be at a disadvantage to the Soviet Union or any other power. If we were to allow the opinion to develop that the Soviet strategic position is markedly superior to ours we would find that political decisions were being adversely influenced. Thus we must always keep in mind the balance of power image that our forces portray to the non-Soviet world. In part, this image affects what and how much we buy for strategic deterrence. In part, it affects how we talk about our comparative strength and how we criticize ourselves.

In summary, the Strategic Deterrence mission is divided into four tactics: *Assured Second Strike*, *Controlled Response*, *Deterrence of Third Powers*, and *Balance of Power Image*.

There is very little overlap between Strategic Deterrence and other Navy mission areas at present. However, significant improvements in enemy ASW technology could reduce the ability of SSBNs to survive without assistance from friendly Sea Control forces. With this exception and the fact that aircraft carriers still possess the potential for nuclear strikes, that mission is performed almost exclusively by forces designed specifically for it.

There is a good deal of overlap in the overall field of deterrence. There is no doubt that our strategic deterrent forces inhibit at least ourselves and the Soviet Union from engaging in non-strategic or conventional warfare. It is also true that the very existence of our Sea Control and Projection of Power Ashore forces deter conventional warfare, over and above whether we consciously employ them in the Naval Presence role. There is very likely even some interplay between our conventional force capability and the way in which our strategic deterrent forces are perceived, e.g., a Sea Control capability is essential to the security of our sea-based strategic deterrent forces. Thus, the boundary lines between the four naval mission areas cannot be precise. More than anything, they each express a somewhat different purpose. Despite these inevitable overlaps and interdependence, we can understand the Navy far better if we carefully examine each mission individually. We must know what each mission's objectives are so that we do not overlook some useful new tactic or weapon and so that we can strike the proper balance whenever these missions compete for resources.

Additionally, we must be careful not to view as rigidly fixed these mission areas and their relative importance. We swung from a primary emphasis on Sea Control with a secondary interest in amphibious assault before and during World War II, to a primary emphasis on strategic deterrence and tactical air projection for the 20 to 25 years following that war. In about the mid-1960s, the dramatic and determined growth of Soviet naval capabilities forced renewed attention to Sea Control. The even more recent national disinclination to engage ground forces in support of allies should perhaps today place more attention on the conventional deterrent mission of Naval Presence. The dynamic nature of world conditions will demand a continuing reassessment of the relation of one mission to another and the comparative emphasis on their individual tactics.

Perhaps this constant flow and counter flow of mission emphasis and tactical adaptation is even more accentuated today than in the past. On the one hand, the pace of technological innovation is forcing this. On the other, the changing nature of world political relationships and domestic attitudes demands a continual updating of naval capabilities to support national policy. Naval officers, as professionals, must understand the Navy's missions, continually question their rationale, and provide the intellectual basis for keeping them relevant and responsive to the nation's needs. Unless we do, we will be left behind, attempting to use yesterday's tools to achieve today's objectives.

Discussion Questions

1. How does Turner divide up the "warfighting" missions of the Navy? Keeping in mind that the article was written in the 1970s, does he miss any key aspects of the Navy and Marine Corps' roles in war?

2. How does Turner describe the "peacetime" missions of the Navy? Are there other elements of how you see the Navy and Marine Corps' job during peace, which Turner either misses or doesn't seem to place enough emphasis on?

3. Does deterrence have to involve nuclear weapons? How does Turner's essay influence the way that you think about deterrence today?

4. Turner's description of naval missions is clearly tied to the Cold War and conflict with the Soviets. Do his definitions and concepts still apply today?

5. At the very end Turner suggests that we should not take these categories too seriously. Why not? What is the use in studying them if we aren't to take them as a procedural standard?

14

GET OFF MY BACK, SIR!

Robert E. Mumford Jr.

(U.S. Naval Institute *Proceedings* 103, no. 8, August 1977)

On the West Coast, a skipper is ordered to terminate his highly successful management incentive program because some of his men have completed their assigned tasks in less than the standard eight hour day and have been allowed to go on liberty. At an East Coast port, all command duty officers are required to be on the quarterdeck between 1600 and 2000 daily to ensure that the liberty party is in acceptable attire. In Washington, a Navy civilian employee is reprimanded for a security violation because she failed to "sign off" her safe at close of business, even though her safe was properly locked. What do these seemingly unrelated events have in common? Very simply, they illustrate the most pervasive and insidious management problem in the Navy today: the means/ends inversion, a focus on activity in lieu of goals. Procedures are stressed to the exclusion of substance.

There are many ways to describe The Problem, any one of which provides the flavor, but none of which seems to fully explain its extent. In traditional Navy jargon, excessive rudder orders are being issued, seniors telling juniors not only what they are expected to achieve, but how to reach that goal. Some management consultants would tell us that we have lost sight of our objectives; others call it micromanagement or "Big Brotherism."

It requires no special management background to recognize that we have a problem in the Navy. The very size of type commander regulations indicates that something is wrong. Exasperated skippers have suggested that John Paul Jones could not have defeated the *Serapis* if he had been burdened by so much paper. If one takes the time to go beyond the bulk of regulations and examine the substance, the full impact of The Problem becomes obvious. In every publication of regulations the author has examined, there are numerous examples of extremely detailed guidance. It is either so obvious as to be demeaning, or it establishes procedures that are unnecessary for accomplishing worthwhile goals.

These examples indicate that our people in command are not just being given goals to reach; rather, they are being told "how to" in great detail. One logically needs then to ask, "Is this really a problem?" Aren't military people supposed to do what they're told? Isn't this the way it has always been? Is the organization really being damaged by detailed guidance from above? If you want the answers that count most, go to the people on the cutting edge, fleet commanding and executive officers. They may express themselves in different words, but their consensus is clear: they feel overwhelmed and stifled by excessive direction. They are frustrated, angry, and depressed by the realization that what should be the most rewarding years of their lives—the professional peak of their careers—are not all that satisfying. Some have described themselves as puppets, being moved by strings from above. Having thought that they would be able to exercise their creative capacities, they find that they are being forced into doing things the way someone else thinks best. Instead of concentrating on combat readiness, skippers and execs are forced into meeting administrative check-off lists and fitting themselves and their commands into a mold of standardized operation that is uncomfortable at best.

There have been many cases in recent years of top-performing officers refusing commands. Worse, some of those who took command admit in private that they would resign if they could do so gracefully. The Navy, shocked and dismayed by this, seems ready to believe that we have somehow bred a line of timid officers who want to shrink from responsibility. It is always more comforting to blame the individual than to accept the unhappy conclusion that something may be wrong with the organization. What is lacking is not acceptance of responsibility (in most officers), but rather the lack of an opportunity to be creative and independent.

More than just commanding officers are affected. Junior officers seem deeply troubled and turned off by The Problem. Many express their deep frustration and discouragement by exchanging the blue and gold for mufti at the first legal opportunity. It was not without good cause that one of the important initiatives of the early Seventies was to put "fun and zest" back into the system. In the author's judgment, that effort largely fell flat. It is a rare skipper who has not been told by a young division officer or a department head that he doesn't consider the prestige and power of command to be worth the "hassle." More often than not, the officers who express this thought are among the most talented and ambitious on board. We have created a gap between the image with which we recruit officers and the reality of their existence. The romantic image is of a man who goes to sea, leads other men, exercises discretion and power—an independent thinker and doer, an individual in an era of massive organizations. In reality, he is closer to a colorless cipher, conforming to countless paper requirements in order to survive.

We are developing a corps of officers who look for answers in publications but can't fight their own ships. They know how to conform but not create, interpret but not innovate. And we delude ourselves that this is sufficient. Because we have the peacetime capacity to control fleet units in the remote areas of the globe, we assume that these communications will be present during wartime. Thus, the qualities of independence, initiative, and judgment are no longer quite so important. We continue to pay lip service to these characteristics, but our actions belie our words. Our inspection and promotion systems reward those who precisely follow the methodology ordered from above. We seldom, if ever, measure results instead of procedures.

In addition to hurting retention, adversely affecting officer development, and causing dissatisfaction, The Problem detracts from the achievement of the Navy's raison d'etre: combat readiness. Behavioral scientists for years have reported that motivation is best achieved (after the basic needs have been met) by permitting people a good deal of latitude in their vocational environment. By participating in goal development and determining the course to reach those goals, "ownership" develops, and people have a personal stake in ensuring successful accomplishment. Indeed, one of the conceptual foundations of the Navy's own Human Resource Availability is increased commitment through development by the crew of unit goals and the steps to reach them. What the institution has blessed within units during one week of an 18-month cycle, however, is inconsistent with standard practices toward units during the entire cycle. An examination of fleet and type commander goals reveals a number of items which are oriented toward compliance with procedures rather than outcomes. Full use of training devices is an example.

Determining the cause for this devitalizing problem which permeates the entire organization is difficult at best. Undoubtedly, there is no single reason, but rather a cluster of norms, values, pressures, and constraints have contributed. There is no easy target to point to as scapegoat; it is all of us and none of us. While venting one's spleen against staff personnel may provide some measure of satisfaction and ameliorate temporarily the ill effects of a complaining ulcer; it does little to identify the real culprit(s). Some possible factors may be suggested.

Perhaps the largest factor contributing to The Problem is a downward spiraling phenomenon whose elements are failure, distrust, direction, and overload. The cycle typically begins with an acknowledged failure at some level. When a senior is put under excessive pressure by his senior, overreaction can occur, with the result that subordinates are no longer trusted to accomplish their jobs. Assuming that some will fail without guidance, the senior issues directives to prevent another disaster in the area in question. These are followed by inspections to ensure that the senior's program has been implemented and by command attention to preclude embarrassment. The more these programs are directed from above, the more an officer's time at the unit level is dominated by compliance with "how to's" and the less time is spent on achieving the goals themselves. Eventually, one's capacity for supervision becomes overloaded, an important item receives less attention than it warrants, another failure occurs, and the cycle is reinforced and repeated. The number of inspections and "assist" visits being imposed on our units suggests that we have reached criticality. Apparently, however, efforts are being made to reduce the number of such visits.

"Excessive staff echelons in the chain of command" is often identified as a major structural deficiency, and it may be one cause of The Problem. As directives depart each level, there is a tendency to interpret and provide policy guidance. Very often, this guidance includes added "how to's." What begins as a relatively simple objective at the four-star level may end at the unit level as a detailed plan of attack, completely foreclosing any opportunity for individual initiative. It is unreasonable to assume that it will be otherwise, without conscious effort. C. Northcore Parkinson, originator of the famous Parkinson's Laws, told us years ago that work expands to meet the time available. Thus, when staff positions are filled with energetic, bright officers, those officers are going to find something to do with their time. Directives follow directives, and commanders at each level feel it is necessary to issue implementing instructions. But paper alone proves neither loyalty nor effectiveness.

The necessity for a major change can result in The Problem. One example that comes to mind is the equal opportunity issue. While many thoughtful and dedicated people at all levels recognized that the Navy had major racial problems, insufficient progress was being made to satisfy ethical and legal demands. In the face of undesirable racial incidents, dramatic action was deemed necessary. The decision was made in Washington to require certain organizational changes in each unit, such as creation of the Minority Affairs Representative and the Human Relations Council. One can quibble endlessly whether these were necessary when a chain of command was functioning, but the point is that commanding officers were being told how to achieve a very admirable and essential goal. One result was that many officers still resent the program, despite being personally committed to equal opportunity and treatment.

In the author's opinion, a primary cause of The Problem is that—short of combat—we have trouble judging performance, despite 200 years of experience. For a variety of reasons, the surface community seems to have the most difficulty in this area. Our ships are seldom really evaluated against each other or by an objective minimum standard. And even our Battle Efficiency E competition involves a large measure of subjectivity. Because it is often easier to establish and monitor evaluative criteria around procedures than objectives, we rely on these factors to judge units. How are combat readiness, reliability, and casualty control measured? Who does the judging?

We know from past failure what doesn't work. For years there was competition between units which used certain exercises gleaned from Ship Exercises (FXP-3). But ships from the same squadron usually evaluated each other. Not unexpectedly, results were often compromised through mutual interests. A squadron commander could not be expected to be objective either. The more ships in his squadron that achieved departmental Es and other awards, the better he looked. When the author was a shipboard department head, he was the senior inspector for an amphibious battle problem on board a ship in the same squadron. The performance of the inspected ship was judged marginal (including a number of clear safety violations), but she received the annual amphibious assault award after the grades were elevated by the squadron commander. Self-evaluated exercises meet the needs of a training program, but they can hardly be used to determine the achievement of acceptable levels of performance. We have few measurable goals, and those that do exist, we often discount.

It appears that the Navy may be reluctant to accept the results of legitimate, objective competition. Humans in all walks of life believe that they can subjectively judge who is the best performer, yet that judgment often mirrors those who are the most liked. When a subordinate who is out of favor demonstrates success, the senior is often made very uncomfortable and surprised. He must then either reevaluate his assessment of the individual or downplay and ignore the performance. If the Navy as an institution is going to adopt objective criteria for evaluating officer performance, it must be willing to accept the results and reward the winner.

A seductive attraction of standardization can also be a contributing factor to The Problem. There appears to be a strong drive toward standardization in every large bureaucratic organization, irrespective of its function or composition. It does have its benefits and is sometimes necessary, but it is important to understand that standardization should not be a goal in itself. It protects the mediocre and incompetent to some degree and usually prevents gross errors. But it stifles the creative impulse of the most talented managers and precludes discovery of improved methods. Standardization is most beneficial when applied to technical problems but is often counterproductive in managing people.

What is the solution for The Problem? Just as there is no single cause, there is no one easy answer. An institution as large as our Navy cannot be changed overnight. When he was Chief of Naval Operations, Admiral Arleigh Burke reportedly bewailed the amount of energy required to alter the course of the organization by a single degree. There is an incredible amount of momentum accumulated in the habitual ways of conducting routine business, and the Navy has been deeply involved in the "how to" mode for many years. Old ways die particularly hard, and there will be powerful (and sincere) voices of dissent from many quarters if the Navy elects to change its modus operandi. It will be claimed that without detailed guidance, standards of "professional" excellence will not be met, and the readiness of the Navy will suffer, perhaps irreparably, while the "experiment" of concentrating on goals is conducted.

The above notwithstanding, improvement can be realized, and happily, without the necessity for change at the fleet level and above. Leaders at every level can make a conscious decision to get out of the "how to" business. Each can excise from his collection of directives those which contain rudder orders and refrain from getting back into the business with messages and suggestions. Individual people and commands within the Navy can adopt management by objectives, a technique where goals are mutually determined by superior and subordinate, and the subordinate is left to his own devices as to how to reach those goals. His fitness report would reflect how well the objectives were met. Management by objectives is not new to the Navy, and it has some strong advocates, but it often has been abandoned when difficulties have been encountered in implementation. While management by objectives is not the panacea for all Navy management problems, it certainly can contribute to eliminating the feelings of frustration experienced by so many commanding officers.

Of course, for objective-oriented management to be effective, there must be measurable goals. The Navy has developed meaningful objective criteria in some areas. It should continue to establish operational evaluations to determine who is meeting goals and who is falling short. Creating objective criteria and testing procedures is easy in some areas and difficult in others. There are already sufficient exercises and criteria for gunnery and aerial bombardment evaluation, but operations and communications testing is more formidable.

In order to achieve objectivity, special evaluation groups (not in the chain of command) should be established to judge performance. The Board of Inspection and Survey is an excellent example of an existing, no-nonsense, results-oriented evaluation group. Similar teams could be created to judge every facet of naval warfare. But this evaluation should be limited to outcomes, not whether records have been maintained, schools attended, or training programs conducted. Staffs in the chain of command should minimize their current roles of monitoring and evaluation and emphasize support and assistance to the operating forces. The fleet training groups should once and for all be restricted to training. The suggested evaluation groups should judge the final battle problem of a refresher training period. As it is, there is a conflict of interest between training and evaluation, for the judges are personnel from the organization which is charged with training. Complete objectivity does not always result.

One change that could be made overnight to provide commanding officers more latitude and authority would be to modify the restriction on days per quarter that ships can operate. The goal is clearly not to keep ships in port, but to conserve fuel and money. As it is, a ship could theoretically "cowboy" around the ocean for each of its allotted days, squandering fuel and exercising inefficient engineering practices without significant penalty. Why not allot to each ship an equitable amount of fuel and let the ship determine how it is to be expended? A ship with competent engineers, a motivated crew, and an innovative captain can probably figure ways of spending more training time at sea, thus meeting other combat readiness-related objectives.

Closely allied with the limit on days at sea per quarter is the wider problem of the entire quarterly employment schedule. There are usually four levels in the chain of command involved in establishing and changing schedules. The least influential is the ship herself. The number of personnel associated with this process is enormous, and the time and resources required, impressive. It is the author's belief that a simplified system, involving commanding officers to a greater degree, would result in conservation of effort at many levels. Rather than schedule in-port time, upkeep, individual exercises, and other very detailed forms of employment, a ship could be scheduled for COD—commanding officer's discretion. During that time, he could be under way, conducting maintenance, undergoing in-port training, or whatever he deemed appropriate. Imagine the energy that could be saved in not having to process every minor change in schedule. There are undoubtedly many other places in scheduling where a commanding officer can be given more latitude without disrupting the obvious necessity of coordinating and preplanning outside support activities associated with complex multi-unit exercises at sea and major maintenance ashore.

Another graphic example of an area where procedures have become more important than substance—and have eroded the commanding officer' discretion—is individual training. The Navy has implemented the Personnel Qualification Standard (PQS) system in every unit and for most ranks and rates. It is not merely recommended, but required, and many inspections now include the checking of PQS. PQS does, of course, have merit. The materials associated with the program have been developed at great cost and effort and often are of excellent quality. But the system requires considerable officer supervision and paperwork, and it does not necessarily achieve a goal. In today's cliche, what counts is the bottom line, and the bottom line in individual training is whether or not a man knows his job and can do it. If he doesn't, all the systems in use have failed. During inspections, what should be checked is not marks on a schedule but demonstrated knowledge. One unobtrusive measure which could be used would be to review average scores during the previous advancement exams. Another method would be random questioning of both officer and enlisted personnel. During ship visits, one Inspector General of the Navy asked men to demonstrate the use of an oxygen breathing apparatus, reasoning that if the men couldn't take the pressure of an admiral watching, they wouldn't be able to don the equipment in an emergency. As painful as such tests can be for a unit's supervisory personnel, they unequivocally measure results and cannot be "gundecked" by the saltiest operator. We need to eliminate most aspects of command and administrative inspections that deal with procedures and instead concentrate our limited examination time on the real elements of combat readiness.

A far more complicated and radical departure from current practices would be to restore more discretionary financial authority to the unit level. This is clearly a long-term venture which will require substantial in-house planning and congressional approval. Yet it would free the commanding officer from the artificial constraints that now limit his ability to achieve readiness. Instead of funding food, fuel, spare parts, and salaries out of different pockets, a command could determine what element needed budgetary priority. There should be no reason why a skipper could not compensate a man who is doing the work of three petty officers (because of a Navy wide shortage in a certain rating), nor utilize fuel money for spare parts, if that met a higher need. Commanding officers should be given the opportunity to retain funds in a "savings account" status past the fiscal year end. This would replace the current custom of a mad rush to expend funds during the last few weeks of the year. The present feast-or-famine atmosphere not only dictates against prudent fiscal practices at the unit level, it also regularly draws substantial unfavorable publicity to all the services.

What would be required to implement these changes would be nothing short of a major change in fiscal procedures, but this appears technically feasible. Indeed, Dr. Robert Anthony, Assistant Secretary of Defense (Financial Management) proposed a very similar concept a decade ago. The Navy did considerable research on the plan, nicknamed Project Prime, and attempted a shipboard pilot program. However, the effort proved unsuccessful, largely because of a lack of congressional support. Laws limiting discretion in the expenditure of public monies were neither repealed nor modified, and therefore new budgeting and obligating procedures could not be used, and the project was abandoned. Despite past problems, increased pressures on the armed services for improved management may now permit another attempt. Neither DoD nor Congress should object to modified budgeting if it can be demonstrated that the change would result in improved readiness. (Retention, quite clearly, is a major factor in the readiness equation.)

The above suggestions for reducing rudder orders in all their various forms by no means constitute an all-inclusive list. Valuable ideas for the establishment of a goal-oriented Navy will likely be triggered, however, in the minds of every officer with a modicum of fleet experience. Major change will come to the institution only when the cause for widespread dissatisfaction is recognized and accepted and the commitment is made to find a solution. The objective should be an environment of reasonable decentralization with clearly understood goals and priorities at every level. Diversity of styles and methods should be tolerated if not encouraged. Perhaps most importantly, occasional failures should be accepted as the price of developing initiative, innovation, and bold leadership. It should be a system where restraint is exercised in imposing procedures, where sophisticated communications are properly used as a tool instead of a means to tighten control. If this occurs, the Navy will once again be noted for its independent, resourceful seafaring captains, invigorated by modern leadership skills and strengthened by advanced technology. In short, to eliminate The Problem, we must learn again that men are unique, capable, and responsible creatures and that commanding officers can thus be trusted. With that trust, our skippers will no longer be muttering under their breath, "Get off my back, sir. I can hack it." And they will hack it.

Discussion Questions

1. Has anything really changed since this article was printed? If not, why not?
2. Can people really be trusted to do their jobs with a minimum of "how-to" direction? Why or why not?
3. Which of the author's proposed solutions is most compelling, and what would be required for it to work in today's Navy?
4. Which groups in the Navy or Marine Corps seem particularly susceptible to "The Problem"? Why? Why not?
5. Are there ways to reform the personnel evaluation and promotion system to alleviate "The Problem"?

15

MORAL LEADERSHIP

James Stockdale

(U.S. Naval Institute *Proceedings* 106, no. 9, September 1980)

Extortion, the squeeze-play drawing out of victims by force or compulsion is dramatized in Godfather movies as an easily recognized, explicit, usually illegal way of conducting business. In reality, though, it is conducted much more frequently in subtler ways—ways which are both more difficult to recognize and more difficult to deal with. And by no means are these ways illegal, at least not in the sense that I use the word. We frequently face extortionary pressures in our everyday life, for extortion is just a concentrated form of manipulation through the use of fear and guilt. We who are in hierarchies—be they academic, business, military, or some other sort—are always in positions in which people are trying to manipulate us, to get moral leverage on us. It is the wise leader who comes to the conclusion that he can't be had if he can't be made to feel guilty. That is as true today in a free environment as it was for me during my years in prison camp. You have got to keep yourself clean—never do or say anything of which you can be made to be ashamed—in order to avoid being manipulated. A smart man, an ethical man, never gives a manipulator an even break. He is always prepared to quench the extortionist's artful insinuation of guilt with the icewater of a truthful, clear-conscienced put-down. The more benign the environment, the more insidious is the extortionist's style. "Then Arthur learned," says the legend, "as all leaders are astonished to learn, that peace, not war, is the destroyer of men; that tranquility, rather than danger, is the mother of cowardice; and that not need, but plenty, brings apprehension and unease."

This is not to suggest that there is only one way to lead, one manner of leadership, one style that best fits all circumstances. Of course not. I have merely said that all styles must be built on moral virtue. On specific leadership styles, I learned much from a talk by a psychoanalyst named Michael Maccoby. With a comprehensive understanding of American history, and after in-depth interviews of more than 200 American leaders of the 1970s, Maccoby concluded that there were four dominant leadership styles in the American past.

Now there are two things to remember as I quickly go over this analysis of Maccoby's. First of all, examples of men who embody each style have always been around and are still around; it's just that the challenges of different historic periods seemed to draw out particular types of leaders. And second, don't look for progress in leadership styles as we walk through this analysis. The leaders as leaders or as men don't get better as we follow the historic process.

From the Declaration of Independence until the credit system started to grow in the 1870s after the Civil War, most American leaders fell into a category he calls "craftsmen." They were "do-it-yourself" guys: self-reliant, strong-willed, cautious, suspicious, harder on themselves than they are on others. Benjamin Franklin was cited as their prototype then, Aleksandr Solzhenitsyn now. Their target of competition was not other men, but rather their idea of their own potential. Craftsmen climbed ladders not to get ahead of others, but to achieve that level of excellence they believed they had within themselves. They are mountain climbers, not players of what systems analysts call "zero-sum-games." They liked to make up their own minds; they did not buy school solutions. Craftsmen were men of conscience.

The industrial revolution and the need of its necessary credit and banking base were met by a new breed of leaders: Maccoby called them the "jungle fighters." Jungle fighters played "zero-sum-games" with gusto; there was just so much business out there and these were the men who knew how to stake out territory and get it. Andrew Carnegie, the steel magnate, was the prototype. Like craftsmen, jungle fighters were also men of conscience. Although they could sit at the board of directors table and figuratively decapitate incompetents with aplomb, they grieved. Characteristically they did not dodge issues; they settled scores eyeball to eyeball, tasting not only the self-satisfaction of authority but also the agony of pity.

After World War I, as the giant businesses the jungle fighters had built became bureaucracies, and as this "public relations" grew into an everyday national preoccupation, those jungle fighters were gradually displaced by the smoother "organization men." Like the jungle fighters, the organization men were paternalistic and authoritarian. But unlike those in pioneers of industry and finance who were motivated primarily by competitive zeal, "organization men," our psychoanalyst believes, were more motivated by a fear of failure. They were, nevertheless, characteristically honest; they were cautious men of conscience. They looked men in the eye when they fired them. They were "men of the heart," possessing qualities with an emotional content: a sense of commitment, loyalty, humor, and spontaneity.

In the early 1960s, a fourth style emerged to take the prominent leadership role. Maccoby identifies practitioners of this style as "the gamesmen." The gamesmen, impatient under the yoke of their paternalistic and authoritarian bosses, and educated more often than not in game-theory-oriented business schools, turned over a new page in leadership practices. The gamesmen believe that if one properly analyzes the "game" of life, the "game" of management, the "game" of leadership, one sees that it is not necessary to frame the problem as a "zero-sum-game." Rather, in their minds, American life can be as a "game" in which any number can play and win.

These gamesmen were relaxed, objective, open-minded, detached, cerebral swingers. Such emotional baggage as commitment or conscience they deemed inefficient and unnecessary. "Play your cards rationally to win and go to bed and sleep like a baby bothered without remorse." Some bothered with love and families; many gave them a tentative try and quit when they found them too burdensome. Maccoby said that there was a theatrical production that typified each of these four ages and that the drama of the gamesmen was portrayed in the movie "The Sting." You might remember that screenplay; in it, fair, competitive cooperative swingers, with the aid of teamwork and technology, destroyed the hung-up, authoritarian "Godfather."

The gamesmen, concluded psychoanalyst Maccoby, were basically "men of the head": cool intellectual types, walking calculating machines. "Men of the head" do many things well, but often have trouble coping with unpleasantness. These self-confident, cool, flexible men don't like to discipline people, they don't like to look people in the eye when they fire them. Moreover, they often crave to be loved, and that is a great leadership weakness. True leaders must be willing to stake out territory and identify and declare enemies. They must be fair and they may be compassionate, but they cannot be addicted to being loved by everybody. The man who has to be loved is an extortionist's dream. That man will do anything to avoid face-to-face unpleasantness; often he will sell his soul for praise. He can be had.

It was in the heyday of these gamesmen that some of their number, the cool, glib, analytical, cerebral so-called defense intellectuals took charge of the Pentagon under the direction of Robert Strange McNamara. At that juncture, I was fortunate enough to take a two-year sabbatical from military service for study at Stanford University. It was there that I started asking myself what truly rules the world: sentiment, efficiency, honor, justice?

The educated man, particularly the educated leader, copes with the fact that life is not fair. The problem for education is not to teach people how to deal with success but how to deal with failure. And the way to deal with failure is not to invent scapegoats or to lash out at your followers. Moreover, a properly educated leader, especially when harassed and under pressure, will know from his study of history and the classics that circumstances very much like those he is encountering have occurred from time to time on this earth since the beginning of history. He will avoid the self-indulgent error of seeing himself in a predicament so unprecedented, so unique, as to justify his making an exception to law, custom, or morality in favor of himself. The making of such exceptions has been the theme of public life throughout much of our lifetimes. For 20 years, we've been surrounded by gamesmen unable to cope with the wisdom of the ages. They make exceptions to law and custom in favor of themselves because they chose to view ordinary dilemmas as unprecedented crises.

Of course, it has been generally toward the above issue that I directed a course at the Naval War College. My formula for attacking this problem—both at the War College and in my present assignment at The Citadel—is the assignment of enough hard-core philosophy (*The Book of Job*, the Socratic dialogues of Plato, some of Aristotle's *Nichomachean Ethics*, Epictetus' *Enchiridion*, enough of Immanuel Kant to understand his concept of duty) and the reading of enough high-quality ultimate situation literature (Feodor Dostoyevsky's *House of the Dead*, Albert Camus' *Plague*, Joseph Conrad's *Typhoon*, and Herman Melville's *Billy Budd*) as to deter self-pity when in extremis. With philosophy as the parent discipline, a discussion of courage might be focused on the writer who most thoroughly treated it, Aristotle. This might lead to the question of the validity of his viewpoint that courage is impossible in the absence of fear, that courage might be defined as a measure of how well one handles fear. How about the relationship between fear and imagination? Conrad has one of his characters state that imagination is the mother of fear. Must not a leader have imagination? If that breeds fear, might that not sap his courage? He surely must have courage above all else . . . etc. From such readings and discussions come understandings and clarifications of those elements of leadership which served in antiquity and those which must serve now.

Leadership must be based on goodwill. Goodwill does not mean posturing and, least of all, pandering to the mob. It means obvious and wholehearted commitment to the helping followers. We are tired of leaders we fear, tired of leaders we love, and most tired of leaders who let us take liberties with them. What we need for leaders are men of the heart who are so helpful that they, in effect, do away with the need of their jobs. But leaders like that are never out of a job, never out of followers. Strange as it sounds, great leaders gain authority by giving it away.

I am firmly convinced that the time I spent at Stanford has been a major force in molding my own personality as a leader. And I am just as firmly convinced that education in the classics and in the principles of human relationships gave me far better preparation for being a prisoner of war than did the traditional survival and evasion training. My ideas on the art of moral leadership received their most profound testing in the stress and degradation—yes, in the extortion environment—of a Communist prisoner of war camp.

The intensity and stark drama of my eight years in North Vietnam provided a quantity and range of leadership challenge that would more than fill an ordinary lifetime. In mere months or weeks, men made and destroyed their reputations. Those behind bars seemed to be scanning reams of data on the problems of good and evil in fast time. The extortion system, powered by our enemy's willingness to torture and impose isolation, quickly drove to the surface issues of moral integrity which at the pace of normal life could take years to fester and erupt into public view.

For united resistance, men had to get on quickly with the business of assimilating knowledge of the character traits of their fellow prisoners. This knowledge had to be more penetrating and more calculating than the sort commonly found sufficient for amicable social life out here in freedom. Is the newcomer emotionally stable? (We had to make a good guess as to whether he had the steadfastness and composure to warrant being trusted with secret material in that torture environment.) Does he have moral integrity? In the privacy of the torture room, will he go to the wall in silence, or do what is so commonplace in the business world nowadays and try to make a deal? Is he sophisticated enough to avoid falling for the interrogator's bait? Will he work his way out on a limb by "gabbing" after that clever interrogator has dangled before him such American-life enticements as: Let us reason together; You are a pragmatic people, meet us halfway?

In the extortion environment one can always better his own position at the expense of his fellows by holding still for the manipulator's setting up of subtle compromises. A loner makes out by making acknowledged or tacit deals. This will never do. The intensity of life in jail clearly illuminated for us prisoners of war the truth that for the greatest good for the greatest number of us, for our maximum happiness, maximum self-respect, maximum protection of one another, each of us had to submerge our individual survival instincts into an ideal of universal solidarity. "No deals" and "Unity over self" became our mottos.

Some of you are doubtless skeptical of the practicability of such ideals which seem to ask more of a man than human nature might be thought to allow. To the skeptics let me say right off that when there is leadership by example, and when there is a commonly shared threat of total estrangement and humiliation, united magnanimous behavior can become a reality. When a man looks at the bottom of the barrel through creeping and growing fissures in the thin veneer of civilization that coats his existence, he suddenly realizes that his slip back into barbarism could come about in weeks. As he peers over the edge of his world, it dawns on him how lonesome and terrible it would be down there without communication, friends, or common cultural ties. He vividly realizes how men, fellow countrymen, need one another for understanding and for sanity. As he sees himself clinging to a receding civilization with his fingernails, it becomes clear to him that "No deals" and "Unity over self" are not goody-goody idealistic slogans; rather they are practical guides to action.

We saw that we had to build and tend our own civilization if we were to keep ourselves from becoming animals. A man must relate to a community, a commonality of communication style, a commonality of ritual, of laws, of traditions, of poetry, of shared dreams, if he is to prevail, if he is to resist. "Man does not live by bread alone." Learning the truth and full meaning of that biblical adage was lesson number one for us in that crucible of pressure. It goes without saying that the first job of leadership is to provide the communication necessary for that civilization, that ritual, those laws, those traditions.

The problem was to improvise a communications system for a prison camp in which everybody lived in solitary confinement, a solitary confinement in silence, a solitary confinement in which the use of torture was considered just punishment for those who break that silence to communicate with their fellows. Our Vietnam enemies gave us two ways to go on this. We could lie low and not communicate and go to seed over the years of silence and solitude. (One starts "looking for a friend" after a couple of years.) Or we could communicate as a matter of duty and take our lumps. Since the dictates of conscience and morality made the latter the only way to go, the problem became how to communicate stealthily. For us, trapped in isolation in Hanoi, the means for that communication was a tap code that would break through the walls of solitary confinement, the walls of silence. (For the mechanics of the code, I suggest reading Commander Everett Alvarez's "Sound: A POW's Weapon," pages 91–93 in the August 1976 *Proceedings*.)

Leadership basics are vividly portrayed in the prison camp example. Prison serves as a useful "test bed" (to use a test pilot expression) in which to study in detail man's behavior under stress, stress of the sort under which many of life's crucial decisions are necessarily made. Mark this down in your book as lesson two: in the high-stress situation, "status" will not carry you as a leader. That is to say, you have to have more going for you than your title, your seniority, your position in your hierarchy, your rank. You cannot get by with performing like a quarterback who is functional only while being protected "in the pocket"; you've got to be able to scramble and improvise, on your feet, and alone. Even this assumes that by the time the pressure is on, you would have earned your followers' respect, and not just their fear or friendship. Unless people respect you as a leader, when the fat is in the fire they'll just listen to your orders and calmly walk away.

Lesson three: under stress, ordinary "transactional" leadership will never cut it. That is to say, transactional leadership propelled simply by the effect of give and take, leadership driven by the base instincts of the marketplace and bargaining table whereby the leader makes an accommodation in the expectation that his followers will make a complementary accommodation, simply will not stand up. This may come as news to you because the "transactional" leader/follower relationship is so much a part of our way of doing business in everyday economic, social, even academic life. But what to us is the ordinary dance of life, the dance propelled by continuous compromise, finds itself floundering under pressure. Inputs are needed from "transforming" leaders. Transforming leaders don't simply analyze what they think their people want and then try to give them part of it and hope they will receive a counter accommodation in return. Transforming leaders instruct and inspire their followers to recognize worthy needs, and they make those needs their wants. They have a way of raising their followers out of their everyday selves and into their better selves, of making them conscious of the high-minded goals that lie unconscious beneath their self-centered desires. In summary, the transforming leader has the wisdom to read the minds of his flock, to understand what they want, to know what they ought to want; and he has the persuasive power to implant the latter into their hearts.

In all that I have been saying, I've made the points that leaders under pressure must keep themselves absolutely clean morally (the relativism of the social sciences will never do). They must lead by example, must be able to implant high-mindedness in their followers, must have competence beyond status, and must have earned their followers' respect by demonstrating integrity. What I've been describing as the necessary leadership attributes under pressure are the bedrock virtues all successful leaders must possess, "under pressure and otherwise." Prison was just the "test bed," just the meat-grinder that vividly illuminated these prime building blocks for me.

THE DAMN EXEC

Stuart D. Landersman

(U.S. Naval Institute *Proceedings* 91, no. 1, January 1965)

The Norfolk wind was streaking the water of Hampton Roads as Commander Martin K. Speaks, U.S. Navy, Commanding Officer of the USS *Bowens* (DD-891), stepped from his car, slammed the door, and straightened his cap. As he approached the pier head a sailor stepped from the sentry hut and saluted.

"Good morning, Captain."

"Good morning, Kowalski," answered Commander Speaks. He took pleasure in the fact that he knew the sailor's name. Kowalski was a good sailor. He had served his entire first cruise in the *Bowens* and did his work well.

The Captain noticed that over his blues Kowalski wore a deck force foul weather jacket, faded, frayed, dirty, and spotted with red lead. "Little chilly this morning," said the Captain as he walked by. "Yes sir, sure is," replied the sailor with his usual grin.

As the Captain approached his quarterdeck there was the usual scurrying of people and four gongs sounded. "*Bowens* arriving," spoke the loudspeaker system, and Lieutenant (j.g.) Henry Graven, U.S. Naval Reserve, gunnery officer and the day's command duty officer, came running to the quarterdeck. Salutes and cheerful "good mornings" were exchanged, and the Captain continued to his cabin.

Lieutenant Graven looked over the quarterdeck and frowned. "Let's get this brightwork polished, chief."

"It's already been done once this morning sir," replied the OOD.

"Well, better do it again. The Exec will have a fit if he sees it this way," said Graven. "Yes sir," answered the OOD.

As soon as Graven had left, the OOD turned to his messenger, "Go tell the duty boatswain's mate that Mr. Graven wants the brightwork done over again on the quarterdeck."

Later that morning Captain Speaks was going over some charts with the ship's Executive Officer, Lieutenant Commander Steven A. Lassiter, U.S. Navy. The Captain had just finished his coffee and lighted a cigarette. "Steve, I noticed our pier sentry in an odd outfit this morning. He had a foul weather jacket on over his blues; it looked pretty bad."

"Yes sir. Well, it gets cold out there, and these deck force boys have mighty bad looking jackets," the Exec said.

The Captain felt the Exec had missed his Point and said, "Oh, I realize they have to wear a jacket, but for a military watch like that, I'd like to see them wear pea coats when it's cold."

Lieutenant Graven was talking with a third class boatswain's mate on the fantail when the quarterdeck messenger found him. When told that the Executive Officer wanted to see him, Graven ended his discussion with, "There, hear that? He probably wants to see me about that brightwork. I don't care how many men it takes to do it, the Exec told me to be sure to get that brightwork polished every morning."

The Executive Officer indicated a chair to Graven and they both lighted up cigarettes. "How's it going these days?" asked the Exec.

Lassiter had always liked Graven, but in the past few months, since he had taken over as senior watch officer, Graven seemed to have more problems than usual.

"Okay, I guess," Graven replied with a forced grin. He knew that things were not as they used to be. It seemed strange, too, because everyone on the ship had been so glad to be rid of the previous senior watch officer, that "damn" Lieutenant Dumphy. The junior officers even had a special little beer bust at the club to celebrate Dumphy's leaving and Graven's "fleeting up" to senior watch officer. Now the Exec was always after him. The junior officers didn't help much either, always complaining about the Exec. Maybe the Exec was taking over as "the heel" now that Dumphy was gone.

"That's good," said the Exec, "here's a little thing that you might look into. These men that stand pier watches have to wear a jacket, but the foul weather jacket doesn't look good for a military watch. I'd like to see them wear their pea coats when it's cold." Graven had expected something like this, more of the Exec's picking on him. He responded properly, got up, and left.

Graven told his First Lieutenant: "The Exec says the pier head sentries can't wear foul weather jackets anymore. If it's cold they can wear pea coats," he added.

"But the pea coats will get dirty and then what about personnel inspections?" asked the First Lieutenant.

"I don't know," Graven shook his head, "but if the Exec wants pea coats, we give him pea coats!"

"Pea coats!" said the chief boatswain's mate, "Who says so?"

"That's what the Exec wants," said the First Lieutenant, "so let's give him pea coats."

"The Exec says pea coats for the pier sentries when it's cold," announced the Chief to his boatswain's mates.

A third class boatswain's mate walked away from the group with a buddy, turned and said, "That Damn Exec, first I got to have all my men polish brightwork on the quarterdeck, now they got to wear pea coats on sentry duty 'stead of foul weather jackets!" Seaman Kowalski's relief showed up at the sentry booth at 1150. "Roast beef today," constituted the relieving ceremony.

"Good, I like roast beef," was the reply. "Hey, how come the pea coat?"

"Damn Exec's idea," said the relief. "We can't wear foul weather gear no more out here, only pea coats."

"Damn Exec," agreed Kowalski, "Captain didn't say nothin' when he came by."

"The Captain's okay, it's just that Damn Exec. He's the guy who fouls up everything," complained the new sentry.

Seaman Kowalski had just gone aboard the ship when Captain Speaks stepped out on deck to look over his ship. The quarterdeck awning shielded the Captain from the view of those on the quarterdeck, but he could clearly hear the conversation.

"Roast beef today, Ski."

"Yeah, I know, and we wear pea coats from now on."

"Whaddaya mean, pea coats?"

"Yeah, pea coats on the pier, Damn Exec says no more foul weather jackets."

"Well that ain't all, we got to polish this here brightwork 'til it shines every morning before quarters, Damn Exec says that too."

"Damn Exec."

Captain Speaks was shocked. "Why 'Damn Exec' from these seamen?" he thought. It was easy to trace what had happened to the order the Captain gave the Executive Officer that morning. It was easy to see that the Executive Officer had passed it along in proper military manner. It was easy to see that the junior officers, leading petty officers, and lower petty officers were passing it along saying "The Exec wants . . ." That's the way orders are passed along. Why? Because "it is easy."

"All ship's officers assemble in the wardroom," the boatswain's mate announced on the loudspeaker system. Lieutenant Commander Lassiter escorted in the Captain. The junior officers took their seats when the Captain was seated. The Executive Officer remained standing. "Gentlemen, the Captain has a few words to say to us today."

The Captain rose and looked around slowly. "Gentlemen, we are continually exposed to words like administration, leadership, management, capabilities, organization, responsibilities, authority, discipline, and cooperation. You use these words every day. You give lectures to your men and use them, but if I were to ask each of you for a definition of any of these words I would get such a wide variety of answers that an expert couldn't tell what word we were defining. Some we probably couldn't define at all. We still use them, and will continue to use them as they are used in the continually mounting number of articles, instructions, and books we must read.

"If I were to ask any of you how can we improve leadership I would get answers filled with these words—undefined and meaningless.

"If we listed all of the nicely worded theories of leadership, studied them, memorized them, and took a test in them, we would all pass. But this would not improve our ability as leaders one bit. I can tell a story, containing none of these meaningless words that will improve your leadership.

"In 1943, I was secondary battery officer in a cruiser in the South Pacific. In my second battle, gun control was hit and I lost communications with everyone except my 5-inch mounts. I could see that the after main battery turret was badly damaged and two enemy destroyers were closing from astern. At the time my 5-inch mounts were shooting at airplanes. I ordered my two after 5-inch mounts to use high capacity ammunition and shift targets to the two destroyers closing from astern. 'But Mr. Speaks, we're supposed to handle the air targets; who said to shift targets?' my mount captain asked.

"There were noise and smoke and explosions that day, but the explosion that I heard and felt was not from a shell, but from those words of the mount captain.

"Those attacking destroyers got a few shots in at us before we beat them off. Maybe those shots found a target and some of my shipmates died. I never found out. There was too much other damage.

"I thought over the battle afterward and realized that this entire situation was my fault, not the mount captain's. I may have been responsible for the death of some of my shipmates because up to that day I always gave orders to my subordinates by attaching the originator's name to it.

"What does that mean? It means that it was the easy thing to do, to say, 'the gunnery officer wants us to shift targets.'

"In this peacetime world you may say that we no longer have this struggle on a life or death basis. Quick response does not mean life or death now, but it might tomorrow, or sometime after we've all been transferred elsewhere and this ship is being fought by people we don't know.

"Whether you're cleaning boilers, standing bridge watch or administering your training program, it's easy to say 'the exec wants' or 'Mr. Jones says.' It's the *easy*, lazy way; not the right way. You can sometimes discuss or even argue with an order, but when you give it to a subordinate, make him think it is an order coming from you.

"Giving orders the lazy way is like a drug. Once you start saying 'the ops officer wants' you will find yourself doing it more and more until you can't get a thing done any other way. Your men will pass along orders that way, too, and it will become a part of your organization right down to the lowest level. When some problem arises and you want action, you'll get 'who wants this' or 'why should we.'

"Each of you ask yourself if you have given an order today or yesterday in the lazy manner. I think almost all of us have. Now ask yourself if that order really originated with the person who gave it to you, or did they receive it from a higher level? We never really know, do we, but why should we even care?

"In almost every unit the 'lazy' ordering starts on a particular level. From personal experience I can tell you that this can be an exact measure of the unit's effectiveness. If it starts at the department head level or higher it's a relatively bad outfit, and if it starts at the chief's level it's a relatively good outfit. You can find the level below which it starts by hearing a new title preceding a primary billet. 'Damn Exec' means that the executive officer is the lowest level giving orders properly. 'Damn division officer' means that the division officers are taking the responsibility for the order.

"Here I am using some of those words, responsibility and authority, those undefined terms we want to avoid, but perhaps we have helped define them.

"To be more specific, every officer does some 'lazy' ordering, but we need to do it less and less. We must try to push the 'damn' title down as far as it will go.

"Let's push the 'damn officer' down all the way to the chiefs and below, then we will have a Damn Good Ship."

Discussion Questions

1. How are these two essays related? To put it more pointedly, what does Landersman's "push the 'damn' title down as far as it will go" have to do with Stockdale's "'transforming' leaders"?

2. What kinds of leaders dominate today's Navy: "craftsmen," "jungle fighters," "organization men," or "gamesmen"? Why? (For self-reflection: using this typology, what kind of leader are you?)

3. Stockdale says that "great leaders gain authority by giving it away," but he does not explain what he means. What do you understand by that? Is it possible?

4. Should the Navy really cultivate a culture that seeks to "push the 'damn officer' all the way down to the chiefs and below"? Do you agree with Landersman that we should not care where orders originate? (For self-reflection: do you give orders "the lazy way"?)

5. Stockdale says that a "transforming leader" should know what his or her flock "ought to want." Do you think he is right? Why or why not?

16

THE BUSINESS OF
THE MARINE CORPS

Gary W. Anderson

(U.S. Naval Institute *Proceedings* 107, no. 8, August 1981)

Since its founding in 1775, the Marine Corps has occupied a unique place in the American military structure. Alternately maligned and lauded, it has survived by providing a useful mix of services to the nation at critical times and places. In recent years, the rapid pace of technological change has led critics to doubt the viability of the Marine Corps' role in amphibious warfare. Because of the Corps' specialized functions of providing amphibious landing doctrine and of seizing and holding advanced naval bases, some critics have argued that without an amphibious mission, there is no need for a separate Marine Corps.

Some marines have become alarmed by this. A lively debate over roles and missions was begun by the famous Brookings Study and has been joined by reporters, military analysts, politicians, and other branches of the services. Professional journals and civilian news publications have offered a multitude of suggestions, ranging from defense of amphibious techniques to proposals for mechanization. During the debate, some terms have been used rather loosely. This is particularly true in the case of amphibious warfare. Amphibious warfare is not a mission. The seizure and defense of advanced naval bases is a mission; likewise, providing a force in readiness is a mission, even if it is only implied. Even providing doctrine for amphibious operations is a mission. However, the seizure of an advanced naval base does not necessarily imply an amphibious operation. Amphibious warfare is a means, not an end. Those who accuse the Marine Corps of casting about for a mission, and even those in the Corps who fear for its survival, have lost sight of that distinction.

A Maritime Creature. The Marine Corps remains an essentially maritime creature. It should exist to complement the Navy's role in using the waters of the world for U.S. purposes when it suits our foreign policy. The only true threat to the continued existence of the Corps would be one which irretrievably separated it from its maritime identification. This is why the assignment of Marine Corps units as a strategic reserve for NATO disturbs so many marines. This fear of misuse, as exemplified by the employment of the Corps in World War I and Vietnam, may be justified.

Of the other potential uses for marines, three may be identified as potential strategies, not missions, for the 1980s. These are the standard amphibious landing, the use of marines as part of a rapid deployment force, or the use of marines in defense of a strategic littoral. These major options include potential use of marines on the NATO flanks. Many observers see these options as being mutually exclusive. On closer observation, this view simply doesn't hold up. Each of these potential uses has a place in the ebb and flow of a future conflict; each has a potential for success, given some fairly moderate retooling of existing and planned Marine Corps organization, tactics, and technology. To get a feeling for the potential integration of these uses, we should examine the strengths and weaknesses of each.

The Standard Amphibious Operation: The much maligned but historically effective amphibious assault is, of course, the Marine Corps' traditional "bread-and-butter play." It still has the advantage of creating an indirect effect on an enemy's maritime flank as well as providing the capability to wage maneuver warfare on a strategic level. In addition to the assault, the other types of amphibious operations have potential in the future. Amphibious raids and demonstrations provide interesting possibilities for a theater commander. Likewise, the evacuation of U.S. nationals remains an important amphibious function. In a May 1980 *Proceedings* article, Lieutenant Colonel William M. Krulak argues against putting so much emphasis on the amphibious role as has been the case in the past. As one of his several reasons, he contends that early air and sea superiority in a war against the Soviet Union would by no means be a certainty.[1] Other critics cite a lack of mobility ashore and inadequate sealift for all elements of the existing marine amphibious force as crippling limitations. While it is true that these are limitations which must be considered and overcome, it is unrealistic to write off the amphibious concept arbitrarily because of them.

One irony of the entire debate is that of the three possible strategies discussed in this essay, the amphibious operation is the only one that is not necessarily tied to the seizure and defense of advanced bases or readiness missions. Historically, amphibious operations are conducted in the latter stages of a conflict when naval support assets have been released from purely defensive considerations. The concept of using amphibious operations at the outset of a large-scale conflict is a new one, and its ancestry is dubious at best.

The relatively new concept of the Rapid Deployment Force has an immediate apparent impact for marines. It is a seemingly natural offshoot of the old "force in readiness" mission. It is well suited to the Marine Corps' long-established mount-out capability. The Rapid Deployment Force is not purely a Marine Corps concept; nonetheless, in most envisioned scenarios, the early seizure of a port or maritime airfield is considered necessary to take full advantage of prepositioned forces and aerial resupply which constitute the heart of the concept. Although this concept might involve the seizure of a facility by a marine air-ground task force if the force were already in the area, it would be more likely to involve early occupation and defense of an already secure airfield or port facility by a marine force augmented by pre-positioned equipment. The Commandant of the Marine Corps made this clear in his white letter number 2-81. As a result, the Rapid Deployment Force/prepositioning concept envisions the defense of an advanced base rather than its amphibious seizure. The unique aspects of the marine air-ground task force are ideal for the seizure or defense of any such lodgement. The Corps' shore party capability is a natural for early and expeditious movement of supplies and equipment ashore.

There are some potential minuses to the concept as viewed by marines. Lieutenant Colonel G. D. Batcheller, in an article in the June 1980 *Marine Corps Gazette*, points out that in many cases these operations would involve power transfer rather than power projection.[2] Here we must remember that the stated mission of the Corps calls for defense as well as seizure. In World War II, the nature of the beast downgraded the defensive aspect; a Rapid Deployment Force scenario might see the reverse of this trend.

A second objection to marines embracing the concept of rapid deployment would be the inability to sustain combat ashore against a mechanized force. While some of this may be answered by increased Marine Corps mechanization, a great deal of the answer lies in picking the proper time and place to fight. A seizure of Iranian oil fields would be more ill-advised than the reinforcement of a friendly airbase in Oman. Although fraught with some danger, it would appear that the rapid deployment concept has a viable potential as a tool in protecting the nation's maritime interests, and this very definitely makes it the business of the Marine Corps.

Littoral Defense: Still other observers have suggested that seizure and defense of littoral choke points might present a very suitable strategy for the Marine Corps. Writing in the September 1979 issue of the *Marine Corps Gazette*, Commander Bruce VanHeertum suggested that this concept be used to provide sea control to deny Soviet fleets the blue water access that they need to conduct sea denial missions.[3] In April 1980, I suggested early occupation of these littorals as a way of ensuring that bloody amphibious operations would not be needed to retake them.[4]

Commander VanHeertum pointed out that Marine Corps aviation could readily be fitted with antiship weapon systems in order to expedite the sea control portions of this strategy. The marine air-ground task force has the structure to conduct the necessary elements of this advanced base defense adequately. It has an air arm with which to challenge the Soviet amphibious task force at sea and a ground element to challenge a landing attempt.

Although this plan is cost-effective and fits within the advanced base and readiness framework of existing missions, it, too, has some drawbacks. Any attempt to relegate the Marine Corps, even temporarily, to a defensive role is bound to come under criticism. These fears are not without justification. History is replete with examples of the dangers in developing a Maginot Line mentality. Even though the proposal is strategically offensive, there is no doubt that a long-term occupation of a littoral could dull the offensive spirit of even the finest troops. Any adoption of this proposal would have to take this into account.

In his June 1980 article in the *Marine Corps Gazette*, Major Roger M. Jaroch, who then worked for the NATO/Europe Plans Division at Headquarters, Marine Corps, pointed out the extreme strategic importance of Iceland and the Danish Straits to NATO.[5] Early occupation and defense of these key choke points by marine forces could be a key point of leverage in a future NATO crisis.

Synthesis: Debate on each of these options, plus several others, has been lively and intense. Senior officers are concerned with their stewardship over the Corps, and more junior officers wonder if it will exist for them to lead 20 years hence. At the same time, civilian analysts such as Jeffrey Record and William Lind understandably want the most bang for the buck.[6] However, if we can separate the combatants for a moment, we may see more synthesis in these views than antithesis. The strong potential exists that each of the three strategies can be molded into a coherent and formidable system of maritime sea control and power projection, built around a flexible net of advanced naval bases. This system would provide a dual capability of providing rapid crisis response while strategically limiting Soviet blue water entry if that capability is needed.

To envision this system, one must understand the types of conflict possible in the next 20 years. Increasingly, the threat of war takes the form of a Third World peripheral outbreak or an intense conflict between the Soviet Union and the United States and its allies. From an American viewpoint, the intense conflict can be divided into an initial defensive stage and a recovery stage. Each of our proposed strategies has a potential use during these various levels of conflict.

Third World Low-to-Mid-Level Conflict: An intervention during a Third World crisis is the raison d'etre of the rapid deployment concept. This could include everything from evacuation of U.S. nationals to a full-fledged campaign for a Middle East nation's territorial integrity. The concept of maritime pre-positioning will provide a large improvement over a marine amphibious unit's present limited capability to intervene effectively in a crisis. The use of these forces in such a context would not detract from their readiness to intervene in a situation of increased intensity.

NATO-Soviet Confrontation—Defensive Phase: A Soviet assault on Western Europe would be very likely to include a massive move by the Soviet fleet into blue waters through the choke points of the Eurasian land mass. If in a time of crisis advanced parties from marine air-ground task forces could garrison these littorals in preparation for their defense, the Marine Corps could provide a formidable deterrent. If the original garrison is the size of a marine amphibious unit and the follow-up force is a marine amphibious brigade, the Marine Corps will present an impressive dagger at the throat of any Soviet naval thrust. This use of marines to provide a sea control weapon would be a tremendous asset in the desperate days sure to follow an initial Soviet strike.

As pointed out by Colonel Krulak, an amphibious operation in the early phases of such a conflict would be unlikely since the Navy would be otherwise disposed in this phase with sea control maintenance. This being the case, I submit that marines would be better used in assisting this sea control function than in being frittered away as part of a strategic reserve. This would also hasten the day when marines could use their unique amphibious potential to drive home against Soviet power.

NATO-Soviet Conflict—Phase II: When sea control is firmly established in U.S. and NATO hands, the full force of our amphibious potential can be used for a wide range of activities. These could include raids and demonstrations to dissipate strength from the Russian front lines; similarly, raids and demonstrations could be used in connection with the evacuation of pockets of resistance bypassed in the initial Soviet thrust. Of course, the greatest potential of amphibious warfare lies in gaining advanced bases to further contain Soviet sea power and to threaten the Soviets' seaward flanks.

The beauty of this concept is that in each case the first step doesn't preclude the second. A Rapid Deployment Force capability doesn't preclude preparing defensive positions on littoral outcroppings. By the same logic, littoral areas provide outstanding bases for further operations. Each strategy provides for maritime uses that are needed; no strategy requires that the others be scrapped if sound planning and implementation are exercised.

Dealing with the Objections: I realize that we live in a world of apparently diminishing resources. When, I was a lieutenant, I bemoaned the Marine Corps' apparent desire to be all things to all people. How then do I square an apparent desire to expand Marine Corps capabilities to embrace all these strategies discussed thus far? The question is legitimate and bears a fairly detailed answer.

In his article previously cited, Lieutenant Colonel Batcheller offered the opinion that the money spent for rapid deployment would be better spent on increasing the Corps' amphibious potential. Here lies the crux of the problem. In an era when the American people are asking for an increased military capability, marines must stop assuming that every capability will come at the cost of yet another capability. Each use listed in this essay will require new equipment and weapon systems. In the wave of self-flagellation by the public and Congress that followed the Vietnam War, an internal juggling of Marine Corps priorities was justified.

There is a danger that as a result of an era of scarcity, that marines might forget how to deal effectively with adequate resources. A disturbing trend in articles by marines of late is to impose constraints that don't exist. For example, in his May 1980 *Proceedings* article, Lieutenant Colonel Krulak suggests that Marine Corps fixed-wing aviation be reduced drastically as an economy measure; other marines, including Lieutenant Colonel Batcheller, fear a dissipation of amphibious assets to pay for the rapid deployment concept. This type of thinking is prudent, but it ignores the increasingly militant mood of the American public. Improvement in one area of force capability need no longer be accomplished at the expense of another if a reasonable necessity for both can be shown. This is the time to develop a strong, dynamic plan and ask for the funds to implement it. If the mood of the Congress and the people is being correctly interpreted, the next five years will be devoted to creating a counterbalance to a decade of neglect in defense. Any limitations which marines place on their future will be self-imposed.

I recently heard a fable about a man so used to hard times that he couldn't stand prosperity. There is no reason for the Marine Corps to emulate that sad story. Indeed, the future begins now.

Notes

1. "The U.S. Marine Corps: Strategy for the Future," pp. 94–105.
2. "Analyzing the RDF," pp. 16–18.
3. "Power Projection as a Part of Sea Control," pp. 28–33.
4. "A Marine Corps Choke-Point Strategy," *Proceedings*, pp. 103–104.
5. "NATO: Past, Present and Future," pp. 29–40.
6. "Twilight for the Corps?" *Proceedings*, July 1978, pp. 38–43.

THE STRATEGIC CORPORAL

LEADERSHIP IN THE THREE BLOCK WAR

Charles C. Krulak

(*Marines Magazine*, January 1999)

Operation Absolute Agility

0611: The African sun had just risen above the hills surrounding the sprawling city and sent its already dazzling rays streaming into the dusty alleyway. Corporal Hernandez felt the sun on his face and knew that today would, again, be sweltering. He was a squad leader in 2d Platoon, Lima Company and had, along with his men, spent a sleepless night on the perimeter. For the past week his platoon had provided security to the International Relief Organization (IRO) workers who manned one of three food distribution points in the American Sector of Tugala—the war-torn capital of Orange—a Central African nation wracked by civil unrest and famine.

The situation in Orange had transfixed the world for nearly two years. Bloody tribal fighting had led first to the utter collapse of the government and economy, and ultimately, to widespread famine. International efforts to quell the violence and support the teetering government had failed, and the country had plunged into chaos. The United States had finally been compelled to intervene. A forward deployed Marine Expeditionary Unit (Special Operations Capable) was ordered to assist the efforts of the ineffective Regional Multi-National Force (RMNF) and the host of international humanitarian assistance organizations that struggled to alleviate the suffering. The MEU's arrival had stabilized the situation and allowed the precious relief supplies to finally reach the people who needed them most.

The Food Distribution Point (FDP) manned by 2d Platoon serviced over 5,000 people daily. The Marines had, at first, been shocked at the extent of the suffering, by the constant stream of malnourished men and women, and by the distended bellies and drawn faces of the children. The flow of food and medical supplies had, however, had a dramatic impact. The grim daily death tolls had slowly begun to decrease and the city had begun to recover some sense of normalcy. Within a month the lives of the Marines had assumed a sort of dull routine. Corporal Hernandez removed his helmet and rested his head against the mud wall of the house in which his squad was billeted and waited for his MRE to finish heating; satisfied that he and his fellow Marines were making a difference.

0633: The dust and rumble of a half dozen 5-Tons pulling into the market square caught the attention of Corporal Hernandez. Escorted by Marines, the convoy brought with it the food and medical supplies that meant life or death to the inhabitants of this devastated neighborhood. With it also came word of life beyond the confines of this small corner of Orange and useful intelligence concerning the disposition of the opposing factions that wrestled for its control. Today, the convoy commander had disturbing news for the platoon commander, Second Lieutenant Franklin. Members of the OWETA faction, led by the renegade warlord Nedeed, had been observed congregating near the river that divided the capital in half and marked the boundary separating the turf of OWETA from that of its principal rival. Nedeed had long criticized the presence of the RMNF and had frequently targeted its personnel for attack. While he had strenuously denounced the presence of U.S. forces, he had, so far, refrained from targeting American personnel. As starvation became less a concern, however, tensions had begun to rise and there was growing fear that open hostilities would break out again and that attack of RMNF and MEU personnel was increasingly likely.

Lieutenant Franklin passed the report to his company commander and then gathered his squad leaders together to review the developing situation. 1st Squad was ordered to move about four hundred meters north and man a roadblock at Checkpoint (CP) Charlie. Corporal Hernandez returned to his position, reluctantly disposed of his uneaten MRE, and prepared his Marines to move out. The movement to the road intersection at CP Charlie was uneventful and took less than ten minutes. The squad had manned the post before and was familiar with the routine. Pre-staged barricades were quickly moved into place to secure the street to vehicular traffic and a triple strand of concertina was strung in order to control pedestrian movement. Corporal Sley and his fire team moved a hundred meters north and established an Observation Post (OP) on the roof of a two-story building that afforded excellent fields of view. By 0700, the squad was in position. At that hour, the city was still quiet, and except for the intel report concerning OWETA activity, there was no evidence that this day would be any different from the previous. The Marines of 1st Squad settled in for another long hot day of tedious duty.

0903: By nine o'clock, the normal large crowd, mostly women and children with baskets in hand, had gathered to await passage through the checkpoint. The Marines' orders were clear: they were to deny access to anyone carrying a weapon and to be alert for any indications of potential trouble. Their Rules of Engagement (ROE) were unambiguous: anyone observed with an automatic weapon was considered hostile, as was anyone who intentionally threatened Marine personnel. The MEU Commander had made this policy clear in meetings with each of the warlords in the early days of the deployment. His directness had paid dividends and to date, no MEU personnel had been wounded by small arms fire. The factions had kept a low profile in the American sector and had not interfered with those convoys accompanied by Marines. Such was not the case, however, in adjacent sectors, where RMNF personnel had frequently been the target of ambush and sniper fire. The Marines had stayed on their toes.

0915: Corporal Sley reported from his position on the rooftop that the crowd was especially large and included an unusually high proportion of young adult males. He sensed an ominous change in the atmosphere. Less than a mile away, he could see the vehicles of Nedeed's gang gathered at the far side of the bridge spanning the river that separated the OWETA and Mubasa factions. He passed his suspicions on to his squad leader, "Something big is about to happen." The day promised to be a break from the routine.

0921: Corporal Hernandez promptly relayed Sley's report and concerns to his platoon commander and learned from Lieutenant Franklin that Nedeed's chief rival—Mubasa—was moving west toward CP Charlie. Mubasa's intentions seemed clear; his route would bring him directly to CP Charlie and an ultimate collision with Nedeed. 1st Squad's position astride the two MSR's placed them squarely between the rival clans. Lieutenant Franklin directed Hernandez to extend the road block to cover the road entering the intersection from the West and indicated that he and Sergeant Baker's 2d Squad were en route to reinforce. Corporal Hernandez could feel the tension grow. The crowd had become more agitated, aware that Mubasa's men were near and concerned that the vital food distribution might be disrupted. The young men had begun to chant anti-U.S. slogans and to throw rocks at the startled Marines. Corporal Hernandez felt the situation slipping out of control and decided to close the road completely. With great difficulty, the barriers were shifted and the concertina was drawn back across the narrow access point. The crowd erupted in protest and pressed forward.

0931: Overhead, the whirring blades of a low flying IRO UH-1 were heard, but failed to distract the crowd. Their curses and chants, however, were drowned out for an instant by the sound and shock wave of an explosion. The helo had apparently been hit by ground fire, possibly an RPG, and had burst into flames and corkscrewed to the ground several blocks east of the OP. Corporal Sley had observed the crash from his vantage atop the building and saw, to his relief, that at least two survivors had struggled from the flaming wreckage. His relief, however, was short-lived. In the distance, he could see Nedeed's men rushing across the bridge. Sley urgently requested permission to immediately move to the assistance of the downed helo crew.

0935: While Corporal Hernandez considered the feasibility of a rescue attempt, the situation took another serious turn; three vehicles loaded with Mubasa's men and followed closely by a INN film crew arrived on the scene. Brandishing automatic weapons and RPG's, they forced their vehicles through the crowd until the bumper of the lead truck rested against the barricade. With their arrival, the already agitated crowd abandoned all restraint. The occasional rock had now become a constant pelting of well-aimed missiles. One had hit Lance Corporal Johnson in the face. The resulting wound, although not serious, bled profusely and added to the rising alarm. Somehow the sight of the bright red blood streaming down the face of the young Marine fed the crowd's excitement and heightened the panic growing within the squad. What had started out as another routine day of humanitarian assistance was rapidly becoming something else entirely. A Molotov Cocktail crashed into the position injuring no one, but contributed further to the confusion. The Marines of 1st Squad looked from man to man and then stared questioningly at Corporal Hernandez. He reassuringly returned the gaze of each man, knowing better than any of them that the fate of the squad, of the wounded IRO personnel, and perhaps, of the entire multi-national mission, hung in the balance. In the span of less than three hours he had watched a humanitarian assistance mission turn terribly wrong and move ever closer to outright disaster. Corporal Hernandez was face to face with the grave challenges of the three block war and his actions, in the next few minutes, would determine the outcome of the mission and have potentially strategic implications.

The Three Block War

The fictional mission described above—Operation Absolute Agility—is similar to many that have been conducted around the world in recent years and represents the likely battlefield of the 21st Century. It also represents, in graphic detail, the enormous responsibilities and pressures which will be placed on our young Marine leaders. The rapid diffusion of technology, the growth of a multitude of transnational factors, and the consequences of increasing globalization and economic interdependence, have coalesced to create national security challenges remarkable for their complexity. By 2020, eighty-five percent of the world's inhabitants will be crowded into coastal cities—cities generally lacking the infrastructure required to support their burgeoning populations. Under these conditions, long simmering ethnic, nationalist, and economic tensions will explode and increase the potential of crises requiring U.S. intervention. Compounding the challenges posed by this growing global instability will be the emergence of an increasingly complex and lethal battlefield. The widespread availability of sophisticated weapons and equipment will "level the playing field" and negate our traditional technological superiority. The lines separating the levels of war, and distinguishing combatant from "non-combatant," will blur, and adversaries, confounded by our "conventional" superiority, will resort to asymmetrical means to redress the imbalance. Further complicating the situation will be the ubiquitous media whose presence will mean that all future conflicts will be acted out before an international audience.

Modern crisis responses are exceedingly complex endeavors. In Bosnia, Haiti, and Somalia the unique challenges of military operations other-than-war (MOOTW) were combined with the disparate challenges of mid-intensity conflict. The Corps has described such amorphous conflicts as the three block war—contingencies in which Marines may be confronted by the entire spectrum of tactical challenges in the span of a few hours and within the space of three contiguous city blocks. The tragic experience of U.S. forces in Somalia during Operation Restore Hope illustrates well the volatile nature of these contemporary operations. Author Mark Bowden's superb account of "The Battle of Mogadishu," *Blackhawk Down*, is a riveting, cautionary tale and grim reminder of the unpredictability of so-called operations other-than-war. It is essential reading for all Marines.

The inescapable lesson of Somalia and of other recent operations, whether humanitarian assistance, peace-keeping, or traditional warfighting, is that their outcome may hinge on decisions made by small unit leaders, and by actions taken at the lowest level. The Corps is, by design, a relatively young force. Success or failure will rest, increasingly, with the rifleman and with his ability to make the right decision at the right time at the point of contact. As with Corporal Hernandez at CP Charlie, today's Marines will often operate far "from the flagpole" without the direct supervision of senior leadership. And, like Corporal Hernandez, they will be asked to deal with a bewildering array of challenges and threats. In order to succeed under such demanding conditions they will require unwavering maturity, judgment, and strength of character. Most importantly, these missions will require them to confidently make well-reasoned and independent decisions under extreme stress—decisions that will likely be subject to the harsh scrutiny of both the media and the court of public opinion. In many cases, the individual Marine will be the most conspicuous symbol of American foreign policy and will potentially influence not only the immediate tactical situation, but the operational and strategic levels as well. His actions, therefore, will directly impact the outcome of the larger operation; and he will become, as the title of this article suggests—the Strategic Corporal.

The Strategic Corporal

Regrettably, the end of the Cold War heralded not the hoped for era of peace, but rather, a troubling age characterized by global disorder, pervasive crisis, and the constant threat of chaos. Since 1990, the Marine Corps has responded to crises at a rate equal to three times that of the Cold War—on average, once every five weeks. On any given day, up to 29,000 Marines are forward deployed around the world. In far-flung places like Kenya, Indonesia, and Albania, they have stood face-to-face with the perplexing and hostile challenges of the chaotic post Cold War world for which the "rules" have not yet been written. The three block war is not simply a fanciful metaphor for future conflicts—it is a reality. Like Corporal Hernandez, today's Marines have already encountered its great challenges and they have been asked to exercise an exceptional degree of maturity, restraint, and judgment.

Marines, of course, have always shone most brightly when the stakes were highest. The NCO's that led the bloody assaults on the German machine-gun positions at Belleau Wood intuitively understood the importance of their role. The Marines of 2d Battalion, 28th Marines, who scaled the fireswept heights of Mount Suribachi needed no one to emphasize the necessity of initiative. The Marines of the Chosin Reservoir, of Hue City, and of countless other battles through the years did not wait to be reminded of their individual responsibilities. They behaved as Marines always have, and as we expect today's Marines and those of the future to behave—with courage, with aggressiveness, and with resolve. The future battlefields on which Marines fight will be increasingly hostile, lethal, and chaotic. Our success will hinge, as it always has, on the leadership of our junior Marines. We must ensure that they are prepared to lead.

How do we prepare Marines for the complex, high-stakes, asymmetrical battle-field of the three block war? How do we develop junior leaders prepared to deal decisively with the sort of real world challenges confronting Corporal Hernandez? The first step of the process is unchanged. Bold, capable, and intelligent men and women of character are drawn to the Corps, and are recast in the crucible of recruit training, where time honored methods instill deep within them the Corps' enduring ethos. Honor, courage, and commitment become more than mere words. Those precious virtues, in fact, become the defining aspect of each Marine. This emphasis on character remains the bedrock upon which everything else is built. The active sustainment of character in every Marine is a fundamental institutional competency—and for good reason. As often as not, the really tough issues confronting Marines will be moral quandaries, and they must have the wherewithal to handle them appropriately. While a visceral appreciation for our core values is essential, it alone will not ensure an individual's success in battle or in the myriad potential contingencies short of combat. Much, much more is required to fully prepare a Marine for the rigor of tomorrow's battlefield.

An institutional commitment to lifelong professional development is the second step on the road to building the Strategic Corporal. The realignment of the Recruit Training and Marine Combat Training programs of instruction reveal our reinvigorated focus on individual training. Those programs remain the most important steps in the methodical process of developing capable Marines. Our Formal Schools, unit training and education programs, and individual efforts at professional education build on the solid foundation laid at recruit training and sustain the growth of technical and tactical proficiency and mental and physical toughness. The common thread uniting all training activities is an emphasis on the growth of integrity, courage, initiative, decisiveness, mental agility, and personal accountability. These qualities and attributes are fundamental and must be aggressively cultivated within all Marines from the first day of their enlistment to the last.

Leadership, of course, remains the hard currency of the Corps, and its development and sustainment is the third and final step in the creation of the Strategic Corporal. For two hundred and twenty-three years, on battlefields strewn across the globe, Marines have set the highest standard of combat leadership. We are inspired by their example and confident that today's Marines and those of tomorrow will rise to the same great heights. The clear lesson of our past is that success in combat, and in the barracks for that matter, rests with our most junior leaders. Over the years, however, a perception has grown that the authority of our NCO's has been eroded.

Some believe that we have slowly stripped from them the latitude, the discretion, and the authority necessary to do their job. That perception must be stamped out. The remaining vestiges of the "zero defects mentality" must be exchanged for an environment in which all Marines are afforded the "freedom to fail" and with it, the opportunity to succeed. Micro-management must become a thing of the past and supervision—that double-edged sword—must be complemented by proactive mentoring. Most importantly, we must aggressively empower our NCO's, hold them strictly accountable for their actions, and allow the leadership potential within each of them to flourish. This philosophy, reflected in a recent *Navy Times* interview as "Power Down," is central to our efforts to sustain the transformation that begins with the first meeting with a Marine recruiter. Every opportunity must be seized to contribute to the growth of character and leadership within every Marine. We must remember that simple fact, and also remember that leaders are judged, ultimately, by the quality of the leadership reflected in their subordinates. We must also remember that the Strategic Corporal will be, above all else . . . a leader of Marines.

Conclusion

And what of Corporal Hernandez? While his predicament is certainly challenging, it is not implausible. What did he do? First, he quickly reviewed what he knew. He was certain that Lieutenant Franklin and 2d Squad would arrive within a matter of minutes. He knew that the crash site was located within the adjacent RMNF unit's sector and that it manned checkpoints astride Nedeed's route to the downed helo. He knew that any exchange of gunfire with Mubasa's gunmen would likely lead to civilian casualties and jeopardize the success of the humanitarian mission. Second, he considered what he did not know. He was uncertain of either Nedeed's or Mubasa's intentions, or of the feasibility of a rescue attempt. Based on these considerations and myriad other tangible and intangible factors, he completed a rapid assessment of the situation—and acted. Corporal Sley was directed to maintain his position atop the building and continue to monitor Nedeed's progress and the status of the casualties. Hernandez then switched frequencies and contacted the Marine liaison with the adjacent RMNF unit and learned that they had already dispatched medical personnel to the helo crash site, but were unaware of Nedeed's movement and would now because of Hernandez's warning reinforce the appropriate checkpoints. By the time that transmission was completed, Lieutenant Franklin had arrived with the additional squad. With them came a neighborhood leader who had previously acted as an interpreter and mediator. Mubasa's men, apparently uncomfortable with the shift in odds, began to slowly withdraw. The mediator, a recognizable and respected figure in the community, was handed a bullhorn and addressed the crowd. Within minutes the situation was diffused: Mubasa's men had departed, the crowd was calmed, and RMNF personnel had reached the crash site. For a few tense minutes though, the fate of both 1st Squad and the overall mission had hung in the balance and on the actions of a young Marine leader. As would be expected, our Strategic Corporal—firmly grounded in our ethos, thoroughly schooled and trained, outfitted with the finest equipment obtainable, infinitely agile, and above all else, a leader in the tradition of the Marines of old . . . made the right decision.

Discussion Questions

1. How are these two pieces connected? Explain.

2. What is the Navy analog—that is, the business of the Navy and the Petty Officer 3rd Class—if any? Explain how that would help us understand the fleet.

3. Anderson wrote his article at the height of the Cold War, and Krulak just before the start of the Long War. What has changed and what has remained the same? How does that affect the Marine Corps today?

4. How might these articles be applicable to the cyber domain or other twenty-first-century challenges?

5. How do these articles help us understand the relationship between the Navy and Marine Corps? Are the Navy and Marine Corps separate services who happen to operate together frequently, or are they something else?

17

MISSILE CHESS

A PARABLE

Wayne Hughes

(U.S. Naval Institute *Proceedings* 107, no. 7, July 1981)

> It's a great huge game of chess that's being played—all over the
> world—if this is the world at all . . .
>
> —*Through the Looking Glass*, by Lewis Carroll

Peacetime military planning is governed by analogy. The essence of readiness is combat training, which in peacetime is a sterile imitation of wartime experience. Strategy and tactics derive so much from extrapolations from the past that it is a popular half-truth that military men prepare for the last war. Weapons are designed in the mythological paper world of systems analysis and are tested in the tepid environment of safety-first.

In this peacetime world of pseudo-realism, fleet exercises and war games are the best simulations we have of the wartime world of blood, sweat, and courage. Yet fleet exercises are infrequent and expensive and have their own constraints: "Orange" commanders, for instance, will think like Americans, in spite of their best efforts to "think Red." War games are even greater abstractions, of which the most realistic and time-consuming will leave plenty of doubt over the influence of the "random number generator" and other artificialities.

Still, there are clues. After nearly all these exercises and games, the exercise reports say, in effect, "Missile magazine capacity might have been a problem." It is a vast understatement. The Israeli-Egyptian naval war of 1973 was characterized by deception, countermeasures, and tactics in which success or failure hinged on who had the last weapons remaining. The aircraft carrier has long been the backbone of U.S. Navy tactics for two reasons: aircraft radius of action and the capacity for sustained combat. An attack aircraft may rearm; a missile is on a one-way trip. To highlight their formidability, missiles have been likened to pilotless kamikazes. But the comparison also highlights their weakness: a missile can be used only once.

Let us imagine a test of the role that missile capacity will play in naval combat. We will keep the test absurdly simple and the analogy so remote that there can be no danger of inferring unwarranted conclusions. Let us devise a war game that is simple, replicative, and with characteristics that are generally understood by most military men.

Let us play chess.

We will make one change. We will give each piece two "shots." Each pawn and piece will have two chips, and when it takes another piece it spends one chip. After it has captured twice, it is out of weapons and becomes a passive participant— useful, you will learn when you play, to block and interpose but without the power to destroy. All the other rules of chess hold: castling, capturing *en passant*, checking and mating. A pawn reaching the eighth row is promoted and rearmed with two weapons.

Missile chess is different from regular chess. Just as the warrior who adapts to new weapons defeats the warrior who will not learn, so the missile chess player who understands the consequences of his new constraint will defeat the expert at classical chess. Pawns, armed like queens and rooks, become 8 feet tall, like a man on the frontier with a Colt .45. A knight, bishop, or any other piece may capture his way into a mating move and be powerless to execute the coup de grace. End games hinge on who has armed pawns and pieces remaining on the board.

There are untold variations. Missile Kriegspiel is one in which both sides maneuver without knowledge of the enemy's moves and a referee adjudicates, and if you believe that war is not war without the fog of uncertainty, then try it. But the most subtle change is to let both players distribute their 32 missiles among their pieces in any way they choose. Here we come to the nub of it. What is a winning distribution of offensive power? An effective approach is to arm the chessmen according to their mobility and maneuverability. Let us give the White king two missiles for self-defense, the majestic queen six, the formidable rooks four each, the bishops and knights two, and each of the pawns one. With this balance, White will usually defeat Black, whose missiles are uniformly allocated two per piece. White must husband his queen and rooks until their greater capability can be brought to bear, so that as the game opens out toward the end, their sustained offensive power can be decisive. Black must rely heavily on his pawns, which are hampered by their lack of mobility. Black must be willing to sacrifice any piece or pawn to get at and trade off for White's queen and rooks. But as often as not, when Black achieves a breakthrough, he finds that his pieces are out of weapons and have become derelicts on the chessboard.

Does White resemble the U.S. Navy, with the great sustained offensive power of its aircraft carriers represented by the queen and rooks? Whatever one believes about the aptness of the comparison, it is evident that our Navy has not achieved the same balance that we have ascribed to the White chessmen. For the next several years at least, the U.S. Navy will have its offensive strength heavily concentrated in its carriers. It is a queenly strength unparalleled in range, sustained destructive power, and mobility. But we have 13 queens and 300 other pieces. Our 300 other warships are substantially less well armed for offense than White's bishops, knights, and pawns. To draw the analogy with the U.S. battle fleet more closely, one would have to:

- Superimpose the king on the queen, because the tactical commander rides the carrier.
- Remove the missiles from the bishops and knights, and devote them, like cruisers and guided missile destroyers, to the defense of the aircraft carriers—the rooks and queen.
- Remove half of the White pawns, to symbolize the diminishing number of surface combatants that we will have when they are armed with Harpoon, and, ultimately, Tomahawk.

One does not have to play missile chess to sense that the White chessmen so armed would lose. Their offensive power has been over-concentrated. When hapless White feels the frustration of having so much power bottled up in two rooks and a king-queen, harassed and nibbled at and finally destroyed by the relentless pursuit of Black's pawns and pieces, then he will see Through the Looking Glass what Alice saw:

"Look, look!" she cried, pointing eagerly.

"There's the White Queen running across the country! She came flying out of the woods over yonder—How fast those Queens can run!"

"There's some enemy after her, no doubt," the King said, without looking around. "The wood's full of them."

All of this presses the analogy too far, of course. Moreover, we have excluded all thought of amphibious warfare ships, minecraft, and many submarine and antisubmarine forces which would play out their roles on another gameboard. And yet . . . and yet . . . the essence of wisdom remains. One cannot play missile chess without the haunting premonition of an impending disaster for our Navy and our nation if we do not more quickly distribute our offensive power into more ships.

Stalking the marble halls of Washington are men who have a phobia against aircraft carriers. Let them not misconstrue the meaning of missile chess. Missile chess is not a parable against sea-based air power; it is a parable in favor of a balanced battle fleet. To remove sea-based aviation would be to remove the queen. Let us set aside the parable and speak plainly about a balanced fleet on its merits. It is a force which might have its offensive power distributed roughly as follows.

Such a battle force will continue to have as its nucleus one or more carriers, the number driven by the extent of the threat in the offing and the tactical circumstances. Smaller carriers in greater numbers would be pleasant to contemplate, but the facts are that economies of scale drive carrier efficiency, and given that the carriers can be reasonably safeguarded, bigger ships offer disproportionately greater combat strength. Carrier aircraft with their awesome range and power of repeated strikes have no rival for sustaining the attack.

But the enemy (which, in these days of first-rate technology in the hands of second-rate countries, need not be the Soviet Union) cannot be allowed to believe it is home free if it incapacitates one or two ships. Therefore, we should add Harpoon- and Tomahawk-carrying missile ships in numbers of, perhaps, six per carrier. These ships, being numerous, must be inexpensive, if $100–200 million can be thought of as inexpensive. They cannot be expected to have much more defensive armament than point defense. They depend for their survival on the carriers' fighters, on yet-to-be-described antiair warfare missile-armed ships (AAW), and, one would hope, on active and passive electronic countermeasures. In the nature of the war, all will not survive: their role might be likened to the battle fleet's destroyers of the 1920s and 1930s. Their missiles should carry both conventional and nuclear warheads. These new "destroyers" present the enemy with an impossible targeting problem. They have no sustained firepower, yet they threaten to survive a surprise attack from the sea and assure a devastating counterattack; to present a massive nuclear retaliatory threat to the enemy ashore; or to pave the way for carrier air power by nonnuclear precision first strikes on airfields and command and control centers. Like pawns on a chessboard, individually their offensive capacity is limited, but collectively they are a powerful, threatening force.

Third, there should be ships with Aegis and other surface-to-air missile ships, three or four or more per battle group, depending again on the mission and the threat. In the narrow sense, the AAW missile ships defend the carriers. In a broader sense, their purpose is to present the enemy with an insoluble dilemma. If the opposing fleet tries to take out the AAW ships first, our battle force's offensive missile ships and attack aircraft will destroy it. If the enemy aims at the carrier and the "destroyers," the Aegis ship and her companions will survive to forestall the missile threat. The AAW missile ships, like knights and bishops, will absorb attacks that would otherwise fall upon the queen.

The fourth component of the future battle force comprises attack submarines in direct support. Armed with missiles, increasingly they should be appreciated as much as an offensive component of battle force combat power as they are as a defensive component. They heighten the discomfort of the enemy in the same way the hypothetical destroyers do. Their roles are verisimilitudinous to destroyers in the sense that the former are more survivable and freer to roam the seas, but the latter are much cheaper per weapon carried and more easily commanded.

Finally, let us remove the battle force commander from the carrier. It sounds inefficient to build a ship the foremost purpose of which is to carry the officer in tactical command. But when the added complication imposed on the enemy of having to deal with a fifth kind of target is appreciated, then a specialized flagship makes sense. Our five battle force components each in a different way will be imperative targets for immediate destruction. The enemy is presented with an impossible coordination problem. Nor is it any longer axiomatic that the officer in tactical command can command best from his carrier. In this balanced force the offensive capability is dispersed throughout the force. If the carriers are lost, the battle may be lost, but it is folly to think that the battle will be over. The king should not be chained to his queen.

Here, then, are five components of a battle force whose offensive power is distributed and balanced. We have not entered explicitly into the antisubmarine warfare question. Suffice to say in passing that the concept of spreading the offense for the sake of survivability against air and surface missiles will serve as well to dilute the threat from submarine-launched missiles.

Having constructed a new battle force, let us evaluate it in three sets of circumstances. The first is the bread-and-butter mission: to project power in a war in which the Soviet Union is passive. As before, the carriers will move in to project their formidable, sustained, striking power. The other components are largely extraneous, with the officer in tactical command back in his carrier, submarines detached, surface combatants few in numbers, and logistics support ships the tail that may wag the dog. But this comfortable pattern of operations is obsolescent. Increasingly our prospective antagonists, in the Middle East, for example, will be well armed with some share of sophisticated weaponry. Soviet forces may be present, and they, unlike heretofore, cannot be discounted or ignored. Therefore, in many, if not most crisis or limited war situations, elements of the other four battle fleet components—guided missile cruisers, destroyers, attack submarines, and a flagship—will be needed. In old-fashioned terms, we should sacrifice some efficiency in power projection for the sake of sea control.

Second, the battle force must deal with a localized direct confrontation with the Soviet Union itself: Black's pieces painted Red. Mark how that over the course of the last decade changes have taken place. It is reasonable to imagine circumstances in which we may be outnumbered by Soviet naval forces on scene. This is no time to be confronting a Red Navy with only one or two ships that can hurt it. The Soviets must know that if they attack they will assuredly suffer and may lose. In addition, Red naval forces are configured for nuclear attack. Ours are not. The change—the new element—is that the United States no longer has strategic weapon superiority. A fundamental shift occurred when the Soviets became free to contemplate a theater nuclear attack in an atmosphere of strategic parity. If there is such a thing as a theater nuclear war that can be contained, then it is most likely to occur at sea, simply because vital national interests will be less threatened and the homeland will not have been struck. Likely or not, the temptation to the Soviets will be to redress their naval conventional weapon inferiority with their nuclear weapon superiority. The way to reduce the temptation is to eliminate the asymmetry, by spreading an offensive nuclear weapon capability through our battle groups.

Finally, there is the mission of deterring a major war with the Soviet Union. The battle fleet helps deter today by posing a substantive conventional weapon threat to the Soviet homeland. One should not view its potential as hollow on grounds that the war would escalate into a nuclear exchange. One should view the U.S. battle fleet as helping to dissuade the Soviets from starting and winning a war without nuclear weapons because we have no conventional response. Our conventional naval offensive power has a value we should cherish. To put its value in perspective, it is well to consider how the peacetime battle fleet has paid for itself by evoking a massive response on the part of the Soviet Union. Contrary to those who argue that the battle fleet engenders a naval arms race, our carrier battle groups have diverted resources that could otherwise have been devoted to the Red Army and Air Force.

Since the end of World War II, the Red Navy has been charged with, and frustrated in, its responsibility to defend the Soviet homeland against our carrier striking power and our strategic submarines. For them, defending against the threat of the U.S. Navy has been a running sore, involving many false starts and the expenditure of vast resources at less payoff than the United States has had in return for our substantial naval investments. Because of the U.S. Navy, Soviet naval strategy has been focused on defense. Sobering indeed is a moment or two of reflection on what would be the potential of their navy to cut off our military reinforcement to NATO, hazard the very ingress and egress of our ballistic missile submarines, interdict and harass our economic trade partners the mere symbol of which is Saudi Arabia, and without firing a shot create untoward mischief anywhere in the world, all of which would befall if there were no deployed battle groups.

Our suspicion must be, moreover, that offensive power represented exclusively by our 13 carriers is a problem the Soviets now have nearly solved. There should be few more important national military objectives than to raise the specter again of the power of our Navy to inflict mighty damage on the Soviet homeland. The way to accomplish this is to distribute our striking power more evenly through the ships of the fleet.

The burden of this essay is that the circumstances under which naval battles will be fought are rapidly changing, that the U.S. Navy's offensive power is over-concentrated in a small number of ships, and that we are not adapting quickly enough to these new circumstances. But the essay is not the parable of naval conflict. The parable lies in playing missile chess. There is a vividness that emerges from the play of the game that words cannot describe. How the asymmetry in firepower leads White and Black to dissimilar tactics. How both sides suffer from a prospective shortage of weapons and must constantly decide whether to capture or wait for a better, or more critical, opportunity, an opportunity which, sometimes, comes too late. How the knights and bishops not only capture, but threaten and distract, and sell themselves dearly in exchange for missiles that the enemy can ill afford to lose. And how, in the end, White's queen and rooks will sweep the chessboard clear if they survive, and of Black's all-consuming search for ways to keep this from happening.

Of course, missile chess is just a game. Chess in comparison with the powerful analogical tools at modern man's disposal for the simulation of war must, in the end, be treated as a bit of whimsy. You are advised to embrace missile chess as mere diversion. If the play insinuates something more: inferences, perhaps, that cannot be shaken . . . reflections . . . conclusions that no simple game on 64 squares can possibly justify . . . if these things come to pass, well, you have been warned.

———

Note: In Through the Looking Glass, *written by Lewis Carroll, the kings, queens, and knights that Alice encountered were White and Red. The simile between Red and the U.S. Navy's most capable competitor is almost irresistible, but we will stay with White and Black, not just because that is modern chess convention, but especially to emphasize that the U.S. Navy has commitments that extend beyond confronting the Soviet Union.*

OPERATION PRAYING MANTIS

THE SURFACE VIEW

J. B. Perkins

(U.S. Naval Institute *Proceedings* 115, no. 5, May 1989)

For the escorts of Battle Group Foxtrot, preparations for the 18 April 1988 Operation Praying Mantis began in the southern California operating area ten months earlier. From this first underway period as a unit, the Battle Group Commander, Rear Admiral Guy Zeller (Commander Cruiser Destroyer Group Three), had insisted on a rigorous set of exercises to prepare for the upcoming tour on station in the North Arabian Sea (NAS). Initially, the ships drilled hard at interpreting rules of engagement (ROE) and at devising means to counter small high-speed surface craft (e.g., Boghammers) and low, slow-flying aircraft—both of which abound in and around the Persian Gulf. We later added exercises stressing anti-Silkworm (an Iranian surface-to-surface missile) tactics, boarding and search, Sledgehammer (a procedure to vector attack aircraft to a surface threat), convoy escort procedures, naval gunfire support (NGFS), and mine detection and destruction exercises.

We practiced in every environment—in the Bering Sea during November, throughout our transit to the Western Pacific and Indian Ocean, and on station in the NAS. During the battle group evolution off Hawaii in January, we executed a 96-hour Persian Gulf scenario, with a three submarine threat overlaid. We conducted live, coordinated Harpoon missile firings in southern California and off Hawaii, dropped Rockeye, Skipper, and laser-guided bombs (LGBs) on high-speed targets off Point Mugu and Hawaii and drilled, drilled, drilled. By late March, each ship had completed dozens of these exercises, and we were considering easing the pace and working on ways to make the exercises more interesting, as the day approached when the *Forrestal* (CV-59) battle group would relieve us. Such philosophic discussions ended abruptly when the USS *Samuel B. Roberts* (FFG-58) hit a mine on 14 April.

Four battle group ships en route to a port call in Mombasa were turned around, and the USS *Joseph Strauss* (DDG-16) and USS *Bagley* (FF-I069) raced north, refueled from the USS *Wabash* (AOR-5) and steamed through the Strait of Hormuz at more than 25 knots to join teammates, the USS *Merrill* (DD-976) and USS *Lynde McCormick* (DDG-8). They, and their Middle East Force (MEF) counterparts, the USS *Simpson* (FFG-56), USS *O'Brien* (DD-975), USS *Jack Williams* (FFG-24), USS *Wainwright* (CG-28), USS *Gary* (FFG-5 I), and USS *Trenton* (LPD-14), repositioned at high speed as the plan was developed. In the NAS, the USS *Enterprise* (CVN-65) closed to within 120 nautical miles of the Strait of Hormuz. Her escorts, the USS *Reasoner* (FF-1063) and *Truxtun* (CGN-35), were stationed to counter the potential small combatant threat in the Strait, and the air threat from Chah Bahar.

On 16 April, I flew with Lieutenant Commander Mark "Micro" Kosnik—my one-officer "battle micro staff"—from the Enterprise to Bahrain at the direction of Commander, Joint Task Force Middle East (CJTFME), Rear Admiral Anthony Less, to assist in planning and executing the response. We were joined on the flagship, the USS *Coronado* (AGF-11), by the MEF Destroyer Squadron Commander and began working on the plan with the CJTFME staff and other players. The objectives were clear:

- Sink the Iranian *Saam*-class frigate *Sabalan* or a suitable substitute.
- Neutralize the surveillance posts on the Sassan and Sirri gas/oil separation platforms (GOSPs) and the Rahkish GOSP, if sinking a ship was not practicable.

There were also a number of caveats (avoid civilian casualties and collateral damage, limit adverse environmental effects) to ensure that this was in fact a "proportional response."

It was a long night, but by 0330 on 17 April we had developed a plan. We formed three surface action groups, each containing both battle group and MEF ships, that were to operate independently but still be mutually supportive. Surface Action Group (SAG) Bravo was assigned Sassan (and Rahkish), SAG Charlie, Sirri, and SAG Delta, the *Sabalan*. The *Gary* was our free safety, a lone sentinel on the northern flank protecting the barges. Each SAG commander had an objective and a simple communications plan to direct our forces, to coordinate if required, and to report to CJFTME.

Both GOSPs were to be attacked in the same fashion: we would warn the occupants and give them five minutes to leave the platform, take out any remaining Iranians with naval gunfire, insert a raid force (Marine reconnaissance unit at Sassan/SEALs at Sirri) on the platform, plant demolition charges, and destroy the surveillance post. Colonel Bill Rakow, Commander of Marine Air-Ground Task Force (MAGTF) 2-88, and I developed a plan to coordinate NGFS and Cobra landing zone preparatory fire and discussed criteria for committing the raid force, which included the possibilities of die-hard defenders, secondary explosions, and booby traps.

At first light, as SAG Bravo approached the Sassan GOSP, the *Trenton* began launching helos, including the LAMPS-III from the *Samuel B. Roberts*, which we used for surface surveillance. The GOSP appeared unalerted as we came into view from the southwest and turned to a northerly firing course. Our gun target line was limited by a United Arab Emirates oil field three nautical miles south of Sassan and a large hydrogen sulfide tank on the northern end of the GOSP. H-Hour was set at 0800; at 0755, we warned the Sassan GOSP inhabitants in Farsi and English.

"You have five minutes to abandon the platform; I intend to destroy it at 0800."

This transmission stimulated a good deal of interest and activity among a growing group of Iranians, milling about on the roof of the living quarters. Several men manned their 23-mm. gun and trained it on the *Merrill* about 5,000 yards away, but many more headed for the two tugs tied up alongside the platform. One tug left almost immediately, and the other departed with about 30 men on board soon afterward. The VHF radio blared a cacophony of English and Farsi as the GOSP occupants simultaneously reported to (screamed at) naval headquarters and pleaded with us for more time. At 0804, we told the inhabitants that their time was up and commenced firing at the gun emplacement. This was not a classic NGFS mission; I had decided on airbursts over the GOSP to pin down personnel and destroy command-and-control antennae, but to avoid holing potential helo landing surfaces.

At the first muzzle flash from the *Merrill's* 5-inch mount 51, the Iranian 23-mm. gun mount opened up, getting the attention of the ship's bridge and topside watch-standers. The *Merrill* immediately silenced the Iranian gun with a direct hit, and encountered no further opposition. After about 50 rounds had exploded over the southern half of the GOSP, a large crowd of converted martyrs gathered at the northern end. At this point, we checked fire and permitted a tug to return and pick up what appeared to be the rest of the Sassan GOSP occupants. Following this exodus, the

Merrill and the *Lynde McCormick* alternated firing airbursts over the entire GOSP (less the hydrogen sulfide tank), and we watched the platform closely for any sign of activity but saw none. As this preparatory NGFS progressed, Colonel Rakow and I selected 0925 as the time to land his raid force. In a closely coordinated sequence, the ships checked fire, Cobra gunships delivered covering fire, and the UH-1 and CH-46 helos inserted the Marines via fast rope. It was a textbook assault, and I caught myself stopping to admire it. Despite some tense moments when Iranian ammunition stores cooked off, the platform was fully secured in about 30 minutes, and the demolition and intelligence-gathering teams flew to the GOSP. About two hours later, 1,500 pounds of plastic explosives were detonated by remote control, turning the GOSP into an inferno.

Meanwhile, the fog of war had closed in periodically. First, a United Arab Emirates patrol boat approached at high speed from the northwest. We evaluated it as a possible Boghammer—a popular classification that day. It could be engaged under the ROE, but we just identified it and asked it to remain clear. Later, we reconstituted SAG Bravo and headed north to attack Rahkish GOSP, for no ship had yet been located and sunk. A Cobra helo crew, our closest air asset, evaluated a 25-knot contact closing from the northeast as a warship. This quickly took shape as a "possible Iranian *Saam* FFG," and the *Merrill* made preparations to launch a Harpoon attack. We then asked for further descriptive information and ultimately for a hull number. The contact turned out to be a Soviet *Sovremennyy*-class DDG. The skipper, when asked his intention, replied with a heavy accent, "I vant to take peectures for heestory." We breathed easier. Shortly after that, SAG Bravo was instructed to proceed at full speed to the eastern Gulf, in response to Boghammer attacks in the Mubarek oil field. That ended our participation in the day's fireworks.

At the Sirri GOSP, the sequence of events began essentially the same way they did at Sassan. SAG Charlie gave warnings on time, most of the occupants departed on a tug, and the *Wainwright*, *Bagley*, and *Simpson* commenced fire about 0815. Sirri was an active oil-producing platform, however, and one of the initial rounds hit a compressed gas tank, setting the GOSP ablaze and incinerating the gun crew. Thus, it became unnecessary to insert the SEAL platoon.

With the primary mission accomplished, SAG Charlie patrolled the area. About three hours later, they detected the approach of an Iranian Kaman patrol boat, which the *Bagley*'s LAMPS-I identified as the *Joshan*. As the patrol boat closed, the SAG commander repeatedly warned the Iranian that he was standing into danger and advised him to alter course and depart the area. When his direction was ignored, the U.S. commander requested and was granted "weapons free" by CJTFME. He then advised the *Joshan*:

"Stop your engines and abandon ship; I intend to sink you."

After thinking this communication over, the *Joshan*'s CO apparently decided to go out firing and launched his only remaining Harpoon. The three SAG Charlie ships, now in a line abreast at 26,000 yards, and the *Bagley*'s LAMPS simultaneously detected the launch and maneuvered and launched chaff. The Harpoon passed down the *Wainwright*'s starboard side close aboard (the seeker may not have activated) and was answered by a volley of SM-1 missiles from the *Simpson* and the *Wainwright*. Four missiles fired; four hits. An additional SM-1 (a hit) and a Harpoon (a miss, probably resulting from the sinking *Joshan*'s sudden lack of freeboard) were fired, and the patrol boat was eventually sunk with gunfire.

SAG Charlie had still more opportunities to modify the Iranian naval order of battle when an F-4 made a high-speed approach just prior to the sinking of the *Joshan* hulk (SAG Bravo also detected approaching F-4s, but those dove to the deck and departed as they reached SM-1 range). The *Wainwright* is SM-2 equipped. As the F-4 continued to close, ignoring warnings on both military and internal air defense circuits, the SAG Commander fired two missiles and hit the Iranian aircraft. Only the pilot's heroic efforts enabled the Iranians to recover the badly damaged aircraft at Bandar Abbas. At this point, SAG Charlie was through for the day, as well.

For SAG Delta, it had been a frustrating night and day of following up intelligence leads and electronic sniffs as they tried to locate the *Sabalan*. Various reports had held her in port or close to Bandar Abbas with engineering problems. The tempo picked up when the U. S. civilian tug Willy Tide and a U.S. oil platform were attacked by Iranian Boghammers near the Saleh and Mubarek oil fields. The *Joseph Strauss* provided initial vectors that assisted the A-6s in locating and destroying one of these high-speed craft and chasing the others onto the beach at Abu Musa Island. Following this successful tactical air engagement, an Iranian *Saam*-class frigate, the *Sahand*, was discovered proceeding southwest at high speed toward the Mubarek and Suleh fields, perhaps as part of a preplanned Iranian response to the GOSP attacks. Another CVW-II A-6 detected her when it flew low for a visual identification. Pursued by antiaircraft fire, the A-6 evaded and reattacked with Harpoon, Skipper, and a laser-guided bomb. This brought the *Sahand* dead in the water as SAG Delta closed on the position at high speed. The *Joseph Strauss* conducted a coordinated Harpoon attack with the A-6's wingman, achieving near-simultaneous times on target in the first-ever coordinated Harpoon attack in combat.

Although this was the SAG's final participation in the day's attack on Iranian forces, their location in the crowded waters of the Strait of Hormuz-closest to the Bandar Abbas naval base and airfield-led to several tense moments. Reports of Iranian Silkworm antiship missile firings and the apparent presence of targeting aircraft caused the SAG to fire SM-1 missiles at suspected air contacts and in several other near engagements. Because of the concentrated efforts of both Battle Group Foxtrot and SAG Delta assets—with special credit going to the E-2C and F-14 aircrews—however, there were no blue-on-blue or blue-on-white engagements. These results reflect an extraordinary degree of discipline on the part of ship and air crews, as well as a bit of good luck, in this area jammed with so many oil platforms, neutral naval and merchant ships, small craft, and civilian aircraft.

As the sunset on 18 April, all objectives of Operation Praying Mantis had been achieved. There were no civilian or U.S. casualties, and collateral damage was nil. The Iranian war effort had been struck a decisive and devastating blow. Tactics and procedures that had been honed over the previous nine months had been dramatically validated, but a number of lessons were (re)learned which should be reviewed by commanders in future "proportional responses" of this sort. They include:

- KISS: Keep It Simple, Stupid. Simple plans, with clear objectives and a minimum of interdependence and rudder orders from higher authority are most effective.
- Force Integration: Pairing up disparate forces (e.g., at least one MEF and one battle group ship in each SAG; co-locating SAG and MAGTF commanders) is essential in a joint—or multiple task group—operation.
- Surface Surveillance: Air assets, fixed wing and helos, are essential to force protection, targeting, and battle damage assessment. Visual identification is almost always required; especially in areas with high white and blue shipping densities.
- "Proportional" responses: Classic contingency plans do not contain such options and should. The order to respond will leave little time to plan and collect intelligence.
- Linguistic support: The Farsi linguist was indispensable; both in communicating with the Iranians and in gleaning intelligence from clear radio circuits.

- GOSP destruction: This was not classic NGFS since the goal was to clear the platform, not destroy it. Their distinctive construction makes shooting off platform legs a non-starter and a waste of ammunition (we fired 208 rounds total at both Sassan and Sirri). Airbursts were effective for this mission but mechanical time fuse ammunition was in short supply.
- Warnings: Warning an armed GOSP—or worse, a warship—prior to opening fire may register high on the humane scale, but it clearly ranks low in terms of relative tactical advantage. We should rethink this requirement.
- Missile performance: SM-1 in the surface mode worked very well (five fired; five hits), which is better than my earlier experiences. With its high speed, it should be the weapon of choice in a line-of-sight engagement. Harpoon performance was good, and its use as a "stopper"—even at relatively short range and in proximity of other shipping—was validated.
- Fog of war: Karl von Clausewitz was right; it is always there. Commanding officers need to think through, talk through, and exercise in as many scenarios as possible with their watch teams. There is no cookbook solution to the problem of deciding when to shoot and when to take one more look first.

Most of us believe in the deterrent value of sea power and hope that by such strength we will successfully avoid conflict. Should deterrence fail, however, and hostilities occur, each of us wants to be there to act swiftly and decisively. Such was the opportunity presented to the ships and aircraft of Battle Group Foxtrot and the Middle East Force on 18 April 1988, and their crews did themselves, and all Americans, proud.

Discussion Questions

1. Hughes focuses a good portion of his article on the idea of fleet design in the potential fight with the Soviet Union. What would a balanced battle fleet look like today? What would be its main components?

2. What would "missile chess" look like today? Would it be "missile chess" or something else? What if the game were "cyber chess"?

3. How are these two articles related, if at all?

4. Would people who thought about naval combat through the lens of Hughes' ideas or who had played "missile chess" be well prepared for Operation Praying Mantis? Why or why not?

5. Did exercises greatly aid those who commanded and operated in Operation Praying Mantis? Explain.

18

NAVIES AND THE
NEW WORLD ORDER

Geoffrey Till

(U.S. Naval Institute *Proceedings* 131, no. 3, March 2005)

A s the Merchant of Venice remarked: "Thou knowest that all my fortunes are at sea." Shakespeare might not have been a maritime strategist, but the words he gave Shylock are as true now as they were then—perhaps more so, given mankind's growing reliance on the resources of the sea and the dependence of international trade on the capacity to move people and goods across its face. On top of this, we have to accept the rise of the perceived importance of the sea as an environment, both for the future enjoyment of its resources and for the physical health, even future, of the planet and all life on it.

The Result: A System Exists

These interests all intersect; the result is a global sea-based system based on the merchant ship and the container. The system essentially is transnational. Typically, a merchant ship is owned by one shifting international conglomeration, insured by another; the cargo is owned by a third; and the crew comes from all over. When it is attacked, it is hard to tell who is being hurt beyond the crew. It may seem curious to expect state-based entities such as individual navies to protect other people's property, especially when it is not easy to tell who those "other" people are.

But this way of looking at the sea-based trading system is not new. Alfred Thayer Mahan himself was aware of it:

> This, with the vast increase in rapidity of communication, has multiplied and strengthened the bonds knitting the interests of nations to one another, till the whole now forms an articulated system not only of prodigious size and activity, but of excessive sensitiveness, unequalled in former ages.[1]

Whether we like it or not, this sea-based trading system is turning us into a single world society. We are all stakeholders in its success, but some are more willing and better able to defend that stake against anything that threatens the system. The United States and the Europeans are obvious contenders, but only somewhat less obvious are maritime sea-based trading countries such as India, Singapore, and Japan. It is increasingly clear that, in the words of Singapore's recent defense statement,

> We depend on the world economy for a living. We will have to work more actively with others to safeguard peace and stability in the region and beyond, to promote a peaceful environment conducive to socio-economic development.[2]

The same might be said of China. At the moment, its exports amount to some 6% of the world total, but according to some estimates, by 2020 its population will need 900 million tons of grain a year; the most it will be able to produce is some 615 million tons. This gigantic deficit can be met only by trading it in with greatly expanded exports. To survive, China has to trade even more than it does now. Instead of seeing globalization merely as a threat, China is beginning to see it as a safeguard and is talking of assuming more responsibility in its protection, simply because it has to.

Threats to the System

As Mahan also spotted, it is a system under permanent threat. Sometimes the threat is unintended, the accidental effect of local wars and disturbances. Sometimes it is the result of criminals and others seeking to exploit the system for their own benefit. Sometimes, and more insidiously, the threat proceeds from different and hostile value systems, involving wholesale rejection of the assumptions of economic rationality that underpin the system.

Nor should the environmental aspects be forgotten. According to many analysts, global warming could be more of a threat to international stability than international terrorism. Three thousand died in the twin towers; 138,000 in the 1991 cyclone in Bangladesh. The physical health of the ocean is both a cause and a consequence of an incipient environmental crisis. The United Nations declared 1998 the Year of the Ocean to draw attention to the fact that much of the world ocean is in a state of near crisis, environmentally. And marine environmentalists point out that neglect of this will imperil mankind's ability to use the sea in all the other ways just mentioned. If this goes, everything goes.

Sea Power to the Rescue?

Just as the sea is central to the system, so maritime power is to its defense—hence, the growing importance of navies and coast guards. Partly, it is a matter of spreading ideas and values in the ways mariners always have—only in this case the ideas that matter are those that facilitate stable international trade. It is less a matter of encouraging Western-style democracy than of striking equitable balances between God and mammon, liberty and license, and individualism and community. It is unhistorical, politically counterproductive, and, worst of all, quite unnecessary to argue that the West has a monopoly in the civic virtues that stabilize and encourage trade. Nonetheless, by helping provide the conditions in which the world economy can flourish, navies strengthen the trading values that make the system work and that can, in turn, contribute to correction of the world's democratic deficit.[3]

Naval Contributions

If this is their indirect contribution to a stable future, navies have much to offer in three more-direct ways, too:

Maritime Power Projection. One characteristic of the system is that it has hugely increased the level of economic interdependence and drastically decreased the importance of geographic distance—so that what happens "over there" matters far more to us "here" than it once did. Hence, navies are being required to act together in common cause to project military power ashore, particularly in expeditionary operations at a distance from the home base. Freed in many cases from the requirements of peer competition and the need to fight to make use of the open ocean, navies now can concentrate on exploiting that control. Making use of the vast size and ubiquity of the world ocean and of their own inherent flexibility, navies contribute critically to the military capacity to maneuver at the strategic, operational, and tactical levels. But this requires them, to some extent at least, to shift priorities from the sea to the land, from power at sea to power from the sea.

The U.S. Navy's helicopter carrier *Peleliu* (LHA-5) demonstrated the variety of forms of this in late 2001. In November, with 2,100 Marines on board, she and two other warships took up station off Qatar to help guard a meeting of the World Trade Organization at Doha. Later that month, she was one of the ships that projected U.S. Marines 400 miles inland into southern Afghanistan as part of an international and initially sea-based operation against the Taliban and al Qaeda. Both were clear examples of the way in which cooperative maritime endeavor helps defend a globalized trading system through the projection of power ashore.

Maritime forces have qualities and attributes that make them particularly valuable in the conduct of expeditionary operations. They usually are more flexible and more controllable than their land-based equivalents. They often are more readily available, indeed, first on the spot. They provide a means by which diplomats can slide the intensity of the operation from coerce to compel or deter, to limited conflict and back again. They have increasing reach, and they can sustain operations ashore. They seem to be uniquely useful, in other words, as a means of policing the system.

This does not mean they can do all that is required on their own. Their reach tends to be ephemeral when compared to the long-term effect of boots on the ground. There are innumerable types of instability ashore that are better handled ashore, or can be handled only ashore. And there are instabilities that cannot be resolved by military action in the first place. The current Iraq situation amply illustrates both the contribution and the limitations of maritime and military power.

Accordingly, around the world, and perhaps especially in the United States, Europe, and the Far East, navies are being rebalanced into a more expeditionary format, with emphasis on the capacity to project power (both hard and soft) ashore, in distant places, for long periods of time, in common with others.

To do this, they need not just to develop the means to project power ashore in a timely and discriminating way, but also to have sufficient security at sea to do so. They have to cope with the very different challenges of maintaining sea control in the narrow seas and littoral against everything from shore-based aviation, missiles, and artillery, through mines, coastal submarines, and fast attack craft, to swarming attacks from terrorists on jet skis.

Maritime power projection also mandates a thoroughly joint force, which is much more than the sum of its parts. This requires a shift from looking at general input (Are carrier-based aircraft more or less useful than land-based ones?) to specific output (What is the required effect and how might it best be achieved in this case?). This shift toward effects-based operations is both facilitated by and predicated on network-enabled capabilities that challenge traditional naval ways of doing things and some ancient naval expectations about operational independence and freedom of maneuver.

Dealing with Threats to Good Order at Sea. These threats include terrorism, maritime crime (piracy, drugs, and people smuggling), resource degradation from overexploitation and/or pollution, accidents, the quarrels of competing users (e.g., oilmen versus fishermen versus submariners), and inadvertent involvement in the quarrels of others, such as the 1980s tanker war or jurisdictional disputes such as those in the South China Sea.

These disputes often involve navies acting in defense of national interest, usually as instruments of diplomacy, deterring or cajoling as necessary. Sometimes though, navies may be a means of exerting potentially lethal force against adversaries (the recurrent maritime conflicts of the Koreas in the Yellow Sea, the wary preparations of the navies of China and Taiwan, India and Pakistan). Though navies generally are getting more collective in their responses to challenge, for many, old-fashioned national objectives still are crucial.

In many cases, maritime disorders can be attributed to wider disorders ashore—the crisis in governance in Indonesia increasing piracy rates in local waters, or al Qaeda extending its activities to the sea. The result is a vortex of interconnected threats, such as al Qaeda funding its operations through the drug trade, that need to be considered as a whole.

This calls for defensive and preventative action against smugglers, pirates, snake-heads, polluters, and poachers. Because many of these problems are transnational, local, regional, even global responses rather than just national ones will be necessary. And since many of these threats are in the grey area between civilian and military aspects of sea use, the response also calls for cooperative action by coast guards and navies. Above all, it calls for an all-round oceans policy decided and implemented by properly joined-up governments.

These diversifying maritime threats to the system may well require a shift in emphasis from the military to the civil aspects of sea power. Navies may need to redefine their relationships with coast guard forces, or even produce forces that essentially act as coast guards, which are a crucial component of homeland security as it is now understood.

If the meaning of maritime security is widened like this, and if it is accepted as increasingly important, then all this is likely to have implications for the traditional concept of freedom of navigation. Perhaps sea space will need to be treated more and more like airspace—with merchant ships getting more like airliners, handed from one land-based sea traffic controller to another. The International Ship and Port Facility Code first announced in late 2002 is ushering in a quiet revolution in world shipping and is a major step in this direction. For this and other reasons, the 21st century may prove a very challenging time for navies.

Diplomacy and Coalition Building. A hidden bonus of this sort of collective action is that it encourages multinational naval cooperation, which in turn makes

possible such activities as the current international maritime interception operation in the Gulf and the Proliferation Security Initiative (designed to intercept the
trafficking of weapons of mass destruction even on the high seas). The range and
number of navies engaged in this kind of collective response to common threats is
extraordinary, and likely to grow.

Naval diplomacy in all its forms makes this possible. Through their capacity
to make free use of the comparatively unencumbered ocean and being armed with
weapons and sensors of increasing range, navies have unique advantages as agents
of diplomacy.

They can be a means to compel wrongdoers to do things they would rather not
do (such as Iraq's withdrawal from Kuwait in 1990) or to deter them from committing such acts in the first place. In the tanker war, Western navies deterred attacks
on passing shipping by both the promise of denial (you will not be able to do it)
and the threat of punishment (if you try). All this is critically dependent on naval
presence and the capacity to build and maintain a picture of what is happening
everywhere. Failures in intelligence can be catastrophic in human, political, and
operational terms.

Because for the United States, and certainly for everyone else, pressure on budgets, the growing expense of naval weaponry, and the political costs of unilateralism
mean there is a growing gap) between maritime assets and their potential commitments, and increasing incentive for navies to operate together against common
threats, hence the importance of coalition building and the need for navies to develop
ways of working together. There is nothing new about this. Mahan talked about
maritime multilateralism at the beginning of the last century and advocated "a
community of commercial interests and righteous ideals." But as we move further
into the 21st century, the need for collective maritime action in defense of the common sea-based system on which the whole world depends becomes ever more obvious. At one level, this might not seem quite so obvious to some Americans since
they know they have a relative level of military and naval power probably unparalleled since the end of the Roman empire. Why, they might ask, do we need to slow
down so the posse can keep up—especially when national sensitivities have been
outraged by the horrors of 11 September?

Recent events have supplied the answer. The "system" will survive only if
most buy into it and contribute to its defense. As Amitai Etzioni has so powerfully
argued, national governments and inter-government organizations simply cannot
cope with threats such as international terrorism, the proliferation of weapons of

mass destruction, transnational crime, environmental degradation, humanitarian disasters, and pandemics of infectious diseases. What is called for, instead, is a World community acting together in defense of common interests. Of course, we need to ensure the interests are sufficiently common for everyone—or at least a majority—to accept them as such. If a majority of the world's population were ever to see globalization as it is portrayed by its critics (raw, unrestrained U.S. economic imperialism trampling everything that is equitable and decent), the system would be rejected by too many as indefensible.

But assuming we are talking about a world system from which everyone is seen to benefit, even if not to the same degree, then navies have a huge role in rallying the defenders. This explains the growing emphasis on maritime coalition-building operations ranging from naval visits and cross-training to combined procurement, exercises, and, ultimately, operations such as Enduring Freedom. This activity is by no means confined to large navies; small navies do all this, too. This essential naval diplomacy is one of the factors that keeps the posse together and makes it easier for them to interact with the sheriff.

It is hard to exaggerate the importance of this kind of naval activity and of the need to defend it against its twin enemies. On the one hand, mandarins from the Treasury dismiss it as social junketing, cocktail parties on the water, something whose value is impossible to quantify and hard to justify. On the other, steely eyed war fighters regard it as little more than a distraction from the real business of honing their operational preparedness.

Both are wrong to dismiss the advantages of the "soft" security that such activities help provide. It is still too early to see how events in Iraq will play out, but if things eventually do improve in that tortured country, then success will be the result not just of the warfighting professionalism of the U.S., British, and Australian navies but also of their capacity to contribute to the consolidation of victory afterward.

Because this was a quintessentially political conflict, navies acted as instruments of diplomacy at every step. Before the war, the allied sanctions campaign intercepted more than 900 Iraqi dhows and other smuggling craft in 2003 alone, depriving Saddam Hussein of significant illicit revenue. This depended on effective multinational naval cooperation between the U.S., British, Canadian, Australian, French, Japanese, and Polish navies and on a working relationship with local navies, too.[4]

Diplomacy does not stop when the fighting starts, of course. One incentive for the early amphibious operation against the Al-Faw Peninsula, for example, was to get humanitarian supplies into Umm Qasr as soon as possible. For this reason, minesweeping of that port's approaches became not merely an enabler of maritime operations, but almost their whole point, given the overwhelming need to fight the war politically and to win over world opinion. In the same way, low-level and scarcely remarked allied efforts to reconstitute the Iraqi River Patrol and Iraqi Coastal Defense force are an essential part of winning the peace. And so are the continuing antismuggling and antiterrorist patrols in the Gulf and elsewhere. But all this can hope to work only if the naval forces responsible for carrying it out are used to operating with the locals and with allies from further afield.

Changes and Challenges

There can be little doubt that maritime power is transforming away from its historic fixation on peer competition and that, because of this, the sea and the forces that operate on it are going to be critical for the future development of the new world order. At the same time, these changes and challenges suggest that sailors around the world are having to do some hard thinking about how they cope and the extent to which they need to reconsider some long-standing assumptions. Shylock may have been exaggerating, but there is still a lot in what he said.

Notes

1. Alfred Thayer Mahan, *Retrospect and Prospect* (London: Sampson, Low, Marston, 1902), p. 144.
2. Defending Singapore in the 21st Century, Ministry of Defence, Singapore, 2000, p. 35.
3. Amitai Etzioni, *From Empire to Community: A New Approach to International Relations* (New York: Palgrave, 2004), pp. 13–41, for an interesting discussion of these ideas. For a maritime take, see Peter Padfield, *Maritime Supremacy and the Opening of the Western Mind* (Woodstock and New York: Overlook Press, 1999), pp. 1–5.
4. "British Warship Puts the Squeeze on Iraq," *The Guardian*, 21 December 2003; "U.S. Warships Pinching Persian Gulf Drugs Trade," *San Diego Union Tribune*, 9 February 2004.

FUTURE WARFARE
THE RISE OF HYBRID WARS

James Mattis and Frank Hoffman

(U.S. Naval Institute *Proceedings* 131, no. 11, November 2005)

Thanks in large measure to the experiences of Afghanistan and Iraq, there is less talk in Washington these days about revolutions in military affairs (RMA) or defense transformations based solely on technology. Our fascination with RMAs and transformation has been altered once again by history's enduring lesson about the predominant role of the human dimension in warfare. Our infatuation with technology was a reflection of our own mirror imaging and an unrealistic desire to dictate the conduct of war on our own terms.

Recent conflicts highlight the need to always remember that the enemy is a human being with the capacity to reason creatively. In effect, he has a vote in the competitive process we know as war, and does not have to play by our rules. Certainly there are both revolutionary and evolutionary changes in the conduct of war. Social, political, and technological forces can impact the character of conflict. But they do not—they cannot—alter its fundamental nature.

This is an important distinction as the Pentagon completes the Quadrennial Defense Review (QDR). Relevance is more important than yesterday's dominance. The reasons that some claim dominance in their particular area of expertise or their domain of warfare is that no one is contesting us in that domain. If you want to start arguing about strategic priorities in the QDR, we argue that you look at where our enemies are gathering to fight us. That is relevance. If you want to determine where investments are needed to eliminate risk and have the greatest return in terms of defeating our enemies and saving the lives of Americans, look at combat in the "contested zones" of urban and other complex terrain. We need to create the same sort of dominance we currently hold in the Global Commons to our ground forces in these contested zones.

As you are probably aware, the new National Defense Strategy (NDS) and the Quadrennial Defense Review process are broadening our planning framework. This is a very important step forward. The NDS lays out four emerging challengers or threats: the traditional, the irregular, the catastrophic, and the disruptive.

Defense planning scenarios and force planning have focused on the traditional or conventional challenger in the past. While state-based conventional threats have not disappeared, it is clear that the United States will dominate conventional adversaries for the foreseeable future. Yet interstate war has not disappeared. It is possible that some state may miscalculate our resolve or commitment or some irresponsible state actor could take actions that might require a U.S. intervention of significant scale. Thus, we need to maintain our traditional combat capabilities for major war. This includes a forcible entry capability by an integrated combined arms team. These skills sets are still the foundation or baseline of our capability for other forms of war.

But our conventional superiority creates a compelling logic for states and non-state actors to move out of the traditional mode of war and seek some niche capability or some unexpected combination of technologies and tactics to gain an advantage. Thus, we need to explore the nature of alternative challenges and the corresponding investments we must make to better posture ourselves for a projected world of more unconventional adversaries.

Of course, the greatest probability is the rise of so called irregular challengers. Irregular methods—terrorism, insurgency, unrestricted warfare, guerrilla war, or coercion by narco-criminals—are increasing in both scale and sophistication and will challenge U.S. security interests globally. Such irregular challengers seek to exploit tactical advantages at a time and place of their own choosing, rather than playing by our rules. They seek to accumulate a series of small tactical effects, magnify them through the media and by information warfare, to weaken U.S. resolve. This is our most likely opponent in the future.

But as we look out at the future and formulate future priorities and recommendations about capability enhancements for the Marine Air-Ground Task Forces of the future, we become increasingly convinced that future conflicts will not present the sort of neat distinctions represented by the Office of the Secretary of Defense view of emerging challengers. We expect future enemies to look at the four approaches as a sort of menu and select a combination of techniques or tactics appealing to them. We do not face a range of four separate challengers as much as the combination of novel approaches—a merger of different modes and means of war. This unprecedented synthesis is what we call Hybrid Warfare.

In Hybrid Wars we can expect to simultaneously deal with the fall out of a failed state that owned but lost control of some biological agents or missiles, while combating an ethnically motivated paramilitary force, and a set of radical terrorists who have now been displaced. We may face remnants of the fielded army of a rogue state in future wars, and they may employ conventional weapons in very novel or nontraditional ways. We can also expect to face unorthodox attacks or random acts of violence by sympathetic groups of non-state actors against our critical infrastructure or our transportation networks. We may also see other forms of economic war or crippling forms of computer network attacks against military or financial targets.

The kinds of war we will face in the future cannot be won by focusing on technology; they will be won by preparing our people for what General Charles Krulak, the former Marine commandant, used to call the Three Block War. This is a pretty simple construct. You are fighting like the dickens on one block, you're handing out humanitarian supplies in the next block, and the next one over you're trying to keep warring factions apart. This environment should sound pretty familiar to anyone watching CNN these days. It is not an environment for specialists, who may find themselves in the middle of a firefight that they were not prepared for. This is the kind of complex environment that well-trained expeditionary forces must be prepared to deal with.

We are extending the concept a bit, and beginning to talk about adding a new dimension. We're adding a fourth block—which makes it the Four Block War. The additional block deals with the psychological or information operations aspects. This fourth block is the area where you may not be physically located but in which we are communicating or broadcasting our message.

The Four Block War adds a new but very relevant dimension to situations like the counterinsurgency in Iraq. Insurgencies are wars of ideas, and our ideas need to compete with those of the enemy. Our actions in the three other blocks are important to building up our credibility and establishing relationships with the population and their leadership. Thus, there is an information operations aspect within each block. In each of the traditional three blocks our Marines are both "sensors" that collect intelligence, as well as "transmitters." Everything they do or fail to do sends a message. They need to be trained for that, and informed by commander's intent.

The information ops component is how we extend our reach and how we can influence populations to reject the misshaped ideology and hatred they are offered by the insurgents. Successful information ops help the civilian population understand and accept the better future we seek to help build with them. Our Marine ground and air forces must have the tools and capabilities to get the message across in each block.

Combating our enemies in Hybrid Wars will demand Marines with equal amounts of tenacity, courage, and agility. They will have to be what they have always been, the world's finest expeditionary warriors. We also have to have Marines with the cultural awareness to excel in all four blocks. To this end we are investing significant attention to language and culture training. All career NCOs and officers will be assigned a region or area along the "arc of instability" one ethnic or geographic area. This will hopefully provide us the foundation for the increased intellectual firepower to deal with the interactions between our forces and civilian populations. Our goal is to make certain that they are as good at reading the cultural terrain of an area as they are at reading a traditional map of the physical terrain.

This leads to a point that needs to be underscored during this QDR. We should invest in new systems that better enable our Marines, but it is not our technology that shocks and awes our enemies. It is our capacity to produce highly motivated, innovative, and agile expeditionary warriors. All those who witnessed the Marine in Iraq understand the ultimate meaning of "no better friend, no worse enemy." This will be an even bigger challenge in tomorrow's Hybrid Wars, but no less relevant to victory.

Discussion Questions

1.   Till described the international seaborne economic system and the threats to that system in his 2005 article. What were they, and is his description still valid today? What do you think has changed, and how does that affect the way we should discuss this essay?

2.   How does Till's concept of maritime power and naval missions compare to the one offered by Turner in the previous reading? Why do you think there are differences? What do those differences mean for our concept of sea power today?

3.   What do Mattis and Hoffman suggest is the most likely kind of opponent in the future? What do they mean when they describe "hybrid war"?

4.   Does Till's global system overlap with the challenges that are described by Mattis and Hoffman? Where, or how? Do their proposed solutions interact with one another?

5.   Both of these essays were published in 2005. Do the authors' observations remain valid?

«19»

HOW WE LOST
THE GREAT PACIFIC WAR

Dale C. Rielage

(U.S. Naval Institute *Proceedings* 144, no. 5, May 2018)

*T*he memorial services had finally run their course. Neither of the carriers lost had been homeported at Pearl, but the toll among the destroyers had been more than enough to cast a pall across the island. Having exhausted all the means available and failed, mourning seemed the fleet's remaining task. That and reflection, the admiral thought, as he regarded the letter in his hand—his reflections on where all this could have been averted.

At least for the moment the ceasefire was holding . . . not that the fleet had much left to challenge it with anymore.

———

MEMO: 6 June 2025
From: Commander, U.S. Pacific Fleet
To: Chief of Naval Operations
Subj: Lesson Learned from Recent Naval Actions in the Western Pacific

CNO,

At this point, I expect you are overwhelmed with voices excoriating and explaining the costly reversals we have experienced in recent months. Once the dust clears from the congressional inquiries and the various special commissions, it will be a challenge to sort the wheat from the chaff to discover and implement the real lessons for our Navy. Politics being what they are, of course, that task will fall to our successors. Like you, I am painfully aware I am being retained just long enough to absorb enough blame for what happened to clear the deck for the next commander. Nonetheless I will add my own thoughts to the cacophony, knowing that in my position I can hardly be said to be a disinterested observer.

The tragedy of our defeat—and I deliberately use that term so carefully avoided in our public discussions—is that it hinged on such small factors. At the start of Admiral John Richardson's term as Chief of Naval Operations (CNO), he noted presciently that our margin of victory in high-end naval combat had grown "razor thin." At the time, he assessed that the margin, though thin, remained "decisive."[1] In the years following, however, the margin shifted imperceptibly to favor the other side.

The loss of our margin of victory is all the more painful because in the years leading up to the conflict we said all the right things. In many cases, we were doing the right things as well. In the quiet of the Nimitz House lanai, I find myself asking what we could have done had we known this was coming. If, at the start of our terms, we had seen that we would not leave our posts without a crisis transitioning into hostilities, could we have averted this disaster? Possibly.

Our Navy had noted the changing strategic landscape. CNO Richardson's stark self-assessment started to drive the sea change we needed. Projecting power "from the sea"—our comfort zone for two decades—shifted to a renewed focus on the need to fight on and for the sea. Nonetheless, moving limited resources from the desert to the fleet was a challenge. Every year brought a new fight in the Mideast, which, while never an existential issue for the nation, carried the urgency of real-world operations. Saying no to U.S. Central Command for anything required steeling the soul for bureaucratic battle.

Shifting resources was simple compared to creating an intellectual shift within the force. The "Rebalance" that was a political theme in the past decade helped in that regard, but we must be honest with ourselves—we did not rebalance the force until well after we advertised that we had. We touted having 60 percent of the Navy in the Pacific, ignoring that 60 percent of a smaller force was still a smaller force. We worked hard on getting the narrative right, but our allies and potential adversaries could do the math on the correlation of forces; and they concluded that the numbers had stopped adding up in our favor. No strategic communications could change that reality.

Thus, we entered the previous administration coming off a "long off-season," and we knew we had accrued "off-season habits."[2] As we considered how to get back in shape, it is apparent now that we assumed our own "ten-year rule." Of course, British military planners between the World Wars formally articulated their assumption that they would not face a major war in the next decade. Our ten-year rule was an informal, unspoken assumption throughout the force, and thus harder to challenge. As the balance of forces in the Pacific shifted, that pernicious mental math allowed us the consolation of hope. We assumed that each technological advance our potential adversaries put in the field could be countered by even more ingenious technology resident in our laboratories—technology that would reach the fleet in some future budget cycle. We lost along the way the truth that the imperfect reality trumps the perfect potentiality. When we started taking losses in the Pacific, the scramble to get these tools from the labs into the field became a significant and ultimately ineffective distraction. Some likened the effort to the Germans desperately trying to get their Wunderwaffen into the field to tip the balance at the end of World War II.

In general, we had the intellectual framework needed to prevail. Fleet staffs, warfighting development centers, and the Naval War College had spent hard effort in creating concepts to win against adversary forces tailored to defeat our traditional strengths. The concepts they developed, however, required varsity-level execution. From the tactical to the operational levels, this fight was going to be hard in extraordinary ways. Fighting with limited communications while relying on commander's intent placed a premium on experience in this operational environment and on an intimate knowledge of plans and expectations up and down the chain of command. Unfortunately, at the same time we were creating these concepts, we were also hemorrhaging experience out of the Pacific. Between the Glenn Defense Marine investigations and the fallout of the *Fitzgerald* and *John S. McCain* collisions, there were few places more hazardous to a senior officer's career prospects than the Pacific. While there were welcome exceptions, the general result was a steep relearning process with every senior personnel move.

What we needed to do was break the personnel system, at least in the senior ranks. A century ago, Admiral Sir Jackie Fisher, the First Sea Lord, did something similar, stacking the deck in the Royal Navy with officers who would drive his dreadnought revolution.[3] We had experienced and visionary leaders in the force, but respect for seniority and maintaining the balance of warfare communities in the flag ranks made pushing them to the forefront unpalatable. It was not always so. In 1955, President Eisenhower jumped

Arleigh Burke over 91 senior flags to be the Chief of Naval Operations. In 1970, Admiral Elmo Zumwalt was appointed CNO over 36 seniors. Their successes made them legends. We named ships for them, but forgot how they got their opportunity in the first place.

Once combat was joined, it was apparent that we had not found the right balance between efficiency and effectiveness. The optimized fleet response plan (OFRP) was a fine conceptual model.[4] In execution, it carried two key flaws that contributed to our defeat.

The first was that we were optimizing the wrong metric. Our standard was "deployable," not "combat ready"—at least not ready for the high-end maritime fight. The inherent flexibility of naval forces created the expectation that our forces would be able to do anything across the entire spectrum of military operations. The resulting laundry list of tasks and certifications filled each moment available for training. This meant that each task was completed to the "good enough" standard. At the same time, we created tactical concepts that required precision, flexibility, and exactitude in execution . . . not "good enough."

We designed the OFRP process to create a fleet ready for war, and instead we delivered an industrial process to maximize production of deployable forces.

Second, we created a sustainment phase in the OFRP. This phase was designed to ensure that readiness did not "bathtub." Each deployment cycle was envisioned to build on the previous iteration, ultimately creating the varsity-level performance the challenge demanded. The sustainment phase was also where we planned to keep surge forces, but it was never resourced. Ten years ago, the director of fleet maintenance for U.S. Fleet Forces referred to it publicly as a "sustainment opportunity" because there was no funding associated with it.[5] The years of continuing resolutions, Budget Control Act restrictions, and maintenance deficits left the sustainment phase a shell of a concept. As early as 2017, we were telling Congress that only a third of our F/A-18 Super Hornets were fully mission-capable. The Commander, Naval Air Forces, noted to Congress that we had begun routinely to "cannibalize aircraft, parts, and people to ensure those leaving on deployment had what they needed to be safe and effective."[6]

Thus, when we desperately needed surge forces to replace our losses forward, we filled the gaps with our training cadre—the only aviators with current skills on "up" jets. I remember the video teleconference—I was among those adamant that we needed to surge more carriers soonest. It was a necessary move, recognized as high risk, and I do not see how any fleet commander could have recommended otherwise. The two surge air wings spent themselves dearly before falling before waves of enemy high-end surface-to-air missiles and fourth generation fighters that outnumbered them two, four, even ten to one. The exchange ratios tilted heavily in our favor—even the realistic ones rather than those trumpeted in the press—and will be cited with pride for years. Those numbers belie the hard reality that we did not lose just two air wings. We lost the ability to train naval aviators in quantity for the next decade. We repeated the mistake of the Imperial Japanese Navy air arm, which spent most of its highly trained naval aviators in combat in the first half of World War II without considering the need to train replacements.[7] The new authority to recall retired and separated aviators will help, but even so, it will be years before a new cadre is established.

You and I were not in positions to undo a decade or more of underinvestment. What we could have done was be ruthlessly clear about the situation we were in, and we could have had the fortitude to employ the fleet differently. The irony is that the OFRP structure was created to resource a presence model of force employment. We taught that presence was synonymous with relevance and made "operate forward" a mantra. We embraced forward deployed naval forces (FDNF) as a more efficient way to generate presence. FDNF Western Pacific was a proud force, hardworking and worked hard even by Navy standards. It also evolved into a strategic mistake. With steady improvement of adversary reach and capability, our forces forward had grown vulnerable. They were no longer large or capable enough to offer decisive deterrence or to disrupt or delay sufficiently an adversary. At the same time, they represented such a large percentage of our force, especially our operationally ready forces, that their loss would have been catastrophic.

The logical strategic answer would have been to take a page from the Royal Navy around 1904 and bring the decisive balance of the fleet home, concentrated, protected and able to surge to consequential action. We could have left behind a new "Asiatic Fleet" construct. Like its pre–World War II predecessor, it could have been just large enough to show the flag and signify U.S. commitment, while being ready to spend itself dearly to buy time when needed. That was unthinkable, of course. Our forward presence mantra had worked too well on the interagency elements that would have needed to approve any shift. (Do you remember when fleet commanders could deploy the fleet without inter-agency approval? I do not.) What was a navy for if not to be forward deployed? Barring that solution, we needed to find our Scapa Flow—a wartime station for the fleet that offered relative safety and an ability to preserve and concentrate forces for decisive engagement. As it was, we were busy forward, providing visible evidence of U.S. commitment—visible and vulnerable—when the adversary's sudden opening salvos tore through our forces.

When the battle was joined, we worked to maneuver the fleet as a fleet. The return of fleet maneuver had, of course, been one of our key intellectual epiphanies of the preceding decade. Power projection from secure sea bases was the work of individual formations, whether carrier strike groups, expeditionary strike groups, surface action groups, or submarines. Contesting and securing sea space across a broad area, on the other hand, required the synchronized effort of an entire fleet. Despite that insight, we never carved out the time and place to maneuver as a fleet. The constant press of current operations (Presence! Always more presence!) meant few serving officers had the experience of seeing more than one carrier strike group (CSG) maneuvering together—certainly never for more than a day or two. Our doctrine for doing so dated from the Gulf Wars or earlier.

As we improvised our way through the conflict, we faced the reality that we did not fully enable our maritime operations centers (MOCs). These typically had been exercised as a joint maritime component, providing staff responses to up-echelon combatant commands during command post exercises. Few, if any, played in unit certification exercises, meaning maneuver elements were unfamiliar with the MOCs' role in combat, while the MOCs were left developing their wartime processes on the fly. Not surprisingly, the cadre of reservists who augmented our staffs during exercises did not bring the depth or experience to work without a defined process. As a result, we clobbered afloat units with staff minutiae to support our Power Point habit, while the key insights needed to command languished in an email backlog.

The state of our MOC staffs demonstrated our need to refocus the Naval War College and war games. Yes, elements of the Naval War College were developing cutting edge thought, and overall the curriculum had been "re-marinized." Nonetheless, most students left the college without sufficient grounding in the high-end fight. Practical issues—the need to cater to each combatant command, restrictive security classifications, the difficulty of maintaining currency on a dynamic operational problem—left students better versed in humanitarian and low-intensity mission planning than in fleet-level engagements. The best insights on this fight had been found within the professional planning community, which was disbanded some years ago after being nursed along for a decade.

Similarly, we needed to align our command and control across warfare domains. We decided that fleet commanders could synchronize, command, and control all the tools of naval warfare—except in cyber. I am convinced that the separation between the fleet and its cyber support elements will come to be regarded in the same way the division between Admiral Thomas Kincaid's Seventh Fleet and Admiral Bull Halsey's Third Fleet is regarded today. At Leyte Gulf, the gap between Halsey and Kincaid nearly cost the landing force. Taffy Three saved the Philippine landings. In cyber, there was no Taffy Three for us. If cyber was decisive, it should have been part of the DNA of our operations, not the preserve of a separate chain of command too complex to allow synchronized operations.

After all, the war started in cyber. From the first inklings of conflict, our networks were contested terrain; and we started that fight behind the power curve. Over the years, we created waste and vulnerability using Navy networks as if they were extensions of our personal lives. How much Facebook and YouTube were Navy networks supporting day in and day out? We told ourselves that this was a morale issue . . . that we needed to endure the cyber and security vulnerabilities that came with this usage to retain qualified personnel. The losses sustained by Task Force 70.2 stemmed in part from attacks that leveraged these vulnerabilities. We should have been willing to harden the network in peacetime.

If we were unwilling to talk about not having Facebook, we were hardly going to talk about the losses likely in this fight. We nibbled around the issue, emphasizing toughness in our ranks, but we never created a true crucible in training. The Marines invested time and effort to ensure their people experienced something approximating the physical and psychological stresses of combat in training. In contrast, Navy crews experienced the impacts of combat stress for the first time in actual combat. Any Army psychologist could predict the rate at which untrained individuals will fail to cope during their first time under fire. Our Navy seemed surprised.

We also missed opportunities to tell our commanders frankly that there could be no medical evacuations while sitting in the adversary's weapons engagement zone. The crew of the destroyer USS *Fishburne* earned a Navy Unit Commendation going back for the survivors of the USS *Holloway*. It was a heroic, if unsuccessful, gesture that ultimately cost us a second DDG. The reality is that keeping *Fishburne's* missile magazines afloat and in the fight would have saved more American lives than any successful rescue. The *Fishburne's* commanding officer made that call, but the error was mine for not having that uncomfortable conversation with my commanders before they were faced with such decisions.

History will tell us if this is our Suez Canal crisis moment—the end of U.S. primacy in the international order. Certainly, the ceasefire does not leave us well positioned to reconstitute our forces or claw the U.S. back to relevance in the Western Pacific. That herculean task will fall to others.

"We did as well as we could with what we were given" is hardly a ringing epitaph. For the foreseeable future, however, it will be our refrain, and maybe better than we have earned.

Very respectfully,

Admiral W. T. Door, U.S. Navy

Notes

1. Office of the Chief of Naval Operations, "A Design for Maintaining Maritime Superiority, Version 1.0," January 2016.
2. Remarks of Admiral John Richardson at WEST Sea Services panel, 23 February 2017.
3. Henrikki Tikkanen, "'Favoritism Is the Secret of Efficiency!' Admiral Sir John Fisher As the First Sea Lord, 1904–1910," *Management & Organizational History* Vol. 11, Issue 3, 2016.
4. Chief of Naval Operations, OPNAV Instruction 3000.15A Optimized Fleet Response Plan, November 10, 2014.
5. Megan Eckstein, "Admirals: Fleet Readiness Plan Could Leave Carrier Gaps, Overwhelm Shipyards," *USNI News*, 9 September 2015.
6. Geoff Ziezulewics, "Only One-Third of Super Hornets Ready to 'Fight Tonight' as of October, Admiral Says," *Navy Times*, 9 November 2017.
7. Mark A. Peattie, *Sunburst: The Rise of Japanese Naval Air Power, 1909–1941* (Annapolis, MD: Naval Institute Press, 2001), 190–1.

Discussion Questions

1. Upon what assumptions does this article rest? Do you think they are the right assumptions for thinking about a future conflict?
2. Does the author's use of historical examples have merit?
3. Related to the above, is the action to "bring the decisive balance of the fleet home" indeed the "logical strategic answer" for today's Navy?
4. How else could the personnel system "be broken" to avert disaster and maximize the likelihood of victory? What other changes might the naval services make that would help to keep the problems identified from growing?
5. What metrics do we wrongly optimize? What metric should we optimize? (By the way, what is the assumption underlying the use of metrics?)

Appendix

NOTES ON PUBLISHING
A PROFESSIONAL ARTICLE

Chapter 6 examined how a naval or military professional can develop an idea into an article for publication in order to contribute to the further development of our profession. The following paragraphs offer a clearer picture of what a writer should expect once their article is written: from submission to publication either in print or online. The advice we offer is based on professional writing for a print or online magazine or journal. People interested in blogging can certainly also learn from these ideas. But blogging has a slightly different place in our digital society and frequently has different (sometimes looser) standards.

One of the things that most intimidate authors about publishing a professional contribution is fear they will get something wrong or embarrass themselves through small mistakes. The reality is a typo, an improperly used italics formatting, or a misspelled name is not something most editors care about. If the problems are repeated and glaring, that is different, but a couple of small mistakes are not very important. This is why we encourage working with journals and magazines more than unedited blogs, or blogs run from personal websites. Personally, our work has always benefited from the critical eye of a dedicated editor, whether a paid employee of a publication or a formal volunteer. That kind of sanity check has kept us from embarrassing ourselves when the editor asks "hey, are you sure that is right?" or "what is your citation or link for this fact?" From fixing typos to helping improve the writing in terms of style or house format and challenging flawed logic or argument, editors have always made our work better. Once the article or essay has made it through them or their editorial board, there's a much smaller chance we have embarrassed ourselves, and they help reduce some of that intellectual fear.

Finding a Publication

With a completed draft on the computer screen, it is time to decide where to submit the article. There are many, many options. For naval writers there are the big-time naval professional journals like *Proceedings*, *Naval War College Review*, and MCU's *Journal of Advanced Military Studies*, as well as the magazines published by community organizations like the Tailhook Association (*Hook Magazine*), the Naval Helicopter Association (*Rotor Review*), the Submarine League (*Submarine Review*), or Marine Corps publications like the *Marine Corps Gazette* or *Leatherneck*. The other services have similar venues like *Military Review*, or branch publications like *Armor* and *Infantry Magazine*. There are also online publications about defense and national security issues. Authors must realize every publication has its own niche and its own style. Your manuscript should aim to fit their unique needs.

There are two good rules of thumb for selecting where to send the article. First, make sure you have read articles from the publication you want to target and make sure your article is the kind of thing they publish. Second, find the publication's "contributor guidelines." They all have them, and the editors actually put work into getting them just right. Frequently, these pages are also a wealth of advice on good writing. FOLLOW THE GUIDELINES. (Yes, we just stomped our foot and raised our voices.) Do not let the word "guidelines" fool you; these are the rules for the publication. The quickest way to get rejected by an editor is to send them something clearly violating the rules they have put out in the open. And do not blast the article out to multiple publications at the same time. Pick one, submit, and be patient. Give the editors a couple of days to acknowledge your submission, and even more time before you demand an answer. Some have review processes that take months. Even if the article is rejected, you frequently will get constructive feedback that will help you make it better before sending it to the next publication.

You may decide you are interested in a less formal arrangement and go with a blog such as *USNI Blog* or work with the blog of the Center for International Maritime Security (CIMSEC.org). But deciding where to send your article should be a conscious choice based on knowledge of what they publish and how you fit into their corner of national security or naval professional discussion. You do not need a personal introduction to an editor. Find the email address for submissions, write a brief introductory email (include who you are, title of the article, length, and where you see it fitting in to the publication), attach the article (or just make a pitch if that is what the guidelines say), and hit send.

Working with Editors

Editors are here to make our work better. Sometimes, we don't like to hear their criticism, but it is crucial we listen and consider it. You can push back against an editor's changes or suggestions, but you have to be able to explain why you are pushing back. You can also ask an editor to explain the reasons they have made a particular change. The writer-editor relationship should have plenty of back and forth, with give and take from both sides.

A professional editor will also never talk about the details of the work they do with you. For example, the Editorial Board at the Naval Institute has very strict privilege rules covering what is discussed in the boardroom. Some new writers fear that editors may badmouth them to other publications or with other writers, but that has never been our experience. In fact, we've had many editors try to help by suggesting other publications that might be a "better fit" if they have rejected the work. Editors have also offered to make introductions to other publications for us. While talking with an editor is not quite like talking with a chaplain, respected outlets are run by respectable people. Publishers always want you to come back with good material because it is how they keep their journal up and running.

Incoming Fire

The vast majority of material published today ends up online. Even print journals like *Proceedings* place their articles on their website. Along with this comes the dreaded "comments section." Realize there is no obligation for you to read the comments section. Frankly, most of the time we try to ignore it. For each ego-stroking reassurance that you have offered a brilliant analysis, there is a troll looking for a fight or a pedantic fact checker ignoring the actual point. Sometimes, a genuine expert in your subject might respond with good insight. Most publications want their authors to engage because it makes their website look busy and vibrant. However, the key for any author is to realize that engaging with digital commenters is entirely a personal choice. If you do engage, ensure you remain professional to sustain your credibility, even if the commenter is not or is poorly informed. Just remember, there is no requirement to engage, and there is no requirement that you ignore it.

Pen Names

A number of professional naval journals have a history of allowing the use of pen names. Many excellent digital commentators, like the naval analyst and blogger

"Commander Salamander," use them with skill and for excellent reasons. The first thing to realize is that most publications have a specific policy on the use of pseudonyms. They probably are not going to break their own rules for you, and you better know what they are before you try to submit as "W. T. Door" or "Sailor Timmy." Many blogs also have a policy on it as well. If you decide you need to use a pen name to protect yourself, you may be limiting how seriously your work will be taken and limiting the kinds of publications you can approach.

Personally, we have also found our writing is far better when we do it under our own names. There is less of a temptation to resort to snark and sarcasm and greater incentive to make sure the research is fully and rigorously sourced. We have been talking about writing for professional journals and magazines, and it is uncommon for them to allow pen names. If you are publishing in a respected journal or online publication, the odds are you want some credit for your ideas and for having the guts to get them out there.

Article Length

Follow the contributor's guidelines. Seriously. If the journal or publication says they take feature articles with a maximum word count of 3,000 words, do not send them 4,500 words (professional publishing works in word count, not number of pages). Some will give you a little bit of latitude, maybe 10 percent overage, but not always. It is not the editor's job to turn your over-length piece into something appropriate. You are telling them either you could not be bothered to check the guidelines, you have never read their publication, you just don't care, or you think you are so brilliant the rules don't apply to your ideas. None of these interpretations will help you impress anyone.

From experience and talking with editors, this is an across the board issue. Frankly, most junior personnel tend to follow the rules, but sometimes they do not understand the difference between "departments" in some journals, which may have different limits. Some mid-grade officers, senior officers, and Flag officers, however, have issues understanding that the rules apply to them. One would hope the professors from our professional military education (PME) institutions who encourage officers to use their school papers for articles would help them understand how it works. Yet, in our own work, we have also seen professors who submit articles that are thousands of words over maximum, so sometimes they are part of the problem. Be cognizant of your length and the submission guidelines, and edit if you have to shorten before submitting.

PME/Academic Papers

Papers and assignments written in the professional military education system or from academic work are a great source of material for articles. We have used the work written for class in a number of articles. But a school paper and an article are not the same thing. We've already covered the length issue, and this is a common problem with academic papers. There are also differences in style and tone, occasionally in formatting, and in the types of arguments that will fit at certain publications. Do not simply send a PME product to an editor. Always rewrite and reformat the paper to ensure it fits the publication you are sending it to. The editors will still help you make it better, but it is on the author to make the first effort of getting it right for the publication in question. It should not require mentioning, but the editor is also not interested in the grade you got on the paper. No need to share; the work should stand on its own.

Individualized Submissions

Ensure you are sending the right submission to the right publication. If a certain publication has a name for a "department," or type of article, do not use that same name at a different publication. For example, *Proceedings* has opinion pieces called "Nobody Asked Me But . . .". An author who sends a commentary submission to *War on the Rocks* or *The Strategy Bridge* "for your Nobody Asked Me But section" is immediately off on the wrong foot.

Manuscript Format

Simple freelance manuscript format is the best way to approach an editor. Do not try to impress with multiple fonts, complicated formatting, and so on. Depending on what software they are working with, your fancy format may get thrown off anyway. You aren't applying for a job in desktop publishing; the words in the article are what matter and speak for themselves. Include your name, contact info, word count, and article title; use one font, double space all of the text, and keep a simple paragraph format; and use bold, underline, or italics to set things off, but only sparingly. William Shunn's website, although it is designed for fiction authors, gives a good image of how to set things up (https://www.shunn.net/format/story.html). Avoid PDFs to the best of your ability because the editor will probably want to digitally mark up the piece, and files from the common word processors tend to be more compatible with their publishing software.

Authorship

The concept of authorship is directly tied to the question of personal integrity in the academic world. Almost every university or institution of higher learning has an authorship policy statement. Fundamentally "authorship" is the question: Who belongs on the byline of an article? Who should get credit? This is a question every senior officer looking to publish an article must ask themselves when they think about the staff process that might have helped them produce the article. Senior officers and civilian leaders sometimes have speechwriters who help them. At what point, and in what venues, should these assistants be mentioned for written work? Is a shared byline proper? Or is a mention in the author bio at the end of the article the right place? Something like "LCDR Jones contributed to the writing of this article." Perhaps a junior officer on the staff amassed the research and wrote the first draft of sections of the piece. Do they deserve some credit? These questions do not always apply, but this is a key ethical question in colleges and universities. If we are going to pursue professional integrity in the military services and consider it intellectually, it makes sense for us to examine authorship as well.

Be Cordial

Professional articles on military subjects are not the place for personal attacks or for antagonism. Even if the spark that got you started writing was disagreement with someone else's idea, take a step back and make sure you are writing about the ideas and content and are not being antagonistic. Often antagonism can be unintentional and requires you to look at your own work closely. And some publications do not publish this kind of tit-for-tat writing, so expect rejections if you are writing something focused on a critical response to a particular person or article. You should be focused on new ideas and solutions. It is OK to be constructively critical of another writer, thinker, or publication, but avoid personal or professional antagonism. Try to follow philosopher Daniel Dennett's rules on criticism: aim at the ideas, not the people, and give credit where credit is due.

Cite Your Work

Footnotes, endnotes, hyperlinks . . . they matter. They help prove you have done the research and reading that we discussed earlier in this book. More importantly, perhaps, they acknowledge the hard work of others who have tackled the same or similar subjects and on whose shoulders you are standing. They offer the editor and the reader a chance to check up on you. None of us forms ideas or opinions in a vacuum. Even senior officers have not come to all their knowledge through experience or some kind of intellectual epiphany. We should acknowledge this through good use of notes and links. This does not mean every article must be peppered with quotes from Clausewitz or Mahan. Actually, please don't. You do not have to tackle the great masters or always pick a quote from them. Sometimes it makes you look silly. We know from experience.

So What?

Say something in your article. Identifying a problem is certainly a contribution, but oftentimes it is not enough. It only becomes a good article when you also suggest a solution or a path to a solution. You have to argue for something, not just report on a situation. In the chapter on professional writing, we talked about John Adams' call to "dare to read, think, speak, and write." Professional articles are at their best when they remember that first word. Writers must dare.

The observations offered here are intended as a little bit of what we naval folks call gouge to get started. These are simple observations from our past several years both writing and editing on military and naval subjects. Individual experience will vary. As we say in the navy, if you live by the gouge, you'll likely die by the gouge. But at least it gives us somewhere to start.

While military personnel are commonly lauded for their willingness to take physical risks in defense of the nation, sometimes we are less open to taking the intellectual risks involved in the betterment of our profession. Yes, it is natural for writers to have a certain amount of fear that they might embarrass themselves through a small mistake or problem in a professional article. Taking an intellectual or academic risk is far different than strapping into an aircraft, rigging to dive the boat, or free-falling out of a perfectly good airplane.

The reality is there are a number of things military authors do that are sort of embarrassing from an editor's perspective. Military personnel hold themselves up as professionals but occasionally behave like inexperienced freshman undergraduates when it comes time to submit an article for publication. Most of the issues can be addressed by acting like the professionals we all claim to be. These are not actually hard things to do but generally fall into the GI Joe category of knowledge: knowing is half the battle.

Notes

INTRODUCTION

1. William Sims, "Cheer Up!! There Is No Naval War College," U.S. Naval Institute *Proceedings* 42, no. 3 (1917): 857–60.
2. William Sims, "The Practical Naval Officer," U.S. Naval Institute *Proceedings* 47, no. 4 (1921): 525–46.

CHAPTER 1. RELAX, THERE IS NO NAVAL UNIVERSITY

1. James Ramsay, *An Essay on the Duty and Qualifications of a Sea Officer: Written Originally, anno 1760, for the Use of Two Young Officers* (London: G. Robinson, 1780).
2. Lori Bogle and Joel Holwitt, "The Best Quote Jones Never Wrote," *Naval History Magazine* 18, no. 2 (2004): 18–23.
3. Richard Blake, "James Ramsay's Essay of 1780 on the Duty and Qualifications of a Sea Officer," in *The Naval Miscellany*, vol. 7, ed. Brian Vale, 129–45 (London: Navy Records Society, 2017).
4. Blake, 155.
5. Blake, 197–200.
6. Claude Berube, "The Crucible of Naval Enlightenment," *Naval History* 28, no. 5 (2014).
7. *Constitution and Bylaws of the United States Naval Lyceum: Established at the Navy Yard, New York* (Brooklyn: E. B. Spooner & Co., 1838), 5.
8. Quoted in Berube, "The Crucible of Naval Enlightenment."

9. "Vauc," "Original Miscellany: The Naval Lyceum," *New York Times*, 8 December 1852, https://timesmachine.nytimes.com/timesmachine/1852/12/08/751 23004.pdf?pdf_redirect=true&ip=0.

10. Thomas B. Hayward, "A Star Is Born: The U.S. Naval Institute Proceedings 1874–1879," U.S. Naval Institute *Proceedings* 140, no. 5 (2014); and *The Papers and Proceedings of the United States Naval Institute*, vol. 1 (New York: D. Van Nostrand, 1874).

11. Peter Swartz, "Looking Out over the Promised Land: The Naval Institute Proceedings 1880–1889," U.S. Naval Institute *Proceedings* 140, no. 6 (2014); and Barney Rubel, "The Voice of Mahan: The Naval Institute Proceedings 1890–1899," U.S. Naval Institute *Proceedings* 140, no. 7 (2014).

12. James Russell Soley, *Report on Foreign Systems of Naval Education* (Washington, D.C.: Government Printing Office, 1880), 152.

13. Quoted in James Goldrick, "The Irresistible Force and the Immovable Object: The Naval Review, the Young Turks, and the Royal Navy, 1911–1931," in *Mahan Is Not Enough: The Proceedings of a Conference on the Works of Sir Julian Corbett and Admiral Sir Herbert Richmond*, ed. James Goldrick and John B. Hattendorft (Newport, R.I.: Naval War College Press, 1993), 87.

14. "About the Naval Review," *Naval Review* (n.d.), https://www.naval-review.com/about-the-naval-review/.

15. Peter Hore, ed., *Dreadnaught to Daring: 100 Years of Comment, Controversy and Debate in The Naval Review* (London: Pen & Sword, 2012).

CHAPTER 3. BEING IN DIALOGUE

1. Stringfellow Barr, "Notes on Dialogue," St. John's College, January 1968, https://www.sjc.edu/application/files/7614/9814/1117/Notes_on_Dialogue.pdf.

2. Alfred Thayer Mahan, "The Practical Character of the Naval War College," U.S. Naval Institute *Proceedings* 19, no. 2 (April 1893); and William S. Sims, "The Practical Naval Officer," U.S. Naval Institute *Proceedings* 47, no. 4 (April 1921).

CHAPTER 5. CHEER UP!

1. *War on the Rocks*: www.warontherocks.com; *The Strategy Bridge*: www.thestrategybridge.org; *CIMSEC's Next War*: www.cimsec.org.

2. Three editions of the Ethics Goes to the Movies discussion guides are available at the Stockdale Center's website: https://www.usna.edu/Ethics/publications /books.php.

3. Robert C. Rubel, "Writing to Think: The Intellectual Journey of a Naval Career," Newport Paper #41 (Newport, R.I.: Naval War College Press, 2014).

CHAPTER 6. READ, THINK, SPEAK . . . AND WRITE

1. John Richardson and Ashley O'Keefe, "Read. Write. Fight." U.S. Naval Institute *Proceedings* 142, no. 6 (June 2016).

2. James Stavridis, "Read, Think, Write, and Publish," U.S. Naval Institute *Proceedings* 134, no. 8 (August 2008).

3. David Vergun, "Army Press Gets Soldiers' Thoughts, Ideas Published," *Army .mil*, 15 January 2016, https://www.army.mil/article/161016; and Joe Byerly, "Writing in the Professional Military: I Tried It and Was Not Attacked by Sea Monsters," *From the Green Notebook*, 29 January 2015, https://fromthegreen notebook.com/2015/01/29/writing-in-the-professional-military-i-tried-it -and-was-not-attacked-by-sea-monsters/.

4. Ernest J. King, "Some Ideas about Organization on Board Ship," U.S. Naval Institute *Proceedings* 35, no. 1 (January 1909).

5. J. P. Clark, *Preparing for War: The Emergence of the Modern U.S. Army, 1815– 1917* (Cambridge, Ma.: Harvard University Press, 2017); J. Furman Daniel, *21st Century Patton: Strategic Insights for the Modern Era* (Annapolis, Md.: Naval Institute Press, 2016); and D. D. Eisenhower, "A Tank Discussion," *Infantry Journal* 27, no. 5 (November 1920).

6. John Adams, "VI. 'A Dissertation on the Canon and the Feudal Law,' No. 4, 21 October 1765," *Founders Online*, U.S. National Archives, https://founders .archives.gov/documents/Adams/06-01-02-0052-0007.

7. Michael Howard, "The Use and Abuse of Military History," *RUSI Journal* 138, no. 1 (January 1993).

8. Arnold Samuelson, *With Hemingway: A Year in Key West and Cuba* (New York: Random House, 1984).

9. Emily Temple, "'My Pencils Outlast Their Erasers': Great Writers on the Art of Revision," *Atlantic* (14 January 2013), https://www.theatlantic.com/entertain ment/archive/2013/01/my-pencils-outlast-their-erasers-great-writers-on-the -art-of-revision/267011/.

Index

About the Authors

Benjamin F. "BJ" Armstrong is a permanent military professor at the U.S. Naval Academy. He is a Volgenau Fellow in the School of Humanities and Social Sciences at the Naval Academy. After spending the first half of his career as a search and rescue and special warfare helicopter pilot, he earned his PhD in war studies with King's College London before becoming a naval educator.

John Freymann is a permanent military professor at the U.S. Naval Academy. After spending the first half of his career as a surface warfare officer, he earned his PhD in the history of Christianity from the University of Chicago before becoming a naval educator.